A Brief History of Christianity in Asia:

Beginnings, Endings, and Reflections

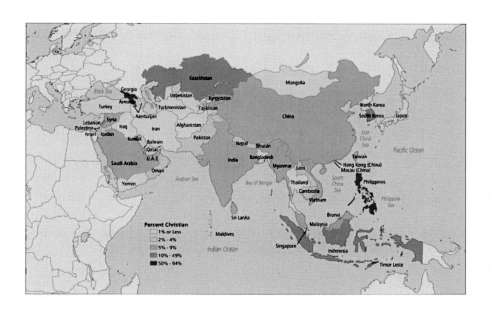

R. LaMon Brown and Michael D. Crane

About the authors:

LaMon Brown (Ph.D.) has been a professor at Serampore College and South India Biblical Institute in India, McGilvary School of Divinity of Payap University in Chiang Mai, Thailand, and New Orleans Baptist Theological Seminary. He has pastored at churches in New York, Georgia and Louisiana. He has authored *Growing Spiritually with the Saints: Catherine of Genoa and William Law* (Peake Road, 1996) and contributed to *Encountering God in the Prayers of Others* (Parson's Porch & Company, 2014).

Michael D. Crane (Ph.D.) has lived in Asia most of his life. He has served on the faculty of two different Asian seminaries. He also serves as a trainer with a global church planting network in Asia. In addition to numerous articles, Michael has written *Sowing Seeds of Change: Cultivating Urban Transformation* (Urban Loft, 2015) and co-authored *City Shaped Churches: Planting Churches in a Global Era* (Urban Loft, 2018).

Cover photo credit to Operation World.

A Brief History of Christianity in Asia:
Beginnings, Endings, and Reflections

Published by
Malaysia Baptist Theological Seminary
40 A-D, Mukim 17, Batu Ferringhi,
11100 Penang, Malaysia
Tel: 604-881 1245 Fax: 604-881 1995
Email: info@mbts.org.my

Printed in Malaysia 2019

Table of Contents

Table of Figures

Preface by LaMon Brown

I am from a small town in the foothills of the Appalachian Mountains in northern Alabama. Growing up I never saw any persons of Asian descent. Perhaps I did when I went to college, but I do not remember actually meeting any. Nevertheless, I have always been attracted to Asia. In high school in the 1960s, it was the story of Mahatmas Gandhi which moved me. When I attended college I was further interested as I studied various courses related to Asian history. Later when I attended seminary, one of my first papers was written on the "Nestorian Christians" of Asia.

After graduating from seminary I had the opportunity to serve God and the Church in India and Thailand. One of my great joys has been teaching Asian Church History. I taught this course for several years at the McGilvary College of Divinity, Payap University in Chiang Mai, Thailand. It was because of that course that this book came to be written.

Other works exist today that speak to the history of the Church in Asia. Perhaps the best known is the two volume work of Samuel Hugh Moffett, *A History of Christianity in Asia.* Any serious student of church history will want to study Moffett's book carefully.

This present work however differs from others in several ways. First, it includes a section on the spread of the Orthodox Church into Asia. Moffett chose to limit his work by omitting this part of the history. Additionally, this work looks at indigenous expressions of Christianity in the 19th and 20th century. While this material is available in a variety of other sources, this is the only book that I know of which includes this material in a book devoted to the history of Christianity in Asia.

The titles of the first two parts are somewhat arbitrary. The first four chapters deal with four expressions of Christianity that have appeared in some ways alien to Asia – at least Asia from India to the Pacific Ocean. They begin with one of the most ancient expressions of Christianity – the Syrian Church of the East. The next three chapters look at a variety of indigenous expressions of Christianity that have been and are found in Asia. All have appeared in the 19th and 20th century – after the coming of European Christianity to Asia. Two other features of the book bear mentioning. It is short. The material is thus suitable for use in settings beyond a class textbook. One does not have to be a lover of history to read these pages.

Finally, the book closes with a series of study questions and opportunities for further reflection. While there are those of us who enjoy the study of history as an academic discipline, a 'study' of Christian history should never remain simply historical. It is my hope that with this short accessible book, Christians will be able to reflect on lessons that have come to us from the stories of our fellow believers living and working in Asia. The story read unreflectively is the story, at best, only half understood.

—R. LaMon Brown, © 2019

Preface by Michael Crane

If you were to look at my face or my passport, you would not see an Asian connection. However, I was born in Taiwan and raised primarily in Malaysia and the Philippines. I've lived most of my adult life in Southeast Asia with my wife and two Asian-born sons. Though I'm not Asian, I'm a son of Asia. It is where I'm most comfortable and where I have sought to live out my faith in Christ.

I've taught church history for many years, lamenting that too little is said of the eastward expansion of the church, that for a thousand years the church thrived deep within the Asian continent and yet few knew this. Too many critics label Christianity as a western religion and I can't blame them, especially after looking at our church history books or lists of most influential Christians. This book comes as a response to the dearth of materials available on the topic.

In August of 2006, I was in Chiang Mai, Thailand awaiting the birth of my eldest when I had the chance to sit in on LaMon's Asian Church History course at McGilvary College of Divinity. It was at that time that he told me of his work of writing this much-needed brief history of Asian Christianity. More recently, LaMon graciously invited me to join him in updating and adding to this work. In other words, LaMon has done the heavier portion of writing, and I get to ride on his coat tails.

It has been a long time coming, but there are now more works devoted to the history of Christianity in Asia than ever before. These newer works have moved beyond a mere retelling of western missionaries going to exotic faraway lands (although the role and contribution of western missionaries cannot be overlooked). They are now telling of the church of Jesus Christ becoming rooted in the diverse soils of Asia and bearing fruit. However, there is not much that seeks to cover this material comprehensively in a short and accessible volume. This is what we have tasked ourselves with here: bringing the rich and complex two-thousand-year history of Asian Christianity into one (hopefully) manageable volume. This means that many events and people of enormous significance could not be included. It is our hope that this short book is the beginning of the readers' long journey of learning about the Asian church throughout the centuries.

Any work like this involves the work of many. My appreciation goes to Malaysia Baptist Theological Seminary (MBTS) for valuing this work enough to publish it. I'm grateful for the ministry and vision of MBTS under the leadership of Dr. John Ong. I'm also grateful to both the libraries of MBTS and Seminari Theologi Malaysia (STM) for their generosity in allowing me to use their resources. I'm ever-thankful for my wife, Karen, and sons, Jaden and Ian, in their patience as I've worked on this project.

—Michael D. Crane © 2019

Introduction

"Just as there is a missional trajectory to all of the Bible, in a similar manner Christian history also has a missional trajectory."

–Scott Sunquist[1]

History will aid us greatly in understanding the struggle of Christianity to take root in Asia, and the reasons that account for the lack of success."

–Melba Maggay[2]

In East and Southeast Asia, Christianity has often been tagged as "western" or "foreign". We will lay aside a more philosophical question of what is foreign and what is indigenous, as there is very little that is purely indigenous in the world. Most of biblical history takes place in western Asia and the first expressions of the church were in the Asian cities of Jerusalem, Samaria, and Antioch. The presence of vibrant forms of Christianity in different parts of Asia have not ceased since those earliest days. It is vital for this history to be known and told. Philip Jenkins states: "We can't understand Christian history without Asia—or, indeed, Asian history without Christianity." [3] Beyond only knowing about this history, it should be instructional and inspirational as we seek to live faithfully in our time in history.

In this book, we aim to offer a brief accounting of the history of Christianity in Asia. Unfortunately, most church history textbooks give little space to the expansion and expressions of Asian Christianity. This book is designed to be

---

[1] China Group, "Xu Guangqi," in *A Dictionary of Asian Christianity*, ed. Scott W. Sunquist (Grand Rapids, MI: Wm. B. Eerdmans, 2001), 5.

[2] Melba Padilla Maggay, "Early Protestant Missionary Efforts in the Philippines: Some Intercultural Issues," in *Asian Church and God's Mission*, ed. Wonsuk Ma and Julie C. Ma (Manila: OMF Literature, 2003), 39.

[3] Jenkins, *The Lost History of Christianity*, 11.

an introductory exposure. Boasting two-thirds of the world population in more than fifty nations or autonomous regions, Asia's immensity is unparalleled. A book of this length cannot explore two thousand years of rich and diverse history in much depth but will give the reader names, places, and resources for further research.

A study of this kind has many limitations. Its brevity is a built-in limitation. The study of Asian Christian history has also faced some challenges that differ from studying Christian history in the West. John C. England summarizes these challenges well. First, original source manuscripts are in highly diverse languages, some of which are no longer in use.[4] In some places, tropical weather has meant few historical documents of any sort have survived. Second, the geography is vast and the terrain is challenging. This has meant access to ancient sites of the church have been difficult for archeologists and historians. Third, the names of places, people groups, and individuals vary according to the era, language, and religious tradition. Ancient records refer to places and people with few clues as to specific locations. Fourth, a number of Christian groups were involved in the Christian expansion eastward. Eastern Christians seldom had state protection that would enable stronger organization and communication.[5] Various Christian traditions established Christian communities in far reaching locations. Theological and liturgical differences add another level of complexity to the rich tapestry of Asian Christian history. These difficulties are not just challenges for the historians, but make it more difficult to recount the movement of the Spirit of God across Asia.

In this volume, we aim to cover key moments and people in the growth and establishment of the church throughout Asia. Regrettably, important people and events and places had to be left out for the sake of brevity. It is our hope that this volume is the inconspicuous hallway that leads the reader to many

---

[4] Even today more than two thousand languages are spoken in Asia, one-third of languages in use globally. Graham Hill, *GlobalChurch: Reshaping Our Conversations, Renewing Our Mission, Revitalizing Our Churches* (Downers Grove, IL: IVP Academic, 2016), 250.

[5] England, "Reclaiming Our Christian History," 22.

beautiful rooms where the stories of the Asian church in each location can be known more fully.

Part One: The Church in Asia: Ancient and Alien

"Since every historical event occurs both in space as well as in time, history cannot, except in some of its more specialized branches, be dissociated from country or place."

–W. Gordon East[1]

"In earliest history, the first Christian centers, Jerusalem, Antioch & Ephesus were in Asia. The first known church building was in Asia, the first NT translation was in Asia. The first Christian king; the first Christian poets; the first Christian state were all in Asia."

–Samuel Moffett [2]

Introduction

Christianity began in Asia. The first church was an Asian church (Acts 2). It started as a movement among the Jews of Palestine. As it took root in far western Asia, it quickly spread west into Europe and North Africa. The first part of this story is found in the Book of Acts which records the beginnings of the church in Jerusalem as well as the journeys of Paul and his companions.

The story of the eastern spread of Christianity is not as well documented but we know that Christians came to Antioch (Antakya in Eastern Turkey) and Damascus as early as the New Testament era[3] before it went to any part of Europe. By 180 CE the Church was established in several places throughout Mesopotamia. At the Council of Nicaea in 325, bishops representing churches in Persia and India were present.

---

[1] East, *The Geography Behind History*, 4.

[2] Moffett, *A History of Christianity in Asia*.

[3] Acts 11:19-26; 9:11

The churches of the west used Greek and Latin in their worship and writings. The churches of the East preferred to use Syriac (a dialect of Aramaic).[4] It is to this Syrian language Church that we first turn in our outline of the story of Christianity in Asia.

---

[4] Most older texts used "Syrian" to refer to the language and as an adjective. Many modern texts prefer to use "Syriac." We have chosen to use "Syriac" as the name for the language and "Syrian" as the adjectival modifier.

Chapter 1: The Church of the East or the Syrian Church

"Founded in the Near East, Christianity for its first thousand years was stronger in Asia and North Africa than in Europe, and only after about 1400 did Europe (and Europeanized North America) decisively become the Christian heartland."

–Philip Jenkins[1]

1.1 Edessa

Edessa was the capitol city of the small Kingdom of Osrhoene. It was precariously located between the mighty empires of Rome and Persia. (Edessa today is the city of Urfa in southern Turkey.)

The kings of Edessa were called Abgar. The Legend of King Abgar tells a story of Abgar V. According to the legend, King Abgar heard of Jesus. Abgar was ill; so he wrote a letter to Jesus asking him to come to Edessa to heal him. Jesus wrote back in reply saying that he could not come. However, he promised that after he had ascended to heaven, he would send one of his disciples to the king.

The legend continues that after the ascension of Jesus, the Apostle Thomas sent one of the 70 disciples (mentioned in Luke 10) to the king. The disciple's name was Thaddeus. In Syriac the name became Addai. Addai healed the king and many people became believers.

While the legend is highly unlikely in many of its details, it is possible that Christianity came to Edessa as early as the reign of Abgar V. Scripture indicates that there were people from Mesopotamia in Jerusalem during the Pentecost season when Peter preached his sermon recorded in Acts 2. Edessa may have been included in that geographical designation. Also, after the

---

[1] Jenkins, *The Next Christendom*, 15.

martyrdom of Stephen, Christians fled from Jerusalem. We know some went to Antioch. It is not improbable that others made their way to Edessa.

However, the first king of Edessa of whom we have evidence of Christian faith is Abgar VIII (177-212 CE). Coins of Edessa, dating from 180-192, bear a symbol of the cross. According to history known to us, Abgar VIII could have been the first Christian king in the world and made Christianity the official religion. By 180 CE the church was already established in many parts of Mesopotamia.

Edessa has some other distinctions. The city chronicle records that in 201 a church building was destroyed in a flood. Thus, it appears that Edessa was the first place to have a Christian worship building. In addition, the first translation of the New Testament into a non-Greek language took place in Edessa. It was translated into Syriac.

The two most important thinkers in the early Syrian Church were Tatian and Bardaisan.

Tatian, who lived in the second century (c.110-180), was a Syrian who studied Greek philosophy among other subjects. He made his way to Rome where he became a Christian. There he studied with Justin Martyr. After Justin's death, Tatian returned to Syria. He died in the city of Edessa.

Tatian's two most important writings are *An Address to the Greeks* and *Diatessaron*. In the first, he sternly rejected Greek culture while affirming the value of Christianity. This distaste for things Greek will surface again in the history of the Syrian Church. It probably played a role in the division of the Syrian Church from the western Greek language churches which would become more or less permanent by the 5th century.

The other writing, *Diatessaron*, is a life of Christ. Tatian translated and edited the four canonical Gospels into one. (The word *diatessaron* means "from four.") This harmony of the Gospels was the most popular version of the Gospels in the Syrian Church until the 5th century. Unfortunately, we do not possess Syriac copies of this work. We only have ancient translations in Greek, Persian, Arabic, etc. Some criticisms were aimed at the *Diatessaron* by Tatian's opponents, but we are no longer able to discern the accuracy of these criticisms. An English translation of an Arabic copy of this work does not reveal any serious discrepancies from the four traditional Gospels.[2]

In the western Church, Tatian was considered a heretic, opposed by Irenaeus, Tertullian, Clement of Alexandia, and others. He was accused of having gnostic tendencies and being the Father of the Encratites–radical ascetics who rejected wine, meat, and marriage.[3] We will see later that the Syrian Church did have a significant ascetic element in it, but it cannot be proven today that Tatian advocated teachings and practices that gave rise to the Encratite movement.

Bardaisan (also written Bardesanes) was another important figure in the early Syrian Church. According to tradition he was born in 154, became a Christian in 179, and died in 222. Bardaisan was a philosopher in the court of Abgar VIII, the Christian king of Edessa. He may have been the first person to write Christian hymns in Syriac.

Bardaisan opposed Marcionism for which he was praised in the West. However, the praise was not without reservation. He was accused of being a Gnostic. While the charge against him may not have been entirely accurate, he apparently did promote a syncretistic form of philosophy that drew inspiration from a variety of sources including Oriental astrology, Gnosticism, Hellenistic philosophy, etc. The expression of this syncretistic mish-mash is not found in his extant writings, but in those of his chief opponent, the 4th century Church Father called Ephrem the Syrian.

Bardaisan's one surviving work is entitled *On Fate* or *The Book of the Laws of the Countries*. This work was actually written by a disciple of his in the form of a series of questions that had been addressed to Bardaisan and answered by him.

In evaluating the theology of the earliest Christian thinkers, it is important to remember that they lived in an era before the establishment of "orthodoxy" had been established. Even the canon of Scripture was still in flux.

---

[2] James Hamlyn Hill, *The Earliest Life of Christ Ever Compiled From the Four Gospels, Being the Diatessaron of Tatian* (Edinburgh: T & T Clark, 2001).
[3] The Encratites were against marriage because they believed that it resulted in more evil people in the world. Butler et al., *Churchfails*, 33.

On Fate's main theme is not heretical. Bardaisan affirmed that human actions are determined by a variety of causes, e.g. nature, destiny, and free-will. He rejected a fatalism that denied the reality of human free-will. He affirmed that while there are other factors that contribute to how we make our decisions and live our lives, Christians have a significant measure of free-will to make right decisions and live right lives.

According to one tradition, Bardaisan was expelled from the church in Edessa because of his heretical ideas. However, two other possibilities exist as to why he left Edessa. He may have lost political favor after the death of King Abgar VIII or he may have been interested in doing missionary work in Armenia, where he died.

Armenia, the kingdom to the north of Edessa, was among the first to adopt the Christian faith as the state religion. Legend surrounds the origins of Christianity in Armenia. There is very little credible documentation about the earliest days of Christianity in the kingdom.[4] Many Armenians were already living in places where Christianity was established, particularly Edessa. There appears to have been an informal spread of Christianity in the southern region around Lake Van in the 3rd century. The nobility remained untouched by the gospel until one young noble, Grigor Lusavorich, returned from studying in a Christian school in Cappadocia. A combination of his influence and organizational skills ensured the faith was firmly established among the leaders, including the ruler, Trdat IV. In 301, Christianity was declared the official religion. The faith of Lusavorich was more formal and hierarchical and pushed down the informal expression of Christianity.[5] Still today, the nation of Armenia remains a lone Christian nation amidst of sea of Muslim nations.

As the church became more established in Asia, it began to reflect values more characteristic of Asia (especially when contrasted with the western church). One example is the sense of hospitality in welcoming women, the elderly, and the poor into the church. We can see this in a document called *Didascalia Apostolorum*, "But if a poor man or woman should come… and especially if they are stricken in years, and there be no place for such, do thou, O bishop, with all thy heart provide a place for them even if thou have

---

[4] Among popular legends are that the two apostles, Bartholomew and Thaddeus, brought the gospel to Armenia. But there is little to substantiate this claim. Payaslian, *The History of Armenia*, 34.

[5] Payaslian, 34–36.

to sit upon the ground."[6] Although not as well known, the early church in Asia exhibited a deep and transformative faith.

1.2 The Church in the Parthian and Persian Empires

The Beginnings and Golden Age of the Persian Church

The Parthian Empire spread from Mesopotamia to the borders of India. According to one legend, Addai brought Christianity into this area near the end of the first century. He came to the city of Arbil (or Abela) which was about 300 miles east of Edessa. Arbil was the capitol of the small Adiabene Kingdom and later became chief city of a province in Parthian Empire. (Today the city is called Erbil and is in the Kurdistan area of Iraq.)

Addai's first convert in Arbil was Paqida, the son of a slave. The date of his conversion is traditionally given as the year 99. Paqida's parents objected to his new faith. To escape persecution, Addai and Paqida fled the city.

Paqida lived with Addai for five years, after which time Addai ordained him and sent him back to Arbil as its first bishop. While the title "bishop'" in modern times is usually reserved for someone who exercises authority over a large number of believers, the title was given in ancient times to those missionaries who were sent to establish a church over which it was supposed they would afterwards exercise the authority of bishop. A modern-day equivalent might be called a church planting pastor.

Paqida is called the first bishop of Arbil. He died in 114, apparently of natural causes.

The second bishop was Samsun. He had been a deacon under Paqida. It was several years after Paqida died before another bishop visited Arbil and ordained Samsun as that city's bishop. He served in that capacity from 120 to 123.

Most of the evangelistic work of this early church took place in the mountains and countryside outside Arbil, as the city was too dangerous for extended work. The predominant religion in the empire was Zoroastrianism. Its priests opposed the spread of Christianity.

---

[6] Moffett, *A History of Christianity in Asia*, 79.

One custom of this area was the offering of a child sacrifice during the Spring festival. This was apparently a local adaptation and not truly part of Zoroastrianism, and Samsun preached against the practice. Because of his evangelistic work many people were baptized.

Our knowledge of the early church in Arbil comes from a document entitled *Chronicle of Arbil*. Here is its description of Samsun's martyrdom.

> Samsun preached to them during two years, and baptized a large number. The Christian faith spread widely in their countryside. When the nobles and Zoroastrian priest heard of this, they put Samsun in chains, tortured him severely, and cut off his head.[7]

In the Parthian Empire, Christians always led a precarious existence. The cities were especially dangerous. Severe persecutions broke out in 160 and 179. However, when the Persians took control of the Empire in 225, the Church experienced a period of peace. In spite of persecution, the Church continued to spread within that Parthian Empire—mostly in the Mesopotamia region. By 225, there were 17 sees (that is, places of a bishop's authority) as well as other bishops scattered throughout the Empire.

Before proceeding to talk about some important persons and events during the 400+ years of existence of the Persian Empire, we need to take a further look at the continuing significance of asceticism in the Syrian Church (hereafter called the Church of the East). We have briefly looked at Tatian and the Encratites. Now we turn to the Sons and Daughters of the Covenant.

This movement began to flourish by the third century and lasted for several centuries. The Sons and Daughters of the Covenant (or simply Covenanters) existed in ascetic communities. They were inheritors of the ascetic tradition that stressed abstinence from possessions, wine, and sex. Some scholars have suggested that this movement was so strong that in this early period only Christians who were not married were considered fully Christian. Those with families would have been on the fringes of the Church. Today, the extent of the asceticism cannot be proven; however, it is true that the elevation of

---

[7] Foster, *First Advance: Church History 1: AD 29-500*, 93.

celibacy was more prominent in the East than in the West. In the East, sexual abstinence was encouraged of married persons as well.

While many (including the authors) would disapprove of this devaluing of sexuality, we should not overlook the positive features of this ascetic movement. Specifically, in the area of missionary outreach, the Covenanters had a great impact throughout Asia. In contrast to the early ascetics in the church to the west, these eastern ascetics were called to preach the gospel and serve the needy. The ascetic was under obligation to "traverse the cities and villages as traveling missionaries, expanding the gospel and strengthening the small communities."[8] This they did; as did later monastic communities of the Church of the East.

Under Persian rule, the situation of the Church at first improved. Although Zoroastrianism became the state religion, Christians were largely left alone.

It was during these early years in the Persian Empire that the Church of the East was established in the capital city of Ctesiphon (about fifty kilometers from modern day Baghdad). We do not know when Christianity first came to Ctesiphon, but a small group of Christians was living there by 270, but they had no bishop. Between 280 and 290, the bishops of Arbil and Susa ordained the priest of Ctesiphon as its first bishop. His name became Papa bar-Aggai.

Without going into the sad details, after much infighting, Bishop Papa attained an agreement, at the Synod of Acacius, that affirmed the primacy of the Bishop of Seleucia-Ctesiphon around 315.[9] Bishop Papa died in 327. The beginning of the national Persian Church as an expression of the Church of the East is credited to the striving of Bishop Papa, however wrongly motivated.

In order to help explain the great persecution that was to engulf the Church of the East in the coming years, it is important to note some of what was going on in the Roman Empire. Although Rome and Persia were not constantly fighting, these rival empires were enemies for several centuries.

---

[8] Moffett, *A History of Christianity in Asia*, 100.
[9] The primacy of a particular bishop meant a higher level of authority over surrounding churches in matters of the faith.

In 311 or 312, Constantine, who was to become the undisputed emperor of the Roman Empire, affirmed an allegiance to the Christian faith. While this was good news for the Christians in the west, it created increasing problems for the Christians in Persia, who remained a minority population. In addition to being opposed by the Zoroastrian religious leaders, they were distrusted as possible supporters of Persia's mortal enemy – Rome. The fact that Constantine wrote a letter to the Emperor of Persia calling on him to protect the Christians in his realm probably only made matters worse.

Representatives from the Church of the East attended the Council of Nicaea in 325. These included Jacob of Nisibis and a bishop from Ctesiphon. These eastern Christians agreed with the majority in rejecting the teachings of Arius. However, the attendance of a bishop from Persia at a council called by the Emperor of Rome probably cast further doubts in the minds of Persian authorities on the Church's allegiances.

In 339, a state-sponsored persecution was promulgated against Christians living in the Persian Empire. On Good Friday, the Bishop of Seleucia-Ctesiphon was forced to watch 100 of his members martyred. Then Shimun (or Simon) the second Bishop of Ctesiphon was put to death only after refusing to pay double taxes and a bribe from the shah in 344. This was the beginning of 40 years of persecution, the likes of which the Church in the west never experienced. In the West, persecution came in short waves and rarely had empire-wide sanction. According to one Greek historian,

> The number of men and women whose names are known as martyred has been counted at sixteen thousand. But beyond those is a multitude too great to be counted whose names have not been listed.[10]

Two important thinkers call for our attention as we move through the 4th century. One of them is clearly a member of that Syrian language Church of the East in the Persian Empire. His name is Aphrahat (Aphraates in Latin).

We know very few details of his life. He was evidently Assyrian by birth from the northern Mesopotamian region. He was a convert from Zoroastrianism and at one time was a member of the Sons of the Covenant.

---

[10] Foster, *First Advance: Church History 1: AD 29-500*, 99.

According to one tradition, he became bishop of Mar Mattai, a monastery east of the Tigris River.

Only one writing of his has survived. Called *Demonstrations* it contains 23 essays that were written between 336 and 345. They deal with a wide range of topics including faith, wars, monks, resurrection of the dead, pastors, Christ the Son of God, persecution, death, and the latter times.[11] Perhaps to keep others from adding to his work, the 23 essays each begin with a succeeding letter of the Syrian alphabet, which had 23 letters.

Aphrahat was not a Greek theologian. He had not learned from the thinkers of the western church like Tertullian and Origen. His language is not influenced by the debates that troubled the west. Thus, in his discussion of Christ, he does not use the two-nature language of the Greeks. In arguing against the Jews who oppose the Christian worship of the man Jesus, Aphrahat affirms that Jesus was indeed a man. However, exalted titles were given to men in the Old Testament. They were even called God or Gods (Ex.7:1; Ps. 82:6). And though the Jews say that God has no son, Solomon is called God's son (2 Sam.7:14) and Israel is called God's first-born (Ex.4:22-23). So applying these exalted names to Jesus is not a novel thing. It is right, Aphrahat affirms, that we should worship Jesus through whom we have known God and by whom our minds were converted from error.

Those of us raised on the two-nature model of Christology may not find this explanation entirely satisfying. However, we should recognize its apologetic character. Aphrahat's discussion is peppered with extensive quotations from the Jewish scriptures in a way that reminds us of the early apostolic preaching.

Syriac is similar to ancient Hebrew in that 'spirit' is a feminine noun. Thus, the old Syrian translation of John 14:26 reads, "The Spirit, the Paraclete, she shall teach you everything."[12] Similarly, Aphrahat regularly refers to the Holy Spirit as female. In writing to affirm the value of virginity, he noted:

> We have heard it from the law that a man will leave his
> father and his mother and will cleave to his wife, and they

---

[11] Donaldson and Roberts, *Ante Nicene Fathers: The Writings of the Fathers Down to Ad 325: Volume 8.*

[12] Burkitt, *Early Eastern Christianity St. Margaret's Lectures, 1904 on the Syriac-Speaking Church*, 88.

will be one flesh; and truly a prophecy great and excellent is this. What father and mother doth he forsake that taketh a wife? This is the meaning: that when a man not yet hath taken a wife, he loveth and honoreth God his Father, and the Holy Spirit his Mother, and he hath no other love. But when a man taketh a wife he forsaketh his Father and his Mother.[13]

While the above passage is used to illustrate Aphrahat's understanding of the Spirit, it also reveals his ascetic tendencies. It is only fair, however, to note that as a church leader, he did recognize the validity of marriage of the normal Christian.

Finally, two quotes from his essay on faith.

Jesus Christ is the foundation of all our faith. And on Him, on [this] Stone faith is based. And resting on faith all the structure rises until it is completed. For it is the foundation that is laid for him upon the Stone, that is our Lord Jesus Christ. And this building cannot be shaken by the waves, nor can it be injured by the winds.[14]

Now this is faith; when a man believes in God the Lord of all, Who made the heavens and the earth and the seas and all that is in them; and He made Adam in His image; and He gave the Law to Moses; He sent of His Spirit upon the prophets; He sent moreover His Christ into the world. Furthermore that a man should believe in the resurrection of the dead; and should furthermore believer in the sacrament of baptism. This is the faith of the Church of God. And (it is necessary) that a man should separate himself from the observance of hours and Sabbaths and moons and seasons, and divinations and sorceries and Chaldean arts and magic, from fornication and from festive music, from vain doctrines, which are instruments of the Evil One, from the blandishment of honeyed words, from

---

[13] Burkitt, 89.
[14] Schaff and Wace, *A Select Library of Nicene and Post-Nicene Fathers of the Christian Church, Second Series*, Vol. 13:346.

> blasphemy and from adultery. And that a man should not speak with a double tongue. These then are the works of faith which is based on the true Stone which is Christ, on Whom the whole building is reared up.[15]

The second key figure from this period is Ephrem (or Ephraim). He is one of the few Syriac writers who is considered a saint by both the eastern and western churches. As we shall see, he was not technically a part of the Persian Church, but his influence in the Church of the East was enormous.

Ephrem was born in 306 in the city of Nisibis (modern Nusaybin, Turkey). His parents were Christian and apparently martyred. He became a Son of the Covenant and never married. He may have been ordained later in life as a deacon.

Bishop Jacob of Nisibis (who attended the Council of Nicaea) started a theological school in which Ephrem became the head teacher. Jacob, from an early age, had removed himself from society by living in wilderness as an ascetic monk.[16] In 306, he was called to serve as a bishop in Nisibis. At this time Nisibis was within the boundaries of the Roman Empire though Syriac was the language of the area.

In 363, The Persians captured Nisibis, but allowed the Christians who so desired to immigrate to the Roman Empire. Ephrem and most of the Christians moved to the Roman city of Edessa. There Ephrem continued a teaching ministry until his death in 373. He died a month after leading the effort to assist the poor during a severe famine.

As already noted, Ephrem was respected in both the east and the west. His orthodoxy was never in doubt. He opposed Arians, Marcionites, Manichaeans, and Gnostics (including the followers of Bardaisan). He wrote commentaries on the Old Testament and the *Diatessaron*, as well a great deal of poetry. Hymns and prayers attributed to him are still used in all Syrian-oriented churches from the Middle East to India.

---

[15] Schaff and Wace, Vol. 13:352.

[16] It is said that Jacob wore no clothes and even refused to warm himself by a fire. Moffett, *A History of Christianity in Asia*, 123.

Apparently Ephrem chose to write in poetic form because heretics were leading people astray by setting their teachings to music that could be sung by the multitudes. Ephrem countered this by writing his own poetry, using the same tunes, and having them sung by a choir of nuns. This earned him the nickname, "the harp of the Holy Spirit."[17]

Most scholars have not been impressed by Ephrem's poetic talents. His poems are filled with fantastic, typological connections. He seemed to have believed it was better to add an image than to omit one. Yet, Ephrem's work of putting his teachings into poetic form and singing set a precedent that has characterized Syrian Christianity ever since.[18] In spite of the tediousness of his writing, his orthodox theology and love of Christ and love for the poor are clear. Ephrem was caring for those sick from the plague when he died in 373.

The Persian Church in the Wake of Severe Persecution

Several events in the fifth century had significant impact on the Church of the East's self-image.

First, in 424, a council of Persian bishops affirmed that the bishops of the Roman Empire had no authority over the Persian Church. This was a confirmation of what had in fact been true for several decades. Nevertheless, the official declaration was important in claiming independence from the western Church.

The second event occurred in 431. A council of bishops meeting in Ephesus condemned the teachings of Nestorius. This caused a division in the Church that has endured until the present day.

Nestorius was a Syrian by birth. He was educated at Antioch and entered a monastery there. In 428 he was appointed as the patriarch of Constantinople. Arriving there, he inflamed the people by refusing to use the title 'mother of God' (Gr, *Theotokos*) for Mary. Having been trained in Antioch, he preferred to use more biblically justified titles like "mother of Christ" (Gr. *Christokos*).

---

[17] Sunquist, *Explorations in Asian Christianity*, 34.
[18] MacCulloch, *Christianity*, 183.

The bishop of Alexandria, Cyril, entered the fray and accused Nestorius of teaching that Christ was two persons – one divine and one human. While this seems not to have been the case, a council was called to Ephesus to settle the matter. To make a long and sordid story short, it may just be noted that the bishops led by Cyril condemned the teachings of Nestorius before the bishops who supported him could arrive from Antioch. In many respects, Nestorius was a casualty of church politics between Alexandrian influence and Antiochan influence.

For the next twenty years the Church continued to be torn by conflicts between the two parties. Finally, in 451, a council of bishops met at Chalcedon (on the Asian side of modern-day Istanbul) and declared that Christ was one person who had two natures – truly divine and truly human. The council affirmed the condemnation of Nestorius's "teaching" although he himself wrote that the decision of the council was in fact what he had taught.[19]

Many of the followers of Cyril rejected the council because they wanted to emphasize the deity of Christ, believing an overemphasis on Christ's humanity detracted from his divinity. This party eventually was called Monophysite, which means "one nature." They taught that Christ had only one nature and that nature was divine.

Thus, the church in the East was fractured into three groups: Monophysites, Nestorians, and those in full agreement with the Council of Chalcedon. Although Monophysites and Nestorians were both condemned because of the council's decision, they remained mortal enemies. Their place of constant struggle was in Syria. Eventually the western part of Syria from Edessa became Monophysite. East of Edessa, the Syriac language churches became Nestorian.

In 486, the Bishop (or Patriarch) of Seleucia-Ctesiphon, Aqaq (or Acacius) called a synod of bishops. At this synod two important decisions were made. First, they adopted a confession of faith that was in effect Nestorian in its rejection of Monophysite theology.

---

[19] Historians are divided on Nestorius' true views on the matter. The lack of primary sources from Nestorius make the matter difficult to settle. For good discussion on Nestorius' Christology, see Justo L González, *A History of Christian Thought: Volume 1: From the Beginnings to the Council of Chalcedon*, 2nd ed. (Nashville: Abingdon Press, 1987), 353–67.

The second decision was the synod's affirmation that priests and bishops could be married. This decision clearly offended the western Church and made the division between them and the Church of the East even wider.

Another event actually preceded the Synod of Aqaq. Around 470 the ancient theological school of Nisibis was reestablished. The founder of the reestablished school was Bishop Barsaume. Barsaume had been a professor at the School of the Persians in Edessa, which may have been started by Ephrem when he moved from Nisibis to Edessa.

In 457, the Monophysites took control of the church in Edessa, so Barsaume and other 'Nestorian' scholars fled. Barsaume became Bishop of Nisibis. He convinced Narsai, the former head teacher of the School of the Persians, to become the head teacher of the new school in Nisibis.

In 489, the Monophysites forced the closing of the School of the Persians in Edessa and the last refuge of Nestorianism in the Roman Empire came to an end. Many of the students of that school were then welcomed at Nisibis. This school eventually became the most important center for theological education in the Church of the East. At its peak in the late 6th century, over 1000 students were enrolled.

Scripture was at the heart of the curriculum. Bible knowledge was emphasized. The students were trained in the literal, historical exegetical method that had been popularized by the school at Antioch. The importance of the Bible is seen in the title of the school director. He was always called simply "Interpreter of Scripture."

Discipline was an important part of student life. In some ways the school resembled a monastery. Upon entering the school, the students had to leave the life of the world. For example, they took vows of celibacy for as long as they were enrolled. They studied from daybreak to dark. From August to October they did various forms of labor to earn their keep. The penalty for breaking any rule was immediate expulsion.

Missions was a primary emphasis. Narsai affirmed the missionary lives of Peter and Paul and the missionary command given to the Church by Christ. Many of the graduates of the school became missionaries to places even further east.

Despite the church never receiving state sanction, the church in Persia persisted over centuries. We gain a glimpse into the Persian church during the mid-to-late 6th century through Mar Aba I, Patriarch of the Church of East Persia. Once an ardent pagan who reviled Christians and joined in their persecution, he was saved through the humble and gentle witness of an ascetic Christian. After studying the scriptures at the school in Nisibis, Mar Aba travelled to Constantinople to preach Nestorianism, and was ultimately appointed Metropolitan in Persia.[20] By this time, the Persian rulers had come to see the Christian population as significant enough to help moderate the control wielded by the Zoroastrian priests. Mar Aba, having Persian noble status and pagan roots in early life, was able to give the church deeper footing in Persian society.[21]

1.3 India, Central Asia, and China

The Spread of the Church into India

No one knows when Christianity arrived in India. Local oral traditions and later written legendary material trace its origins back to the Apostolic age, crediting the Apostle Thomas with bringing the gospel to India is Thomas.

Two different traditions exist relating Thomas to India. One is found in a Syriac language work called *The Acts of Thomas*.[22] It was likely produced in Edessa in the 3rd or 4th century. This work contains much legendary material, but it does correlate with certain historical realities of 1st century northern India.

According to *The Acts*, Thomas was sent to India by the resurrected Jesus. He went as a carpenter and agreed to build a palace for King Gundaphor. He received the money to do so, but gave it away to the poor. When the king asked to see his palace, Thomas told him that he would see it in heaven. The

---

[20] This was no light undertaking, as Emperor Justinian had called for all bishops in the empire to adhere strictly to the conclusions of Chalcedon. Olson, *The Story of Christian Theology*, 244.

[21] Anonymous, "Life of Mar Aba: English Translation with Introduction," ed. Roger Pearse, 2013, http://www.tertullian.org/fathers/life_of_mar_aba_0_intro.htm.

[22] A translation of this work is found in Donaldson and Roberts, *Ante Nicene Fathers: The Writings of the Fathers Down to Ad 325: Volume 8*.

king was not impressed, and had Thomas thrown into prison. Later the king's brother, who had died, appeared to the king in a vision, saying that a palace had been prepared in heaven for the king. Immediately the king released Thomas, heard the gospel, and believed. Thomas led many others to Christ, traveling throughout India before being martyred, possibly near the modern city of Chennai.

It may be noted that *The Acts* contains the ascetic emphasis we have noted earlier as present in the Syrian Church. Thomas was martyred because he had convinced the queen and leading ladies of a southern kingdom to embrace celibacy. The king was incensed and ordered Thomas executed by soldiers.

In the 19th and 20th centuries the discovery of ancient coins and other artifacts established the fact that a King Gundaphor did rule in northern India during the 1st century. Further discoveries in the modern era have also proven that commercial travel from the Roman Empire to India was present during the first two centuries after the birth of Christ. However, there are no inscriptions on his coins which would indicate an adherence to the Christian faith.

The southern tradition which tells of the coming of Thomas to the Malabar coast (modern Kerala) is largely found in the oral traditions of the Syrian Orthodox Church which has long existed in that region. According to this tradition, Thomas arrived by ship in the middle of the 1st century. He converted thousands, travelled across southern India, and was finally martyred at Mylapore by angry Hindu priests. There is a tomb in Mylapore, a city south of Chennai, which is claimed to be that of Thomas.

All one can say is that either tradition is possible, and perhaps they are not mutually exclusive. Today at least 6 different denominations in India with a combined membership of over one million trace their roots back to Thomas.

Other names associated with an early Christian witness to India include Pantaenus, a bishop from Basra named David, John the Persian, and Thomas of Cana.

According to the 4th century Church historian Eusebius, Pantaenus left his position as head teacher at the school in Alexandria and went to India around 180. He reportedly found that the Apostle Bartholomew had preceded him there.

A Syrian document from the 7th or 8th century reports that Bishop David of Basra went to India around 300 to spread the Christian faith. Basra is a city on the Persian Gulf (in modern day Iraq) and would have been a city linked to India by a trade route.

John the Persian's name is listed on the role of bishops at the Council of Nicaea (325) who accepted the council's rejection of Arianism. He was there as a representative of the churches of Persia and India. It may be assumed that Bishop John lived in Persia but had ecclesiastical authority over the churches of India.

In 345 Thomas of Cana, a merchant (perhaps Armenian), led a group of around 400 Syrian Christians to the western shore of southern India (modern Kerala). They probably were fleeing from the great persecution experienced in the Persian Empire at that time. He received formal grants from a local king, which were attested on copper-plates found by the Portuguese many centuries later.

In summary, we can say that a Christian presence was established in India by the 4th century and perhaps much earlier.[23]

The ancient Church in India used the Syriac language and at least by the late 4th or early 5th century, was ecclesiastically connected with the Persian Church. At first they were under the jurisdiction of the Bishop of Rewardashir (a city located on the Persian Gulf). They sent their priests to study in Persia, where their education would have included the traditional teachings of Nestorianism. Centuries later, the Portuguese Catholics would be incensed that the Thomas Christians of India refused to call Mary "the Mother of God."

The church in India continued to grow until in the 7th century a new metropolitanate was created for India itself. Traditionally, a metropolitan had at least 6 bishops under his authority. This gave the church in India greater independence and established a stronger Indian Christian identity.

---

[23] Neill recognizes that Christians in South India are convinced that the founder of the church in India was the apostle Thomas, but there is not sufficient historical evidence to confirm or deny this belief. Neill, *A History of Christianity in India*, 49.

The Spread of the Church of the East into Central and Southwest Asia

The geography of the vast Central Asian land mass made possible the flow of peoples, trade, and ideas. "The open spaces of Central Asia have often been likened to a great sea, so easily do they permit passage without necessary change in the means of transport, and the camel and the horse, both native to the region and capable of domestication, became the ships respectively of the desert and the steppe."[24] The ease of movement held great potential for the spread of the Christian faith across the continent. But this ease of movement for the Christian faith also made it more vulnerable to syncretism and persecution.

While Christians may have existed in Central Asia earlier, it is only in the 6th century that we can be certain of their presence, in the area called Bactria along the River Oxus (present day Amu Darya River), where the Huns (also called Turks and White Huns) lived.

Two events bought the gospel to the peoples of Central Asia. One was the exile of the Persian king after a successful revolt against his reign. The king fled to the Huns. He was not a Christian, but two of those who accompanied him were. They apparently settled there, married locals, and promoted Christianity.

The second event was the coming of Qaradushat (Karaduset, c. 6th century) as a missionary to the region. He was a Nestorian Bishop from Aran, in eastern Armenia. He came with a small group of priests to minister to Roman (or Byzantine) soldiers who had been captured by the Huns and, if possible, to convert the Huns.

These two events combined had an enormous impact. An alphabet for the illiterate Huns was prepared using Syrian letters. The scripture was eventually translated.

Fourteen years later, when Qaradushat died, another bishop came from Armenia. His name was Makarios. He helped to teach the nomadic Huns agricultural methods so they could plant crops and settle down.

---

[24] East, *The Geography Behind History*, 57.

Interestingly, the theological disagreements which were causing such hardship in west Asia, were not considered so important in central Asia during these early missions endeavors. Makarios was a Monophysite (believing in only distinction Christ's divine nature).

Due to the rise of Islam and continuous political turmoil, information about the continuing growth of the Church of the East has to be pieced together. We have letters from the Patriarch of the Church as he sent out more missionaries or established new bishoprics and metropolitans. We also know that Christian merchants plied their trade along a route called the Silk Road that ran from central Persia to China. All of the major cities in central Asia along that route eventually had significant Christian populations – though probably always in the minority. There is archeological evidence of church buildings and Christian monasteries in key cities throughout Central Asia. One church building in the once prominent city of Merv (Mary, its ruins are in modern day Turkmenistan)[25] appears to have been constructed in the 6th century and was used until the 11th or 12th centuries.[26] It had been a major Nestorian center and metropolitan see (similar to the seat of the archbishop) until it was attacked by the "Golden Horde," when untold thousands were killed.[27] Afrasiyab (now Samarkand in Uzbekistan) was the location of the Metropolitan church established in the 5th century; coins with crosses on them have even been discovered in this city.[28] Although archeological exploration has been very difficult in the region for myriad reasons, there is mounting evidence of Christian presence all along the various routes of the Silk Road.

---

[25] Merv was a large and influential oasis city on a Silk road. In the 12th century Merv was possibly the largest city in the world with more than half a million residents. There was consistent Christian presence in the city for at least five centuries. Genghis Khan's army brought a complete end to the city, perhaps killing 700,000 people. The site has been recently excavated after the dissolution of the Soviet Union. Barraclough and Parker, *The Times Atlas of World History*, 101; Herrmann, "A Central Asian City on the Silk Road."

[26] Maria Adelaide Lala Comnemo, "Nestorianism in Central Asia during the First Millennium: Archaeological Evidence," *Journal of the Assyrian Academic Society*, n.d., 27.

[27] Gorder, *Muslim-Christian Relations in Central Asia*, 51.

[28] Comnemo, "Nestorianism in Central Asia during the First Millennium: Archaeological Evidence," 33–34.

Thus, in places now governed by the modern nations of Turkmenistan, Afghanistan, Uzbekistan, Kyrgyzstan, and Tajikistan, the Church of the East had been established. Apparently, a Christian presence had also reached Tibet, for in the 8th century, the Patriarch Timothy I appointed a bishop for that country. By the 10th century monasteries could be found across Central Asia linked to the trade route from Persia to China. Such monasteries served not only for worship and evangelism but also as inns for the Christian merchants traveling through; they also provided medical care and ran schools. In this way Christianity "began to seep into the local life of central Asia."[29]

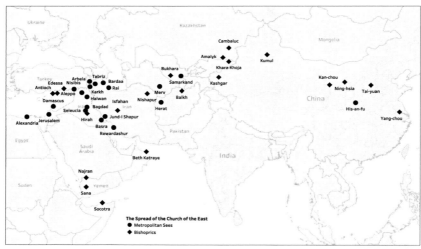

Figure 1: Metropolitan Sees and Bishoprics to the East, ca. 1000[30]

The spread of Christianity even made it to Mongolia. A tribe in Western Mongolia, the Keraits, were converted to Christ in the 11th century and influenced Mongolian elites.[31]

---

[29] Irvin and Sunquist, *History of the World Christian Movement*, 305.

[30] Map was created by Minh Ha Nquyen.

[31] Comnemo, "Nestorianism in Central Asia during the First Millennium: Archaeological Evidence," 27.

Even after Islam swept through the Arab world (Southwest Asia) the church continued to have a significant presence for a few centuries.[32] There were established Metropolitan Bishops who continued serve the church from key cities in the region (i.e. Baghdad and Damascus). The church sought to engage their Muslim rulers with the gospel and even establish the church in the midst of Muslim strongholds.

One figure of note is Timothy 1 (ca. 778-821, sometimes called Timotheus), Nestorian Patriarch in Baghdad who proved to be a gifted diplomat, able administrator, and had a wide vision for the spread of the church. The all-powerful Caliph, based in Mosul, called Timothy 1 into debate. The Caliph said it was a shame that Christians, otherwise respectable would believe that God married a woman and begat a son. Timothy agreed that this was blasphemy, "Who would say such a thing?" He added, "Christ is the Son of God—not, however, 'in the carnal way.'"[33] Timothy went toe to toe with the Caliph on a number of issues, always gentle and respectful, but firm in the Scriptures, Trinitarian doctrine and uniqueness of Christ. Timothy also handled divisions within the church, both of political and doctrinal natures.

Missionary orientation of the church in this time can also be seen in Timothy as he sought to establish churches in places where Christianity did not yet have a foothold. His desire was for Christians to share "the pearl" of the gospel with Muslims and pagans.[34] He appointed a missionary bishop to San'a, Yemen as well as among the Turks and in the Caspian region. During the next three centuries, Christianity continued to grow and formed majorities in Syria, Iraq and Khurasan (modern day Turkmenistan). It was not until the thirteenth and fourteenth centuries that the church in these regions declined.[35]

---

[32] Lewis describes the dramatic shift that took place with Islam: "Within little more than a century after the Prophet's death, the whole area had been transformed, in what was surely one of the swiftest and most dramatic changes in the whole of human history." Lewis, *The Middle East*, 55.

[33] Not all Bishops were as pleasant or tactful in their debates with Islamic clerics. John of Damascus (ca. 675-749) was far more polemical in his disagreement with Islam. In particular, he wrote against Islam, which raised the tensions between Christians and Muslims. Moffett, *A History of Christianity in Asia*, 342–43, 349–50.

[34] Moffett quotes Timothy further: "God has placed the pearl of His face before all of us like the shining rays of the sun, and every one who wishes can enjoy the light of the sun." Moffett, 353.

[35] Latourette, *The Thousand Years of Uncertainty 500 A.D. to 1500 A.D.*, 274–75.

Spread of the Church to China

Around 1625 a carved stone slab was discovered in China, about 50 miles from Xian. It had been erected according to the date on it in 781. It tells about a new religion that had entered China, and describes its beginning and its beliefs. This new religion was Christianity as represented by the Church of the East. Since that time manuscripts have been discovered, containing liturgies and theological writings produced by some of the leaders of this church in the ensuing centuries.

The stone carving (known as the Nestorian Monument), a public monument three meters in height, tells the story of a Persian monk named Alopen (Aluoben) who came to the Chinese city of Ch'ang-an (modern Xian) in 635.[36] At this time, Ch'ang-an, imperial capital of the Tang dynasty, was one of the largest cities in the world and, being at the center of major trade routes, was rather cosmopolitan.[37] The emperor

The Nestorian Monument at Siganfu (Hsi-an-fu). It was set up in the days of the Nestorian Catholicus and Patriarch, Mar Henan Isho (died A.D. 780) and was unveiled on February 4 following (A.D. 781).

Figure 2: Nestorian Monument

---

[36] This stone carving had basic Christian teachings, a history of Christianity in China, and a cultural apologetic for Christianity as good for the Chinese kingdom. One portion included this: "If there is only a Way [Tao] and no Sage, it [the Tao] will not expand. If there is a Sage and no Way, nothing great will result. When a Way and Sage are found together, then the whole Empire is cultured and enlightened." Sunquist, *Explorations in Asian Christianity*, 14.

[37] This vast metropolis was once the capital of the Han dynasty (206 BCE- 220 CE) and emerged again as capital of the Sui dynasty (581-617 CE) and grew to its height during the Tang dynasty (618-906 CE). During the time of the Tang dynasty Ch'ang-

welcomed Alopen and allowed him to build a church and a monastery. Within three years, 21 monks were in China, though it is unlikely that any of these monks were Chinese. One of the works of the early years was the translation of the scripture (or portions of it) from Syriac into Chinese. There is strong evidence of Christian presence in the Uighur region (now Xinjiang, Western China), particularly in the city of Turfan.[38]

Alopen was most certainly not the first Christian to enter China, since Christian merchants had been traveling the Silk Road for many years. In fact, Syrian Christian artifacts have been discovered throughout China, stretching even to the east coast. According to the carved stone, monasteries were built in every province of China.

Although little is known of Christianity in China during this time, we have evidence of the growth of the Church in China as the cities of Dunhuang, Ch'ang-an, and Beijing were designated as metropolitans by the Patriarchs of the Church of the East.

In subsequent centuries the Church in China experienced alternating times of peace and persecution. Finally, in the middle of the 9th century, Confucians instigated the persecution of all 'foreign' religions, including Buddhism and Christianity. All monks were forced to leave their monasteries. By the 10th century Christianity had apparently disappeared from China.

The Church of the East returned to China in the 13th century when the Mongols established their own dynasty over China – and indeed much of Asia. Many of the tribes allied with the Mongols had significant numbers of Christians. In fact, one of the daughters-in-law of Genghis Khan was a Christian.

Four events from this period shed light on the return of Christianity in China by way of Mongolia.

The first is the coming of Marco Polo in the latter part of the 13th century to China. His accounts of his travels in China include descriptions of numerous

---

an was likely the largest and most advanced city in the world and the center an expansive empire. Wright, "Changan," 143–44.

[38] Tang, "A History of Uighur Religious Conversions (5th-16th Centuries)," 40.

Christian communities spread throughout the country. The majority were in the northwest along the old Silk Road, but there were also significant numbers along the coast and in the southeast.

Polo's report encouraged the western Church to send missionaries to the lands of the east. John of Montecorvino (1246-c.1330) was a Franciscan missionary who served in Persia which was at that time ruled by the Mongols. Later he was sent to China, arriving in Beijing around 1294. This was the second event of importance. His work was opposed by the Nestorian Christians; however, he was allowed to build a church in Beijing in 1299. This division of Christians did not help their cause in China.

One of his converts was a ruler of the Ongut tribe who left the Church of the East for the Catholic Church. The Ongut tribe had many Nestorian (Church of the East) Christians among them. The third event begins in 1245 with the birth of a son to a deacon of the Church of the East in a province west of Beijing. The son's name was Mark. It is likely that Mark was of this Ongut tribe.

At the age of 23 he gave away his possessions and became a monk in Beijing. When he was 30, he and another friend started on a pilgrimage to Jerusalem. Because of raging wars, they were never able to reach their goal. They eventually stayed at a monastery in Arbil (Arbela) and made many contacts with the Syrian Christians of Persia.

In an amazing turn of events, the Patriarch died and the bishops chose Mark as their new Patriarch. They were obviously impressed by his holiness and dedication. This was in 1281. Mark was 35 years old and apparently spoke very little Syriac. However, he accepted the position and took the name Yaballah III. He served for 36 years, dying in 1317. He is considered the last great Patriarch of the Church of the East.

Returning to China; it can be said with some degree of certainty that between 1289 and 1320, 72 churches existed in China and in 1330 there were over 30,000 Christians. These figures do not include Catholic numbers, which would have been far fewer.

The fourth event halted the spread of the Christian faith in China. The Mongol dynasty fell in 1368 to the Ming dynasty, a more Chinese-centered dynasty. The Church disappeared for a second time in China. "Indeed," describes Latourette, "so completely did Christianity disappear in China that we do not know either the date or the manner of its demise."[39] We can only assume that the disappearance was a combination of conversions to Confucianism – the religion of the Chinese – and the desolations caused by the war.

1.4 Reasons for the Weakening and/or Disappearance of the Church of the East

The Church of the East completely disappeared from China, Tibet, and Central Asia in the fourteenth century. It became very weak in the Middle East. It only maintained its strength in India. What are the causes of this massive loss of Christianity in Asia? At least five suggestions have been offered to account for this fact.

First, in China, the converts were primarily from nomadic tribes. To the Chinese, it always appeared as a foreign religion; and during the Mongol reign, it was a foreign religion supported by a hated foreign dynasty.

The second reason relates to the strict asceticism promoted by the Church of the East. Celibacy was often presented as the highest form of Christianity. The ascetics were vigorous in doing missions, but their very lifestyle may have discouraged converts. This would have been particularly true among peoples like the Chinese, where family would have been considered the most important fact of life.

Third, in some places it may have been too syncretistic. In the 20th century thousands of ancient scrolls were found in the cave near the Chinese city of Dunhuang. Most of these were Buddhist, Confucian and Taoist texts. However, eight of them were Christian.

Some of these texts show how Christian expression incorporated Syrian names and Chinese images. The following is an example:

> So God caused the Cool Breeze to come upon a chosen
> young woman called Mo Yan, who had no husband, and
> she became pregnant. The whole world saw this, and

[39] Kenneth Scott Latourette, *A History of Christianity: Volume I: Beginnings to 1500*, Rev. ed. (New York: Harper & Row, 1975), 601.

understood what God had wrought. The power of God is such that it can create a bodily spirit and lead to the clear, pure path of compassion. Mo Yan gave birth to a boy and called him Ye Su, who is the Messiah.[40]

This more or less traditional teaching written with Syrian names and Chinese images is also found in the theological section of the Nestorian Monument mentioned earlier.

Other passages contain a confusing blend of Christianity and other religions. Jesus is presented as saying:

So, Simon, if anyone wants to follow the Way of Triumph they must clear their minds, and set aside all wanting and doing. To be pure and still means to be open to purity and stillness – as a result you can intuit the truth. This means that the light can shine revealing the workings of cause and effect and leading to the place of Peace and Happiness. Simon, know this, I carry myself in strangeness in words that can reach out north, south, east, and west. And if I am everywhere in the world, then I don't know who I am. If I am truly in my words, then I don't know what I signify. If a person has a made-up name, no one really knows who he is. Trying to know and to see are irrelevant. Why is this? People struggle trying to figure it all out. This struggle creates the desire to do something. Doing creates movement which creates anxiety: Then it is impossible to find Rest and Contentment. This is why I teach no wanting and doing without doing. It stops you thinking about things which disturb you. Then you can enter into the source of pure empty being.[41]

In contrast, there is no record of the Bible being translated in Chinese.[42] Lamin Sanneh traces the long-term impact of Bible translation around the world. Sanneh avers that good Bible translation was important for the church

---

[40] Martin Palmer, *The Jesus Sutras: Rediscovering the Lost Scrolls of Taoist Christianity* (New York: Ballantine Books, 2001), 75.
[41] Palmer, 190.
[42] Sunquist, *Explorations in Asian Christianity*, 39.

to be planted deep in various soils: "for a good, successful translation vindicates indigenous claims, while a bad, unsuccessful one justifies the charge of foreign incompetence."[43] Indigeneity without syncretism was of critical importance.

The fourth possible reason for the fall of the Church of the East relates to the liturgy. Apparently, the liturgy continued to be expressed in Syriac; this in spite of the fact that even the Persians could not understand it. We do have a few liturgical pieces that were translated into Chinese. That would have been the case in other places, but the basic worship liturgy remained in Syriac. In fact, there are still churches all over the world that use Syriac liturgy in their services.

The fifth reason, and the one that we believe to be decisive, was persecution and war.

Already mentioned was the Great Persecution in Persia, 339-379. Sixteen thousand names of martyrs were recorded, but some estimates suggest that as many as 190,000 Christians were martyred.[44] Although this was far more intense than the persecutions in the Roman Empire, apparently there were fewer apostates in Persia. Nevertheless, persons of great faith were executed, and many of those left alive may have had a weaker faith.

In the 7th century Arabian Muslims conquered Persia. Christians, at first, were allowed to continue their worship. However, they faced severe restrictions. They were required to live in segregated areas and had to wear a special cloth that identified them as being Christian. They were also doubly taxed. Converting a Muslim was unlawful, and converted Muslims faced the death penalty. Enforcement of these restrictions was uneven and depended on the particular ruler. Nevertheless, the cumulative force of this more passive form of persecution had a telling effect, as newer generations found it more convenient to convert to Islam.

Here is an account by a Muslim of how the laws were executed during the reign of the Caliph al-Muqtadir bi-Amrallah (1180-1225):

---

[43] Lamin Sanneh, *Translating the Message: The Missionary Impact on Culture* (Maryknoll, NY: Orbis Books, 1989), 230.
[44] Moffett, *A History of Christianity in Asia*, 145.

He ordered them to hang bells around their necks and to put wooden effigies on their doors in order to distinguish them from Muslim homes. Their homes were not to be of the same height as those of Muslims. He obliged the Jews to wear a badge and a yellow turban, whereas Jewish women were to wear yellow veils and different colored shoes, one white and the other black. They also had to wear iron necklaces around their necks when they entered the bath houses. As for the Christians, they had to wear black or grey garments, a special belt around the waist, and a cross on their breast. They were not allowed to have a horse as a mount, but only a mule, or an ass without a pack or a saddle, which they were not allowed to ride astride, but on one side only. Although all of this has been abandoned, no increase in tax has been enacted, whereas in most [Muslim] countries they are still forced to wear badges and are admitted to none but the most humiliating employments. This, for example in Bukhara and Samarkand the *dhimmis* [minority status given to non-Muslims in part of the Muslim world] clean out the lavatories and sewers and carry away the rubbish and refuse. In Aleppo, which is the closest to us, . . . when the poll tax is to be paid, the person who delivers the sum must be standing and he who receives it must be seated. The former places it in the other's hand so that the Muslim receives it in the palm of his hand, the Muslim's hand being above and that of the *dhimmi* below. The later then stretches forth his beard and the Muslim strikes him on the cheek with the words: 'Pay the dues of Allah, O enemy of Allah, O infidel'. But today, it even happens that some of them no longer come in person before the officials, but send their messengers in their stead.[45]

In addition to these laws, Christians were occasionally persecuted more violently either by local mobs or by the government. In fairness, it should be noted that, when the tables were temporarily turned, many Christians reacted violently toward their Muslim neighbors. In 1258 Baghdad fell to a Mongol

---

[45] Bat Ye'or, *The Decline of Eastern Christianity under Islam: From Jihad to Dhimmitude; Seventh-Twentieth Century*, English Translation (London: Associated University Presses, 1996), 348.

army led by Hulegu, brother of the Khubilai Khan. Hulegu's wife was a Christian, as was the general of his army. When Damascus fell in 1260, local Christians rejoiced. However, their joy was short-lived, for a reduced Mongol army was defeated by the Egyptians, and Syria returned to Muslim rule.

Gradually the Mongol rulers of western Asia, from Russia to Persia, adopted the Islamic faith, thus sealing the fate of the Church of the East.

In this discussion of wars and persecution, final mention must be made of Timur the Great (Tamerlane) who lived from 1336 until 1405. Hailing from central Asia near Samarkand, he wanted to create an Islamic empire and destroy the infidels–a designation that included not only Christians, but also Muslims who did not share his own particular convictions.[46]

Timur established his empire through some of the most destructive military campaigns ever witnessed. Although the empire did not survive his death, the consequences of his rule were evident from the destruction of whole cities in his empire that stretched from northern India to central Russia to the Middle East. The church which had been strong in some of these cities was very nearly decimated.

The decline of the Church of the East, particularly in Persia can be seen by counting the names of churches that appear in official records. In 1000 CE, 68 churches are named. In 1238 CE, when Hulegu captured Baghdad, 24 are recorded. By the time Timur conquered Persia around 1380, only 7 cities are known for certain to contain churches.[47]

---

[46] Timur was destructive to everyone in his path, even Muslims he claimed to represent, but he was devastating to the church in Asia: "From north to south his new empire slashed diagonally through all the major land trade routes that connected Europe, Syria, and Persia in the West to China in the East. Before he died, this son of small tribal sheep stealers, this Machiavellian prince who fought like a common soldier hand-to-hand in battle with his troops, had conquered and murdered and pillaged his way from Turfan to Damascus and from Delhi almost to Moscow and Constantinople. He had subdued both of the great powers of western Asia—Persia and the fast-rising Ottoman Empire of the Turks. He had defeated Egypt in Syria, the White Horde in Russia, and the sultanate of northern India…. He ploughed deep but left no seed in the furrows, only death." Moffett, *A History of Christianity in Asia*, 484–85.

[47] Moffett, 487.

According to researcher David Barrett, there were 21 million Christians in Asia in the year 1200. This would have included not only members of the Church of the East, but also members of the Syrian Orthodox Church (a Monophysite Church also called Jacobite or West Syrian) and the Armenian Church (also technically a Monophysite Church). By 1500 the number had fallen to 3.4 million – or less.[48]

Looking from the time of the Crusades to the present era, we would suggest one other reason for the decline of the Church of the East. It lost membership to Roman Catholic, and to a lesser degree, Protestant incursions. The next section will deal some with this issue.

1.5 The Present State of the Church of the East

The descendants of this great Christian movement are still found in Southwest Asia (the Middle East) and India. However, the vast majority no longer consider themselves to be members of this communion.

In 1552, a conflict in the Church of the East resulted in a number of bishops requesting recognition by Pope Julius III. This permission was granted and the Chaldean Catholic Church was formed in 1553. This resulted in conflict between the Church of the East and the Chaldean Catholic Church. The first Patriarch of the Chaldean Church was tortured and executed by the local government in 1555, at least in part because of the encouragement of the Patriarch of the Assyrian Church of the East (the modern name for the Church of the East).

The animosity between the two churches lasted until the 20th century. Both denominations continue to use a Syriac liturgy.

---

[48] David B. Barrett, George Thomas Kurian, and Todd M. Johnson, eds., *World Christian Encyclopedia: A Comparative Survey of Churches and Religions in the Modern World Volume I: The World by Countries: Religionists, Churches, Ministries*, 2nd ed. (Oxford: Oxford University Press, 2001); Jenkins, *The Next Christendom*, 24.

The Chaldean Catholic Church is the larger of the two. As of 2003 it has a total worldwide membership of perhaps over 1,000,000. Membership in the Middle East is estimated at nearly 750,000, with the majority in Iraq.[49]

The Assyrian Church of the East maintains its religious and cultural heritage, but the numbers are very small. It estimates a worldwide membership of around 400,000. Bishoprics remain in the Middle East and in India, but emigration from the Middle East has resulted in dwindling numbers there. Since 1978, the Patriarch of the Church of the East has had his residence in the United States.[50]

A modern schism in this church occurred in 1968, resulting in the formation of the Ancient Church of the East. Its members total around 75,000 and reside primarily in Iraq and India. The patriarch lives in Baghdad.[51]

The history of the Church of the East in India after the arrival of the Europeans is very complicated. One way to deal with the facts is to list, along with brief notes, the major denominations that come from that tradition.

Two denominations continue to use a liturgy similar to that developed by the Church of the East. The largest is the Syro-Malabar, with adherents numbering around 3,000,000. Emerging as the result of submission to Rome in the 16th century after the arrival of the Portuguese, the denomination has adopted many of the customs and rituals of the Roman Catholic Church. A much smaller group of "Nestorians" continues to exist in India and owes allegiance to the Patriarch of the Assyrian Church of the East.

The remaining groups are descended from a transplanted Syrian Orthodox (Monophysite or Jacobite) tradition.

The "Syrian" or "Thomas" Christians who opposed the Portuguese pressure to submit to Rome had ordained one of their own in 1653 as their Metropolitan. He took the name of Mar Thoma I. ("Mar" means bishop.)

---

[49] Betty Jane Bailey and J. Martin Bailey, *Who Are the Christians in the Middle East?* (Grand Rapids, MI: Wm. B. Eerdmans, 2003), 82–84. The numbers of Christians in the Middle East have shifted significantly in recent years due to wars and anti-Christian militias like

[50] Bailey and Bailey, 132–33.

[51] J. F. Coakley, "Church of the East," ed. Ken Parry, *The Blackwell Dictionary of Eastern Christianity* (Oxford: Blackwell Publishers, 1999), 122–23.

Apparently wanting to make his ordination more legitimate he appealed to three non-Roman patriarchs asking that one of them send a bishop to confirm his title. Historically, the church had related to the Nestorian Patriarchy of Baghdad (the Church of the East). One appeal was sent to Baghdad. The other two patriarchs receiving his appeal were Monophysite, based in Antioch (West Syrian, Jacobite or Syrian Orthodox) and Alexandria (Coptic). A bishop from Antioch was the first to be able to breach the religious blockade established by the Portuguese. Mar Gregorios arrived in 1665 and confirmed Mar Thomas as the Metropolitan. This eventually resulted in these "Thomas" Christians moving from Nestorianism to Monophysitism – though most of the congregants apparently had little realization of that change.[52]

The Syrian Orthodox (Jacobites) number slightly less than 1,000,000 and continue to accept the authority of the Syrian Orthodox Patriarch of Antioch. However, a number of other denominations have emerged from this tradition. A division in the 19th century resulted in the Mar Thoma Church which has a membership of around 750,000. This division was the result of the coming of Protestants to India—more specifically, the Anglicans. Working with the Syrian Christians in Kerala, the Anglicans came with instructions not to seek to replace the ancient Indian Church with a new Anglican one. However, by teaching at the seminary, their "Protestant" theology was presented. Perhaps more importantly, they translated the Bible and the Book of Common Prayer into the local dialect, Malayalam. Today, Anglican ordination is recognized by these churches.

Eventually, a call for reform began to spread, led by Abraham Malpan of Maramon (1796-1846). The reformers wanted a more biblically founded faith, and they wanted to worship in the local language rather than Syriac. Malpan's call for reform resulted in his excommunication. In ensuing years however, some Metropolitans sided with the reformers and others with the traditionalists. Finally, when a court decision in 1888-1889 ruled that all church property and ecclesiastical authority belonged to the Patriarch of Antioch, the split became official.

---

[52] Adai Jacob, "Jacobite Syrian Orthodox Church, India," ed. Scott W. Sunquist, *A Dictionary of Asian Christianity* (Grand Rapids, MI: Wm. B. Eerdmans, 2001), 406. It may be noted that the official view of the Jacobite Syrian Orthodox Church is that it was always under the 'Monophysite' bishop of Antioch except for 1490-1599 when it was under Nestorian bishops.

The Malankara Orthodox church (or Orthodox Syrian Church of Malabar) is independent from the Patriarch of Antioch. Their membership exceeds 1,000,000. The split with the Syrian Orthodox (Jacobites) occurred in the early 20th century and related to rival claimants to the Patriarchy of Antioch – who was at that time appointed by the sultan of Turkey.

The Malabar Independent Syrian church is a small denomination of less than 25,000. It became an independent diocese in the late eighteenth century probably as the result of a dispute between rival claimants to the Metropolitanate.

There is also the Syro-Malankar church which is the modern remnant of another group of Syrian Orthodox who submitted to Rome in the early 20th century. It has a membership over 200,000.

Finally, mention can also be made that some of the Syrian Orthodox reformers in the 19th century despaired of reforming their church, so they joined the Anglican Church which itself eventually united with other Protestant denominations to form the Church of South India.

Chapter 2: Russian Orthodox Growth in Asia

"It is easy...to forget how vast a missionary field the Russian continent embraced. Russian missions extended outside Russia, not only to Alaska (of which we have spoken already), but to China, Japan, and Korea."

−Timothy Ware[1]

2.1 Asian Russia

Christianity's introduction into the Slavic world was a long process. Cyril and Methodius, missionaries to the Slavic people, were to be the foundation and inspiration of at least some of the mission work of the Russian Orthodox Church. Their methodology included the use of local languages, for which they developed an alphabet, in the translation of Scripture and in the writing of liturgies. The scope of this work does not allow us to look at the missionary projects sponsored in the 9th century by Photius, the Patriarch of Constantinople. He initiated work among the Slavic peoples of eastern Europe, including western Russia.[2] It was another century before a prince of Kiev, Vladimir the Great, took Russia into a deep embrace of Christianity.[3]

It is the missionary work east of the Ural Mountains that is more properly considered Asian missions. Nevertheless, we will begin our survey with Stephen of Perm, Apostle to the Zyrians. It is not clear if his work ever took him east of the Urals or not, but those who imitated his example certainly did.

---

[1] Timothy Ware, *The Orthodox Church: An Introduction to Eastern Christianity* (London: Penguin Books, 1964), 194–95.

[2] Stephen Neill, *A History of Christian Missions*, 2nd edition, History of the Church 6 (Penguin Books, 1991), 73–77.

[3] Vladimir converted to Christianity in 1988 and married Anna, the sister of the Byzantine Emperor. "Vladimir set to in earnest to Christianize his realm: priests, relics, sacred vessels, and icons were imported; mass baptisms were held in rivers; Church courts were set up, and ecclesiastical tithes instituted." He took down the idols from the high places, during Vladimir's reign, Russia became unequivocally Christian. Ware, *The Orthodox Church*, 87.

Stephen Khrap was born around 1340 in the town of Ustyug. According to church tradition, his father was a clergyman and his mother belonged to the Komi tribe. The Komi are a branch of the Zyrians who are a Finnish people. In Stephen's day, the Zyrians lived primarily in the northeastern part of European Russia.

Stephen became a monk at an early age. He studied diligently and he mastered the Greek language in order to better understand the Scriptures.

Desiring to carry the gospel to the Zyrian people, Stephen received permission from the Bishop of Moscow to begin missionary work in the area of Perm, he started the work in 1379 CE. Before his death in 1396 CE, he would see a large number of Zyrians baptized into the Christian faith. How did he accomplish this?

One reason for his success was that he had developed an alphabet for the illiterate Zyrian people. Apparently, some of the characters he chose for that alphabet were similar to symbols already used on Zyrian money and craftwork. He translated at least portions of Scripture and other liturgical texts into the Zyrian language. Strangely enough, he was criticized by the Slavic-language Christians for his translation work. They criticized him in spite of the fact that they had received their Scriptures in the Slavic language instead of Greek because of the pioneering work of the disciples of Methodius and Cyril.

Stephen believed that all peoples deserved to have the Scripture in their own language and to worship in their native tongue. This missionary strategy was repeated over and over again as the church spread east of the Ural Mountains into Asia. However, it should be noted that with the Russian national expansion, the old Permian Christian liturgy and indeed even the original Zyrian alphabet passed out of existence by the 16th century. The church was absorbed into the Russian Orthodox Church.[4]

Another cause for his success was his encounter with a local pagan priest named Pamoi (or Pam). This priest followed Stephen around and opposed his evangelistic appeals. Many people respected Pamoi, and therefore would

---

[4] MacCulloch, *Christianity*, 519–20.

not accept Christian baptism. Despite significant animosity, those who opposed Stephen were afraid to murder him because he possessed a letter of protection from the Tsar.

Throughout Christian history the preaching of the gospel was accompanied by displays of God's power. One day, Pamoi challenged Stephen to undergo the tests of fire and water. The test of fire involved walking through a burning structure. The test of water meant swimming under the ice from one water hole to the next. According to tradition, when Stephen accepted the challenge, the priest was startled. Stephen took his hand for the both of them to walk through the fire. Pamoi pulled away and refused to go. The people were so enraged that they wanted to kill Pamoi, but Stephen encouraged them to spare his life and only send him into exile. This they did. Many were subsequently baptized.

Stephen started a number of monasteries and began training local clergy. He opened schools near churches where people could be taught to read the scriptures in their own language.

In 1383, Stephen was consecrated as the first Bishop of Perm. As the leader of the church among the Zyrians, Stephen had always sought the welfare of his people. During a famine he secured food from another city and gave it away to the needy. On another occasion, he helped to withstand an enemy tribe that sought to inflict harm on the Zyrians. He also protected them from the powerful neighboring governments of Novgorad and Moscow. In fact, he died on April 26, 1396 CE while in Moscow on a trip for the benefit of his people. Much to the dismay of the Zyrians, Stephen was buried in Moscow. However, his legacy continued among the Zyrian people.

Of Stephen, it has been said that his work

> was marked by wisdom and breadth of outlook. . .. It was entirely free from political involvements. . . . His whole missionary activity was solid and prudent. He was careful to guard against merely outward success, and devoted himself to the strengthening and deepening of Christian faith among his converts.[5]

---

[5] K. Lubeck, as quoted in Neill, *A History of Christian Missions*, 211.

Peter the Great, ruler of Russia in the early 18th century, was interested in missions and promoted missionary expansion into the Siberian region of Asia. His interest probably had less to do with spiritual concern than with extending his authority over non-Russian people groups. On June 17, 1700, Peter published the following affirmation.

> For the strengthening and extension of the Orthodox Christian faith and for the proclamation of the Christian faith among the idolatrous peoples; also in order to bring the tributary peoples of the neighbourhood of Tobolsk and the other towns of Siberia to Christian faith and holy baptism, his highness . . . decided to write to the Metropolitan of Kiev in the following terms: he should . . . seek out a virtuous and learned man of good and blameless life; this man shall become Metropolitan of Tobolsk, and with God's help shall gradually bring those peoples in Siberia and China who live in the blindness of idolatry, and generally in ignorance, to the knowledge, the service, and the worship of the true and living God.[6]

The man chosen for the task was Filofei Leszczynski. What follows is a brief summary of his work and the work of those who followed him.[7]

In 1702, already middle-aged, Filofei was chosen as the Metropolitan of Tobolsk with responsibility over an enormous area that included Russian possessions in Asia. Filofei conducted missionary trips himself, as well as securing missionaries to go into other regions. His vision spread as for as Kamchatka on the east coast.

According to Stephen Neill, Filofei "was without a doubt a zealous and devoted missionary, and his work was not without result; in his time the number of churches increased from 160 to 448, and he is said to have baptized 40,000 converts."[8]

---

[6] Neill, 213.
[7] Neill, 214.
[8] Neill, 214.

After his retirement to a monastery at the age of 71 in 1721, the work initiated by him ebbed and flowed.

Nevertheless, the growth of the Orthodox Church from the Urals to the Pacific Ocean eventually succeeded as tribe after tribe accepted the Christian faith. For example, by 1750 most of the population of Kamchatka was reported to be Christian.

Several points may be made about this spread of Christianity.

1. It went hand in hand with Russian imperialism.

2. Many conversions may have had little to do with spiritual needs, since formal conversion resulted in exemption from paying tribute to the Russian government.

3. In general, missionaries were still committed to providing religious training in the languages of the various people groups. In the city of Irkutsk, a seminary was opened that gave instruction in Mongolian and Chinese. In many other places, scripture and liturgical material were translated into local languages.

2.2 China

In the latter part of the 17th century, China and Russia engaged in a number of military conflicts. Two of these resulted in Russian captives being taken to Beijing. The first group arrived in 1683, the second in 1685. These Russians agreed to live peacefully, so were not imprisoned. Among the second group was a parish priest, Maxim Leontiev, whom the Chinese government allowed him to start a church.

For ten years, Father Maxim ministered to his small flock, worshipping together in a chapel that had formerly been a Chinese temple. Then he received a letter from the Metropolitan of Tobolsk that allowed the chapel to be consecrated as an Orthodox Church. It was named the Church of St. Sophia. In the letter, an order was given that prayers should be made for the Chinese emperor, and permission granted to begin preaching to the Chinese. Although the dates are not entirely clear, it seems that the first Chinese person was baptized as an Orthodox Christian in 1692 – before the letter was received.

Father Maxim continued to pastor his church until his death in 1712. He lived in Beijing for 27 years. He may have received financial support from the Russian government—a practice that would certainly be common for Orthodox religious leaders in China in later years. His services were also requested by the Chinese government, specifically to accompany Chinese soldiers to war.

For many years after the death of Father Maxim, Orthodox priests continued to work in China. Until 1858, the Orthodox mission was supported by the Russian government. Members of the mission were expected to learn Chinese and act as interpreters for the Russian government in its dealing with China. Russian political concerns overshadowed any interest in evangelistic work, thus the number of baptisms was statistically insignificant.

In 1860, the mission was officially separated from the government. This was in part the result of the Treaty of Tinjin (1858), which allowed representatives of foreign countries to live in China and also provided for the legal residence of missionaries there. It was perhaps this separation that made ordaining Chinese priests more likely. The first was ordained in 1884.

Although there were other missionaries who made significant contributions to the growth of Orthodox missions in China, the name of Innocent Figourovsky is the most well-known. At the age of 33, in 1897, he arrived in China with the title Archimandrite. This is an honorable title for a celibate priest who is the head of a large monastery or a group of monasteries. His success in China can be seen in part by his elevation to Bishop of Beijing (1902-1921), to Archbishop of Beijing and All China (1922-1928), and to Metropolitan of Beijing and All China (1928-31).

Before his arrival, churches had already been started in several provinces. However, by the time he came to China, the church had become more or less moribund. He acted quickly and efficiently to re-energize the work.

He built new church buildings, including the first monastery and nunnery. He promoted Chinese-language liturgy for the daily services. He established businesses that helped the poorer Christians with income. These included a dairy and a weaving factory. During his years, the mission acquired its first printing press. He also sent preachers out of Beijing to spread the gospel. He did not ignore the needy, but established various works of charity.

During the Boxer Rebellion in 1900, many Christians were martyred for their faith. Among those were 222 Chinese Orthodox Christians. Afterward, the Orthodox Church renewed its growth under the leadership of Bishop Innocent.

The following is a quote from a Protestant missionary journal in 1916.

> At the present time the Russian Orthodox Mission in China is composed of the following establishments: Monastery of Assumption in Beijing; Hermitage of the Exaltation of the Holy Cross . . . near Beijing; Nunnery in Beijing; . . . The total number of mission churches is thirty-two. . . . The Mission supports three chapels and five church-yards. . . . There are seventeen schools for boys and three for girls under the control of the Mission, also one Theological Seminary in Beijing. Other establishments maintained by the Mission are: meteorological station, library (recently built), printing office (with more than a hundred volumes of Chinese publications), lithographic works, galvanoplastical establishment, type foundry, book binder's shop, paint shop, carpenter's shop, casting foundry, steam flour mill, candle factory, soap factory, weaver's workshop, bee-hive, dairy house, and brick-kiln.
>
> The Mission has thirty-three male teachers in its schools, four of whom are Russians, and five lady teachers, one of whom is Russian. The total enrollment of boys and girls exceeds 680. During 1915, 583 Chinese were baptized. The total number of baptized Chinese is 5,587.[9]

Statistics, especially rounded statistics, are always questionable, but at the time of World War II and before the Communist takeover, the membership

---

[9] Archimandrite Innocent, "The Russian Orthodox Mission in China," *The Chinese Recorder*, accessed June 15, 2017, www.orthodox.cn/history/1610romc_en.htm.

of the Orthodox churches in China totaled around 200,000. However, only 10,000 of those were Chinese. The majority were Russian refugees.

Today the government of China does not recognize Orthodox Christianity, perhaps for fear of Russian political interference within China. Several congregations continue to meet in Beijing and northeast China, apparently with the tacit consent of the government. The membership is less than 10,000 and mostly elderly. As of 2005, only one priest was available to serve these congregations.

2.3 Japan

In 1861, Nicholas Kasatkin (1836-1912) arrived in Hakodate, Japan as the Chaplain of the Russian Consulate. At that time missionary work was forbidden by the Japanese government. However, Nicholas, who after his death was called "Enlightener of Japan," did not come to work only with the Consulate. He came fully hoping to bring the gospel to the Japanese people.

He diligently studied Japanese language and culture for seven years. However, even before that period of study and preparation was over, he was involved in witness. An event of great significance occurred in 1865. Nicholas was on his way to preach when he was confronted by a man who wanted to kill him and thus stop him from preaching. The would-be assassin's name was Takuma Sawabe.

Sawabe had been born Yamamoto Kazuma in 1833. In 1875 he fled from his home area because he was wanted by the police for selling stolen watches. He moved to Hakodate where he changed his name and married the daughter of a Shinto priest. He led a group that reverenced the Emperor and demanded the expulsion of all foreigners.

Faced with the sword of Sawabe, Nicholas asked why he would want to kill him without first hearing what Nicholas had to say. Intrigued, Sawabe listened. His interest was stirred and he began to study more about Christian belief. Soon other friends of Sawabe joined in this discussion group. They were so impressed by the Christian faith that they began to share Orthodox Christianity with other Japanese.

Finally, in 1868, three of them were baptized by Nicholas behind closed doors at the Russian Consulate, Sawabe was among those them. He was given the name Paul–the name by which he is remembered in the Orthodox Church of Japan. Paul Sawabe and other Japanese converts were faithful to witness in spite of persecutions that included arrest.

Almost from the beginning, Nicholas was involved in translating and publishing. He worked on the Bible, the liturgy, and a number of prayer books.

In 1869, the Russian Orthodox Church officially established a mission in Japan with Nicholas as its head. Assured by a positive report from Paul Sawabe, Nicholas moved his mission to Tokyo, where it was to remain.

In 1873, the persecution of Christians abated. During this time Nicholas started to build a church and a school in Tokyo. In 1875, he ordained Paul Sawabe as the first Japanese Orthodox priest. In 1891, the Tokyo Cathedral of the Resurrection was opened.

In the difficult time surrounding the Russo-Japanese War of 1904-05, Nicholas assigned priests to comfort over 70,000 Russian prisoners of war who were kept in Japanese concentration camps. One writer has noted, that during the war, Nicholas "prayed for the victory of his adopted nation."[10]

Nicholas once said that he considered

> it inappropriate for a missionary to retire unless he is totally unable to serve. I have never tried on a 'robe de chambre' [a dressing gown], not even in my dreams. I would better die on the field where God's Providence destined me to plough and sow.[11]

The mission that he started had, from the beginning, encouraged all converts to evangelize. When he died in 1912, the fruit of his work and the work of

---

[10] Dimitri Brody, "Nicolas Kasatkin," *The Blackwell Dictionary of Eastern Christianity* (Malden, MA: Blackwell Publishers, 1999), 343.
[11] "Nicholas of Japan," *Orthodox Wiki* (blog), 2007, http://orthodoxwiki.org/Nicholas_of_Japan.

other faithful Orthodox Christians included over 30,000 church members in 266 churches. These churches were served by 116 preachers. There were also 48 Japanese priests. Three schools had also opened: an Orthodox seminary, an Orthodox women's seminary, and the Kyoto Orthodox Girls' School.

The Orthodox Church in Japan continued to grow in the years immediately following the death of Nicholas, but a renewal of Japanese nationalism and persecutions restricted their growth. Today its membership is estimated between 9,000 and 10,000.

Chapter 3: Roman Catholic Missions in Asia

"When the Portuguese carried the Cross around the southern tip of Africa and disclosed a new route from Western Christendom to Southern and Eastern Asia they opened a new chapter in the expansion of Christianity."

–Kenneth Scott Latourette[1]

3.1 Early Work

In the 13th century, Europe was frightened at the advance of the Mongol invaders into Russia and Eastern Europe. This was one reason that the Pope wanted to send a mission to the Mongol court—he hoped to dissuade them from further invasions. He also had hopes that conversion of the Mongols would create pressure on the Muslims of the Middle East who would then have to contend with Christian forces on both flanks.

The person chosen for the task was John of Plano Carpini, a Franciscan monk. Upon his arrival at the Mongol capitol in Mongolia in 1245, he presented a papal letter to the ruling Khan. Not only was the Khan unimpressed, he wrote to the Pope suggesting that all of Europe, including the Pope, should submit to the Emperor or face dire consequences. Upon receiving this reply, the Pope decided it would be wise not to publicize it!

John Carpini did report that there were many "Nestorian" Christians in the Mongol lands of Asia. Six to eight years later, another missionary, William of Rubruck, did not report as many, though he did say that Nestorians were found among the tribes allied with the Mongols. He also noted that one Nestorian church was located in the Mongol capital.

The name most associated with this first attempt at bringing Roman Catholic Christianity to the Mongol Empire is John of Montecorvino.[2] He was an Italian Franciscan monk and was the first Roman Catholic missionary to

---

[1] Kenneth Scott Latourette, *A History of the Expansion of Christianity: Volume 3: The Centuries of Advance, 1500 A.D. to 1800 A.D.* (Grand Rapids, MI: Zondervan Publishing Company, 1967), 247.

[2] See Chapter One.

reach China proper. He arrived in the summer capital of the Khan (modern day Beijing) in 1294.

Perhaps the most influential Christian in China at that time was Prince George of the Ongut tribe. He was, of course, a member of the Church of the East. Therefore, the Nestorian Christians were incensed when John converted him to the Roman Catholic faith.

John constructed the first church in 1299. By 1305 he reported 6,000 converts. It is unknown how many of these were children. In 1306 he erected the second church building and began a training school for some of the boys who had been baptized. They were taught Greek and Latin, as well as the Roman services and hymns. John reported that the Emperor enjoyed their chanting. He wrote, "I strike the bells at all the hours, and perform the divine Office with a congregation of babes and sucklings. But we sing by heart because we have no service-book with notes."[3]

In 1313 three bishops arrived to assist John. Four others had started the trip with them, but had been martyred by Muslims along the journey. The church continued to grow. The Roman Catholics received financial grants from the Emperor (as did other religions).

John died in 1330 and thus did not witness the demise of Christianity in China. The Chinese rebelled against their Mongol masters and defeated them. In 1368 the Ming Dynasty was established. In 1369 all Christians were expelled from the capitol city.

Christianity, both Roman Catholic and the Church of the East, quickly disappeared from China. The vast majority of Christians of both branches were not ethnic Chinese. The Chinese saw the Church of the East as a religion supported by the Mongols, and the Roman Catholics as a religion of Europeans. Neither, therefore, held much interest for the Chinese.

---

[3] Moffett, *A History of Christianity in Asia*, 457.

3.2 Francis Xavier

Francis Xavier has been called "the greatest missionary since the time of the Apostles."[4]

Xavier was born in Spain in 1506. He joined with Ignatius Loyola and others to form the Society of Jesus or the Jesuits. One of the goals of this new order was missions. Xavier became their first missionary.

Supported by both Pope Paul III and King John III of Portugal, Xavier was sent to India, to his first station in the Portuguese colony of Goa on the west coast. He arrived there in 1542.

Despirte the fact that Goa already had a multitude of priests, Xavier found much work still needing to be done. He was active in preaching and ministering in the hospitals. He also focused on teaching children. As Xavier would walk the streets ringing a bell, children would hear the sound and gather around him. When enough had come, he would take them to a church and teach them elements of the Roman catechism.

While he had some success in Goa, greater accomplishments awaited him on the southwest coast of India. Years before, many of the local pearl fishermen had converted to the Roman Catholic faith. However, without priests to minister to the faithful, the work had almost disappeared. Xavier went there and revived the work among this caste, called Paravas.

He had a number of documents translated into Tamil, the local language. These included the Creed, the Lord's Prayer, the Ave Maria, and the Ten Commandments. Xavier, himself, memorized these, but learned no further Tamil.

He concentrated on converting children, believing that they could more easily influence their parents and, if properly trained, they could become effective leaders.

From his letters, we can see how important the children became in his work.

---

[4] Antonia Astrain, "Francis Xavier," *The Catholic Encyclopedia* (New York: Robert Appleton Company, 1909), www.newadvent.org/cathen/06233.htm.

> As it was impossible for me to meet personally the ever growing volume of calls . . . I resorted to the following expedient. I told the children who memorized the Christian doctrine to betake themselves to the homes of the sick, there to collect as many of the family and neighbors as possible, and to say the Creed with them several times, assuring the sick persons that if they believed they would be cured. . . . This way I managed to satisfy all my callers, and at the same time secured that the Creed, the Commandments, and the prayers were taught in the people's homes and abroad in the streets.[5]

The children, he wrote,

> detest the idolatries of their people, and get into fights with them on the subject. They tackle even their own parents if they find them going to the idols, and come to tell me about it. When I hear from them of some idolatrous ceremonies in the villages . . . I collect all the boys I can, and off we go together to those places, where the devil gets from them more despiteful treatment than their worshipping parents had given him honour. The little fellows seize the small clay idols, smash them, grind them to dust, spit on them and trample them underfoot.[6]

When Xavier left India in 1545, the work among the Paravas had been firmly established. He had started churches in several villages and had baptized thousands. He was also remembered as one who consistently cared for the poor and sick.

In 1545, Xavier travelled to Malacca, a major trading city in Malaysia; then, in 1546, he made his way to the Molucca Islands of modern day Indonesia. Once again, he was called on to strengthen languishing work. The last priest had died several years earlier. Xavier visited several of the islands, preaching and teaching. He again insisted on the importance of translating Catholic

---

[5] Ruth A. Tucker, *From Jerusalem to Irian Jaya: A Biographical History of Christian Missions*, 2nd ed. (Grand Rapids, MI: Zondervan, 2004), 61.
[6] Tucker, 61.

doctrine into the local language. This included the Creed, various prayers and a number of hymns.

It has been claimed that in his travels during this time that he reached the Island of Mindanao of modern Philippines. However, this has never been proven.[7]

In 1547 Xavier was back in the city of Malacca. There he met a Japanese convert named Anjiro (or Yajiro).

Anjiro's story is compellingly told by Moffatt.[8] Anjiro, who was later baptized Paul of the Holy Faith, was from an upper-class family on the southern Japanese island of Kyushu. He was involved in a fight among youth in which someone died. He fled the area to avoid a charge of manslaughter. At first, he stayed in a Shingon Buddhist temple, but could find no peace. Later he boarded a Portuguese ship headed for Malacca. The captain was a Christian. Anjiro unburdened his heart to the captain, speaking of his sense of unforgiven sin. He was ready to become a Christian. The captain told him that when he got to Malacca, he should ask a 'holy priest' named Francis Xavier about these things. When they reached Malacca, however, Xavier had left for the East Indies (Indonesia), and Anjiro reluctantly took ship to return home to Japan. In spite of his intention, a storm forced his ship to make port in China, where he met another Portuguese acquaintance and was persuaded to try again to find Xavier back in Malacca. This time, at last, he met the missionary, and there in Malacca the mission to Japan was born.

First, however, Anjiro and Xavier both went to Goa. There Anjiro received some instruction in the school Xavier had founded for the training of Asian Christians. Xavier also strengthened the Church in India by sending new Jesuit missionaries to the places where he had earlier established Christianity.

Xavier, two other Jesuit priests, and Anjiro went to Japan in 1549. As had been the case everywhere he had gone, Xavier travelled the land preaching. Also, as before, he had Catholic documents translated – this time into Japanese.

---

[7] Astrain, "Francis Xavier."
[8] Samuel Hugh Moffett, *A History of Christianity in Asia, Vol. II: 1500-1900* (Maryknoll, N.Y: Orbis Books, 2005), 69.

One change from his earlier mission work was his decision that Japan needed to see Christianity as more compatible with the upper classes. This strategy worked as, eventually some of the local rulers gave him permission to promote Christianity in their territories. Over time, some even professed the Christian faith.

One of the problems faced by Xavier was translating Christian material into Japanese. He discovered that Anjiro had translated "God" as *dainichi* which was the name of a Buddhist deity. It is possible that some early converts assumed that Christianity was a new Buddhist sect. When Xavier discovered the mistake, he did two things. First, he had "God" translated by using the Latin, *Deus*. Second, he sent one of his brother Jesuits into the streets proclaiming, "Do not worship Dainichi."[9]

When Xavier left Japan he entrusted around 100 converts to the two Jesuit brothers who had accompanied him.

In 1552, Xavier returned to Goa. While there, he mediated a problem that had arisen between the head of the Jesuit mission there and the school Xavier had started. His time in Goa was short because he had decided that China would be the next country to which he would carry the Catholic Faith.

As he waited in a ship off the coast of China, trying to determine the best way to proceed, he became ill. He was taken to the small island of Shangchwan, perhaps to rest from the rolling of the ship. There, on December 3, 1552, he died.

While some might want to withhold the title "greatest missionary since the apostles" by which this story began, they would be hard-pressed to find another missionary who touched as many lives in as many different places in a mere 10 years as did Francis Xavier.

3.3 Matteo (Matthew) Ricci and the Jesuits in China

Matteo Ricci was born into an Italian aristocratic family in 1552. Although his father sent him to study law, Ricci had other more spiritual interests. He joined with Jesuits and began to prepare himself for missionary work. In

---

[9] Moffett, 72.

addition to the normal studies of theology, he also studied subjects like mathematics, astronomy, and geography which he thought might be helpful to him in his future work.

In 1578 Ricci and a number of other Jesuit missionaries made the trip to Goa. Ricci worked for four years there, much of it spent in teaching. However, he wanted a different kind of missionary work and was delighted when the head of the Jesuit missionary work in Asia appointed him and Michele Ruggieri to open up work in China.

That man's name was Alessandro Valignano. His official title was Visitor to the Eastern Missions of the Society of Jesus and Vicar-General for the Jesuits in India. That title meant that he was over all of the Jesuit missionary work in Asia. In his journal, Ricci attributed the founding of Chinese Christianity to Valignano. So, it is appropriate before attending to Ricci's work there that we look for a moment at this very influential person.

Valignano was an Italian who joined the Jesuits in 1566. He was appointed Visitor in 1573. He arrived in Goa in 1574. In 1578 on his way to Japan, he stopped in the city of Macau which had become a Portuguese colony a few years after the death of Xavier.

There, in spite of the fact that there were many Chinese Christians in the city, the Jesuit missionaries were working primarily with the Portuguese, not the Chinese. Valignano was appalled. He insisted that the missionaries learn to read and use the Chinese language.

Valignano expressed the same strategic sentiments when he arrived in Japan. He turned the mission upside down by demanding that instead of turning Japanese converts into Europeans, the Jesuit missionaries had to become more Japanese. They were expected to learn Japanese and to adopt the etiquette and customs so important in Japanese culture. Valignano's leadership in Japan had high-yielding results; within thirty years there were 300,000 Christians, as well as hospitals, schools, seminaries, and local clergy. Tides shifted swiftly in Japan in 1614 when an edict declared Christianity illegal. Here begins two of the darkest centuries for Christians in the land. Many thousands were tortured to the point of apostasy, and thousands more endured severe torture until death. Thousands more took their faith underground, passing on the faith secretly, one generation to the next, until 1865.

Both in terms of China and Japan, Valignano encouraged his missionaries to accommodate to local languages and customs as long as they did not conflict with Catholic doctrine. Valignano approved of Ricci and others wearing the clothing of Confucian scholars and studying the Confucian Classics.

Two additional emphases of Valignano are worth noting. He encouraged the missionaries throughout Asia to disconnect from the colonial aspects of Western trade and Portuguese politics. He also prohibited the Jesuit missionaries from participating in the Inquisition which had been introduced in India in 1560.

Now it is time to look more closely at the work of Matteo Ricci in China.

In 1583, Matteo Ricci and Michele Ruggieri received permission from the Governor of Guangdong Province to live in the city of Zhaoqing, a city to the north of Guangzhou (Canton).[10]

Ricci and Ruggieri worked together for several years before Ruggieri returned to Europe in 1588, hoping to encourage the Pope to send an emissary to the Chinese Emperor to request permission to preach Christianity there. He was never able to see any of a succession of Popes before he died in 1607.

Other Jesuits joined Ricci, but he would be considered the head of the Jesuit missionary work in China.

Ricci's goal was eventually to move to Beijing and influence the Emperor and the royal court to become Christian or at least give permission for Christianity to be proclaimed within the Empire. Several moves brought him near Beijing. Finally, in 1600 or 1601 the Emperor sent for him and he was able to enter the holy city.

In his early years in China, Ricci had worn a Buddhist robe thinking this would be winsome to the people. Eventually realized that was not the case. Instead, he began wearing the clothing of a Confucian scholar. He hoped to

---

[10] Ruggieri had lived in a Buddhist monastery in Guangzhou for a few months prior to this
time.

secure a place in China for Christianity by influencing the important scholars of that day.

The scholars and government officials were impressed by Ricci's learning, though he was careful never to appear patronizing. The Chinese especially appreciated Ricci's map-making ability, his expertise with watches, and his knowledge of astronomy and mathematics.

Among the gifts Ricci presented to the Emperor through an intermediary were a variety of clocks, an atlas, a harpsichord, and several paintings of Christ and the Virgin Mary. Whenever one of the clocks would stop, the Emperor would send for Ricci to fix it.

Although Ricci never converted the Emperor (in fact he never met him), he was influential in the conversion of a number of Chinese intellectuals. Two of these need to be mentioned.

The first was Xu Guangshi (or Guangqi). He was converted by Ricci in 1603 and was baptized as Paul. (He is also known as Paul Hsu.) He was converted largely because he was impressed by the moral teachings of Christianity which he believed exceeded his own Confucianism.

Eventually Xu rose to a position of great influence in government service. With the death of Ricci, Xu became the unofficial leader of the Christian Chinese community. He was also a protector against those who sought the expulsion of missionaries. On one occasion he wrote a letter to the Emperor in defense of the Christians. He wrote that Christianity had

> ...serving God [*Shangdi*] as its foundation, saving souls as its goal, practicing love and kindness as its method, changing evil to good as its way, repentance as its discipline, blessing in heaven as the reward for doing good, eternal punishment in hell for doing evil, that all their teaching and precepts are the best according to both the principle of heaven and humankind, helping people to do good and shun evil with sincerity.[11]

---

[11] China Group, "Xu Guangqi," 913.

The other person was Li Zhizao. For several years, Li resisted Ricci's desire that he convert. He was impressed by Ricci's scientific knowledge. Eventually, he accepted the superiority of Christianity to the idolatry found in his own form of Buddhism. However, it was several years before he was willing to give up his extra wives and accept Christian baptism. Finally, just months before Ricci's death, Li submitted and received baptism and a new name, Leon. (He is also known as Leon Li.)

In spite of his earlier hesitation, Li became an important part of this early Christian church, spreading the Faith in his home province and protecting missionaries when they were harassed by other officials. Li and other scholars assisted the missionaries with their writing and translating.

It was also Li who understood the significance of a newly discovered monument. In 1625, he received a copy of the inscription on the monument. He realized it was a reference to Christianity having been in China almost a thousand years earlier. He was ecstatic. This was, of course, the famous 'Nestorian' Monument.

Returning now to Ricci, we can consider a summary of his missionary methods in China.

First, in matters of dress and appearance, he wanted to fit into Chinese society better than the normal Europeans. Initially, he shaved his head and wore the clothes of a Buddhist monk. Gradually, he came to realize that Buddhism was not greatly respected by the higher classes which he hoped to reach. So, he changed to wearing the clothes of a Confucian scholar.

Ricci believed that only by securing a place among the upper classes would Christianity be safe in China. It is worth noting that Christianity had entered China before – twice by the Church of the East and once by the Roman Catholics. Every time it had later disappeared. From the time of Ricci to the modern day, Christianity has indeed had a place in Chinese society and life. This strategic interest in the upper classes should not be taken as an unwillingness to minister to the poor and needy. In fact, the first person baptized by Ricci and Ruggieri was a poor man who had been left beside the road to die. They took him in. His condition was incurable, but he heard their words of faith and heaven gladly and received baptism before he died. It should be pointed out that contrary to the methods of some earlier Jesuit missionaries in Asia, Ricci and his co-workers normally discouraged quick baptisms, wanting to be more certain of genuine conversion.

The second area concerns language and writing. It helped that Ricci was a master linguist and had a prodigious memory. He memorized large sections of the Chinese classics and could write hundreds of Chinese characters.

He decided to use Mandarin because it was the language of the scholar and court. He also sought to find classical terms to translate Christian doctrine. At first he used *Tien Chu* (Lord of Heaven) [also transliterated as *Tianzhu*] as a synonym for God. Later he will simply use *Tien* (Heaven) [also transliterated as *Tian*] for he came to believe that it had theistic connotations in the original Confucian context. He also used *Shangdi* (or *Shang-Ti*) which meant ruler or king.

At this point a quick survey of his writing and translating work is appropriate. He did some of both in scientific areas which greatly impressed many scholars. Also with the help of Xu he translated the first six chapters of Euclid's *Elements of Geometry*. However, it was his more religious writings that made a lasting impact on the Church.

The first was a treatise on friendship. He wrote this in part because of the great value that Chinese culture of that day placed on friendship and personal relationships.

However, his greatest literary work was entitled *The True Meaning of the Lord of Heaven*. It was completed after nine years of labor in 1603. In this work, he attempted to present a rational account of the Christian Faith. Ricci had little respect for what he considered superstitious Buddhism or Taoism. He also believed that Neo-Confucianism, which included a mixture of Buddhist and Taoist ideas, had contaminated the original Confucianism. It was this original Confucianism which he believed was compatible with Christianity. So, this book erects some bridges between Christianity and Confucianism.

Among the topics covered in the book were the existence of God, creation, providence, human nature, the human soul, demons, transmigration, heaven and hell, celibacy among Catholic leaders, and a short section on the incarnation and redemption. The work was apologetic. It was for the interested intellectual. It was written in a Chinese literary form as a dialogue between a Chinese scholar and a European scholar. For many centuries this book was the most important writing for the Catholic Church in China.

The third area of methodology had to do with ceremonies. Briefly stated, Ricci believed the ceremonies honoring Confucius and ancestors were cultural and not religious. They were a means of reinforcing family values which were so important in Chinese society. Therefore, he allowed Chinese Christians to participate in those ceremonies.

When Ricci died, there were around 2500 Chinese Catholics and of the 18 Jesuits working there, 9 of them were Chinese. The respect Ricci had among the Chinese was such that the Emperor allowed him to be buried in Beijing using a plot of land that belonged to a eunuch of the court. "His Chinese name – Li Matou – is the best-known name of missionaries who have served in China among both Christian and non-Christian Chinese."[12]

Before leaving the Jesuit work in China, we need to consider the Rites Controversy concerning the methodology of Ricci and like-minded Jesuits.

It is important to note that not all Jesuit missionaries agreed with Ricci's methods. However, a consensus was reached at a Jesuit conference in 1628 that included some of the influential Chinese leaders. The term *Shangdi* as a translation for God was rejected and the term *Tianzhu* was affirmed. Participation in Confucian ceremonies was also allowed, though with some restrictions.[13]

However, the greater objections came from other Catholic orders which had entered China beginning around 1631. Some of the conflict was 'national'. The Jesuits were supported by the Portuguese crown, while the Dominican and Franciscans were supported by Spain. (The Papacy eventually bypassed both national institutions and assumed direct control of the missionary enterprise.)

A significant part of the conflict related to an understanding of missions. The Franciscans and Dominicans had come from the Philippines with the desire

---

[12] Ralph Covell, "Ricci, Mateo," ed. Scott W. Sunquist, *A Dictionary of Asian Christianity* (Grand Rapids, MI: Wm. B. Eerdmans, 2001), 705.

[13] It is worth noting that Ricci had also had restrictions, e.g. converts could not say prayers to the dead and they could not attend ceremonies honoring Confucius in which animals were sacrificed.

to eradicate any non-Christian influences in national cultures. The Jesuits were more accommodating. The non-Jesuit orders complained to the Pope about the Jesuit practices. This led to a papal judgment against the Jesuits in 1645. The Jesuits appealed the judgment. A new Pope heard their appeal and sided with them in 1656.

The competing opinions continued to fly back and forth, while the Catholic Christians suffered occasional persecution under later Ming emperors and then the new Manchu dynasty.

Eventually an Emperor came to the throne who would tolerate Christianity. He was Kangxi of the Manchu dynasty. He announced a partial decree of toleration in 1671 and followed in 1692 with a complete decree of toleration. The Jesuits appealed to this Emperor to settle the issue.

Kangxi agreed with the Jesuits that the Chinese rites were only memorial and not religious. He also affirmed that when Confucians worshipped Tian, they were not worshipping the sky. This declaration was sent from the Jesuits to the Pope in 1700.

Pope Clement XI was angry that the Chinese Emperor had been consulted. He sent a decision back to China in 1704 in which he rejected the use of *Shangdi* and *Tian* for God. He would allow only *Tianzhu*. He also refused permission for any Christians to worship at ceremonies honoring Confucius or ancestors, thought he did not forbid them from attending.

There is no need to follow the permeations of this conflict down through the years. Suffice it to say that in 1745, Pope Benedict XIV brought the controversy to a close in an edict that allowed only *Tianzhu* to be used and forbidding Christians to be involved in civil ceremonies that were tainted by superstition. Ecclesiastical authorities would have the final say concerning whether or not a ceremony was 'tainted by superstition'.[14]

---

[14] This edict was effectively overturned in the 20th century, especially through Vatican Council II when Catholic churches were encouraged to learn from the native genius of each and every culture throughout the world. A detailed article on "Ancestor Worship" and a Christian response can be found in Reginald E. Reimer, "Ancestor Worship," ed. Scott W. Sunquist, *A Dictionary of Asian Christianity* (Grand Rapids, MI: Wm. B. Eerdmans, 2001).

Two historians have raised issues related to this controversy which may be sources for continuing reflection.

According to R.G. Tiedemann, some Jesuits and members of other orders

> had established themselves in increasing numbers in the provinces. Here the missionaries concentrated not primarily on the conversion of the ruling class, but worked among the common people. In the towns and villages they came face to face with Chinese popular religion, with its beliefs in miracles and exorcism, the worship of images, practices of divination and acts of healing performed by holy men. The indigenous inhabitants were accustomed to worshipping a vast pantheon of popular deities. The practice of ancestor worship was ubiquitous, as was that of geomancy (*feng shui*). Having been exposed to the realities of popular beliefs and practices, the provincial missionaries were less willing to make the same efforts at accommodations as the court-based Jesuits in Beijing.[15]

Concerning the papal decision to reject the Jesuit practice of accommodation, Samuel H. Moffett writes,

> Much can be said in defense of either side of the controversy. On the one hand, the papal position protected the integrity and purity and uniqueness of the Christian faith, all of which are fundamentally important to its very identity and survival. But on the other hand, the severity of the papal decree unavoidably stigmatized Christianity in China as foreign and non-Chinese, impeded its communication across cultural barriers, and brought persecution upon the Chinese churches and led to the breakup of the most successful missionary society that Catholics had ever had in China. The pope was the better theologian, and the Jesuits were the better missionaries.[16]

---

[15] R. G. Tiedemann, "China and Its Neighbors," ed. Adrian Hastings, n.d., 379.

[16] Moffett, *A History of Christianity in Asia, Vol. II*, 129.

3.4 Robert de Nobili

Robert de Nobili was born in Italy in 1577. His family was a distinguished one, including his uncle, the Cardinal Roberto Bellarmine. His immediate family had great hopes that Nobili himself would rise up high in ecclesiastical circles. His interest in missions effectively eliminated this hope.

Around 1596 he joined the Jesuit Order and, requesting missionary service, he was sent to India. He arrived in India in 1605 and was assigned to the Fisher Coast in southeast India. There he learned Tamil. After seven months he was appointed to work in Madurai – a significant city inland from the Fisher Coast.

He was not the first missionary to the city. Another had preceded him by several years. However, De Nobili was disturbed to discover that after years of work in the city of Madurai all of the native Christians belonged to the lower castes. He was determined to change that, wishing to reach those from higher castes as well. To do so he undertook to structure his life so that he could impact the high caste Brahmins. His new methods worked. Within four years over 100 higher caste Hindus converted to the Christian, several of whom were Brahmin.

His methodology can be outlined under three headings: self-identity, language, and customs.

Concerning his self-identity, he wanted to separate himself from the Portuguese and, indeed, from the lower caste Christians. A single word had been used to identify a Portuguese and/or a Christian. (Indian Christians were thus connected to the Portuguese.) It was the word *parangi* deriving from the word for foreigner in Persian, *farangi*. Because the Brahmin would have no contact with lower classes, De Nobili had to make it clear that he was a Christian, but not a *parangi*. A one point he posted a manifesto outside the little house where he had come to live. It read,

> I am not a *parangi*. I was not born in the land of the *parangis*, nor was I ever connected with their race . . . I came from Rome, where my family holds the same rank as respectable *rajas* in this country . . . The law which I preach

> is the law of the true God . . . Whoever says that it is the
> law of the *parangis*, fit only for low castes, commits a very
> great sin, for the true God is not the God of one race, but
> the God of all.[17]

To solidify his identification with the Brahmins he lived at least for a time
as a sannysasi. He wore the saffron robes of the priestly caste. He became
known as Tattuwa Bhodacharia Swami which means the Teacher of Reality.

Concerning languages, he was blessed with great linguistic ability. He
learned the basics of common Tamil in seven months. Then when he moved
to Madurai, he learned the higher literary form of Tamil. The Brahmins who
visited him were all amazed at the fluency of his language. They had never
heard any European speak Tamil so well.

In addition to Tamil, he learned some Telugu and was also able to study the
sacred language of Sanskrit. He was even able to convince a Brahmin friend
not only to teach him Sanskrit, but also the Vedas. He was probably the first
European to hear the details of Vedic lore, for it was against caste rules for
any but a Brahmin to read the Vedas.

Using his expertise in languages, he wrote in all three. Unfortunately, none
of his writings in Sanskrit or Telugu have survived. His principal work in
Tamil was his "Larger Catechism," though he also wrote a number of other
books on theological subjects, apologetics, and religious disputations.
Additionally, he composed hymns.

One significance of his writing and teaching was that he tried to find
terminology different from that which was being used by other missionaries
and Christians. De Nobili's goal was to communicate the Christian message
using terms and categories Hindus could understand.[18] Some of his words
are still used in the Church today.[19]

---

[17] Neill, *A History of Christian Missions*, 288.

[18] Louis Luzbetak, *The Church and Cultures: New Perspectives in Missiological
Anthropology* (Maryknoll, NY: Orbis Books, 1988), 92.

[19] Todd M. Johnson, "Contextualization: A New-Old Idea, Illustrations from the Life
of an Italian Jesuit in 17th-Century India," *International Journal of Frontier
Missions* 4 (1987): 17–18.

The third area for consideration is that of custom. This connects with his presentation of self-identity, but can be considered separately. In order to be able to reach the Brahmin, Nobili had to make many accommodations. He became a vegetarian. He hired a Brahmin cook and would only invite Brahmins to eat with him. As already noted, he wore the saffron robe. He also wore sandalwood paste on his forehead and the cord across his chest which indicated a high caste. He avoided all wine and strong drink – the exception was the wine of the Eucharist. Before saying mass, he would give himself a ceremonial washing. He followed all of these and other customs and, of course, allowed for his converts to do the same. Imitating Paul's missionary methodology, he said, "I too will make myself Indian in order to save the Indians."[20]

The adoption of these customs caused conflict in the mission. Perhaps even more controversial was his insistence that the Brahmin converts be separated from the low caste Christians. This included separation during worship. In the ensuing century among Jesuits this involved separate buildings. In other cases, the Christians might worship in the same building, but there would be a dividing wall between them and they would enter through separate doors.

Although he had opponents within the mission, his approach was generally approved by the authorities, at least during his lifetime. He also had a few other Jesuit missionaries who adopted his methods.[21]

It should be noted that Nobili was not unconcerned for the lower caste Indians. In fact, he would often leave his house at night to minister to them. Eventually he found at least a partial solution to the problem of his divided Indian Christianity. It was the *pandaram*.

---

[20] As quoted in Moffett, *A History of Christianity in Asia, Vol. II*, 21.

[21] Geneviève Lemercinier, "The Effect of the Caste System on Conversions to Christianity in Tamilnadu:," *Social Compass* 28, no. 2–3 (1981): 254–57. As with the Chinese Rites Controversy, the controversy over Nobili's methods, which were labeled the Malabar Rites, continued until the mid-eighteenth century. At that time, most of his methods were still allowed. However, with the suppression of the Jesuits by the Pope later in that century, the practice of having special 'Brahmin' missionaries ceased.

In the complicated Hindu structure, the pandaram were another level of ascetic priests. They were not as high as the Brahmin, but they were able to deal publicly with all castes, and even with the outcastes.[22]

De Nobili suggested to his superiors that they establish two classes of missionaries in India – the Brahmin and the pandaram. This was agreed upon and the first pandaram missionary started work in 1640. As might be expected, the pandaram missionaries had much greater success numerically.

De Nobili's final years were spent in near blindness and ill health.[23] In 1644 one of his colleagues wrote,

> What a man is this Fr Nobili! What a model for all missionaries! The older he grows, the more he adds to the authority of his life and to the splendour of his apostolic virtues. Almost blind and loaded with physical weaknesses, he works as though he were the most eager and stalwart of young missionaries, his zeal supplying the strength which is lacking in his body.[24]

In the 1640s he and other Jesuits and Indian converts suffered imprisonment because of opposition from Hindus. In 1646, around the age of 70, he was ordered by his superiors to move from Madurai to Jaffna in Ceylon. We do not know why. Later in 1646 he was told to move to Mysore where he remained until he died in 1656.

In those last years in Mysore, four of his Brahmin Christians remained with him till the end. He used his final ten years in dictating more writing. This he did almost to his final day. He died on January 16. His burial place is unknown.

The mission to which De Nobili belonged reported large numbers of conversions. By the end of the 17th century, the number of converts stood between 90,000 and 150,000, most of them were from the lower castes. This was the first Roman Catholic success not connected to Portuguese influence.

---

[22] Lemercinier, 256; Neill, *A History of Christianity in India*.

[23] When Nobili first arrived in India, he became ill and almost died. Afterwards his health was never very robust.

[24] Neill, *A History of Christianity in India*, 296.

3.5 Alexander de Rhodes

"My sole ambition in my travels has been the glory of my good Captain Jesus Christ and the profit of the souls He conquers. I traveled neither for the sake of riches, nor for knowledge, nor to amuse myself. Through God's mercy, I sought no other pearls than those Jesus Christ glories to set in His diadem, no other knowledge than that which St. Paul preached...no other amusement beyond giving joy to the angels by converting not a few sinners."

–Alexander de Rhodes[25]

Alexander de Rhodes was born in Avignon, France. His family had connections with the Jesuits, so it was not surprising that in 1612, he joined the Society of Jesus with the expressed purpose of doing missions in Japan.

After about four years of study, he left for Macao in 1616. However, he did not arrive there until 1623. His voyage was interrupted by a two-year illness in Goa. Additionally, a number of other places were visited before docking in Macao.

By the time of his arrival in Macao, Japan had just expelled all the missionaries. De Rhodes' plans were changed. In 1624 he was appointed to work in "Cochinchina".[26] There he was to reinforce Jesuit work that had begun in 1615.

At this time southern Vietnam was called Cochinchina and northern Vietnam was called Tonkin. A king ruled over all of this area, but he was largely powerless. Lords from two competing families held the real power. Tonkin was ruled by the Trinh family and Cochinchina by the Nguyen family.

---

[25] As quoted in Reg Reimer, *Vietnam's Christians: A Century of Growth and Adversity* (Pasadena, CA: William Carey Library, 2011), 17.
[26] Later the French will designate Vietnam by three terms: Tonkin in the north, Annam in the central area, and Cochinchina in the south.

In 1627 de Rhodes and another Jesuit moved to Tonkin. They were not the first missionaries to the north. The first Catholic missionary may have arrived in 1533, but certainly by 1583 the Franciscans were working in the north.

Just as de Rhodes was making his way to Tonkin, war broke out between the rival families. This war between Tonkin and Cochinchina lasted intermittently until 1672. This complicated matters for the missionaries who were often suspected of being spies for one side or the other.

After a circuitous trip de Rhodes arrived at the port city of Cua Bang on March 17, 1627. He and his party stayed for 15 days. Several people were converted. Among them was a magician who had been troubled by demons. He came to Rhodes for help. De Rhodes advised him to remove the 25 altars from his house and sprinkle the house with holy water. This he did and was freed from the demons. He afterwards asked for baptism.[27]

Eventually within the year, they were allowed to settle in Hanoi, the capitol city of Tonkin. A number of conversions followed including the Lord's sister, her mother, and 17 other members of the royal family. Between Christmas of 1627 and Easter of 1628, 500 persons were baptized. Within a few short months, the number of Christians was around 1600.

All of this did not occur without opposition. De Rhodes and the Church were opposed under three headings. First, many of the persons, especially in positions of authority, were upset because of the insistence of Christians on renouncing concubines. Second, because the missionaries baptized many persons who were dying, the missionaries were accused of killing them. The third reason was entirely political, related to the rivalries between the two "countries." Finally, the Lord of Tonkin banished the missionaries from his territory in 1630.

Within 3 years, de Rhodes and those with him had baptized 4700 persons. What were some of the reasons for this remarkable success?

---

[27] Peter C. Phan, "Rhodes, Alexandre De," ed. Scott W. Sunquist, *A Dictionary of Asian Christianity* (Grand Rapids, MI: Wm. B. Eerdmans, 2001), 699.

First was his insistence on learning the Annamite (Vietnamese) language. When he arrived in Vietnam, he was greatly disappointed that almost all of the missionaries were preaching through interpreters. He believed that learning the local language was important for the success of the Christian enterprise.

He is respected in linguistic circles for helping to develop the Annamite written language as well as producing an Annamite – Portuguese Dictionary. He also developed a Latin – Annamite Catechism for use with new believers.

The second reason for his success was his insistence on training national evangelists. Although his authorities in Macao were opposed to the idea, Rhodes believed that training nationals to work alongside missionaries was essential for the work. They obviously knew both language and customs better than missionaries ever could.

De Rhodes was a culturally sensitive person. He had noticed how Buddhist families would send their children to be taught by Buddhist monks and Confucian families would choose Confucian scholars as their children's teachers. It was then quite natural to develop a system where Christian families could send their most promising offspring to study with the Christian priests.

At least five of these young men are worth mentioning in this short section on de Rhodes. Their Christian names were Francois, Andre, Antoine, Ignace, and Vincent. The first four were converts from Tonkin.

Francis had been a Buddhist monk for 17 years. After his baptism, he wanted to stay with Rhodes. He was given the task of copying the catechetical lessons and teaching them to others. In 1630 or 31 he became the first Vietnamese Christian to be martyred.

Andre was impressive. Even before he was enlisted as an official worker he had brought 112 persons to de Rhodes for baptism. He had taught them the faith. Laboring later in Cochinchina, Andre volunteered himself to the authorities to be executed in the place of his older colleague, Ignace. This was in 1644. Rhodes himself witnessed this great sacrifice.

Antoine apparently was the only one of the five to not be martyred. However, it was not because he was slack in his work. He was converted at the age of 30 and resigned from his career in military service to work for de Rhodes.

Ignace was especially beloved by De Rhodes. He was converted in 1628. Ignace resigned his captaincy in the military and worked diligently with Rhodes. In 1629 he helped de Rhodes teach and baptize 600 converts in one place. Later in the south, he and Rhodes were imprisoned. Rhodes was released and banished from the country. Arriving a few months later in Macao, he learned that Ignace had been beheaded. This was in 1645.

These first four persons formed the core of believers who studied with de Rhodes and became co-workers with him. The training place was called the House of the Lord of Heaven. It functioned like a seminary. Eventually 100 persons were joined to this fellowship of learning. This enterprise was supported by the local churches, not by mission funds. At some point these four and perhaps others took vows of celibacy, poverty and obedience.[28]

This training strategy was a remarkable success. Within one year after de Rhodes and the missionaries were forced to leave Tonkin, the national workers had baptized 3,340 persons and started 20 churches.

De Rhodes had gone to Macao where he remained for 10 years. He returned to Cochinchina in 1640. He worked intermittently there for the next four years. He faced imprisonment and expulsion on several occasions. One story has been told that reflects his fearlessness and commitment to evangelism.

One time he was imprisoned for 22 days. During that time, every evening a Japanese Christian would bring a ladder that allowed Rhodes to climb over the prison wall. He would minister to the Christians and do evangelism during the night before returning to the prison in the early morning hours. During this three-week period, he baptized 92 persons.[29]

Also, during these four years in the south, he trained nationals as he had done in Tonkin. 10 men were chosen who made religious vows as the earlier group had done. Afterward, Rhodes was expelled in 1643. When he returned in 1644, he found that the nationals had baptized almost 300 persons who were

---

[28] Phan, 701; Moffett, *A History of Christianity in Asia, Vol. II*, 45.
[29] Phan, "Rhodes, Alexandre De," 701.

dying – baptism being too important to abandon in the absence of ordained missionaries.

As already noted, the time of severe persecution and martyrdom began in 1645. In addition to Ignatius, Vincent (the fifth person mentioned above) was martyred. Both were beheaded. Additionally, at the same time, seven other Vietnamese Christian workers each had a finger chopped off of a hand.

In total, Rhodes spent only about 7 years in the country today called Vietnam. His methods and his commitment brought great results. When he was forced to leave, his heart remained there.

In 1649, he returned to Europe hoping to convince the Pope to create a national hierarchy for Tonkin and Cochinchina. In 1652, the Pope offered Rhodes the new position of Bishop over his beloved people, but he declined, knowing that his return there would only bring problems for the church. So, instead of that, he was made the head of the mission with recruitment responsibilities. He went to France where he laid ground work for more missionaries being sent.

Part of his success was reflected in the creation of the Paris Society of Foreign Missions (La Societe des Missions Etrangeres de Paris or MEP). This was a mission society of 'secular' priests or lay missionaries instead of priests from monastic orders. One of the founders of this society was Francis Pallu, who was appointed by the Pope in 1658 as the Bishop of Tonkin. In the same year Lambert de la Mott was appointed as Bishop of Cochinchina. The MEP was responsible for establishing a seminary in 1666 in Ayutthaya, Siam (modern day Thailand), to prepare Chinese, Vietnamese and others for the priesthood.

Politically and ecclesiastically, the Portuguese were angered by the rising influence of France in a part of the world that they counted as their own. They opposed any return of Rhodes to East Asia. The Jesuits, under pressure from Portugal, finally sent Rhodes to Persia in 1654. He served there until he died in 1660.

The Catholic Church continued even in the midst of persecution by the Vietnamese rulers, often because of political concerns more than anything else. A series of edicts in the nineteenth century made "the perverse religion of the Europeans" illegal. Severe persecution broke out in several periods

(1833-1840; 1851-1863; 1868-1888). During this time, thousands of Christians were publicly shamed, had property taken, and imprisoned. They were shamed by being forced to wear a wooden yoke called *cangue*. Many Vietnamese Christians were sent to their death for their faith in Christ, faithful to their last breath.[30]

---

[30] Reimer, *Vietnam's Christians*, 19.

Chapter 4: Protestant Missions in Asia

"Within a few months of this time of consecration the impression was wrought into my soul that it was in China the Lord wanted me. It seemed to me highly probable that the work to which I was thus called might cost my life; for China was not then open as it is now."

–J. Hudson Taylor[1]

4.1 Introduction

The Protestant Reformation was born in the 16th century. Protestant missions did not begin in earnest until the 18th century. Why? In their polemics against the Protestants, the Roman Catholics pointed to their own far-flung mission enterprises. Several reasons have been advanced as to why the Protestants were so slow to become engaged in missions.

First, the Protestants used their time and personnel to spread Protestantism in Europe. They were fighting – sometimes literally – against the Roman Catholic Church which had dominated Europe for centuries.

Second, they were not united. There was much discord between the various reformers and what would later evolve into denominations and sects. So, their energies were not only devoted to the struggle against Rome, but against one another.

Third, the sea lanes were controlled by the Catholic nations of Portugal and Spain. Any would-be Protestant missionaries would have had practically no access to Asia by sea or, because of Islam, by land. This only changed when England and the Dutch became competitors with Portugal and Spain.

Fourth, unlike the Roman Catholics, the Protestants did not have a ready-made force to send for missions. Most of the early Roman Catholic missionaries belonged to religious orders.

---

[1] M. Geraldine Guinness, *The Story of the China Inland Mission* (London: Morgan and Scott, 1893), 58.

Fifth, the ecclesiastical situation in Germany was a mitigating circumstance. There, the ruler of each area was considered responsible for the spiritual welfare of his people. They followed his lead in faith and worship. Each ruler was responsible for his own dominion and not for anyone else's.[2] In other words, it was assumed if you were born in a particular jurisdiction, then you followed the religious beliefs of that jurisdiction.

Sixth, certain doctrinal issues delayed the surge of Protestant missions. Many believed that Christ would return soon. This made a prolonged mission enterprise to Asia seem impractical. Others accepted a current understanding that the Great Commission in Matthew 28:19-20 had been given to the Apostles and fulfilled by them. To go a "second" time into all the world seemed presumptuous, for the Age of the Apostles was over.[3] The Calvinist doctrine of election was another factor. Against William Carey's call to missions, one Calvinist pastor is reported to have said, "Young man, sit down; when God wants to convert the heathens, He'll do it without your help or mine."[4]

In spite of these deterrents to missions, some attempts were made. John Calvin supported the sending of missionaries to Brazil as part of an attempt to establish a Reformed colony town. It failed. In the same 16th century, the King of Sweden promoted missions to the Lapps in the northern region of his country. Early success was very limited.

In the 17th century, the German Lutheran Justinian von Welz wrote pamphlets encouraging the Protestant churches to do missions around the world. He was ridiculed and largely rejected. He was ordained by the Dutch church and went to the South American Dutch colony of Surinam. He died of disease after only two years there.

---

[2] This idea of each ruler being responsible for the spiritual welfare of his people (*curius regio, eius religio*) stems from an ecclesiastical system that was tied to the state. Neill, *A History of Christian Missions*, 188. It is worth noting that several of the forerunners of Protestant missions were from free church traditions (i.e. William Carey was a Baptist).

[3] Martin Luther demonstrates this view "No one has any longer such a universal apostolic command, but each bishop or pastor has his appointed diocese or parish." As quoted in Gustav Warneck, *Outline of a History of Protestant Missions*, 1906.

[4] Andrew Walls, *The Missionary Movement in Christian History: Studies in the Transmission of Faith* (Maryknoll, NY: Orbis Books, 1996), 246.

The work of Moravian missionaries in Africa, Greenland, and the Americas is also worthy of mention. This work began in the early 18th century under the influence of Count Nicholas von Zinzendorf.

Asia was even on the mind of some. George Fox, the founder of the Society of Friends (Quakers), commissioned 3 missionaries for China, but they never reached their destination.

4.2 Lutheran Pietism and Missions

This is not a book on Doctrine or European Church History, so I will give only a brief summary of the background to the mission work of the Pietist movement.

Jacob Spener (1635-1705) and August Hermann Francke (1663 – 1727) were German Lutherans who advocated, among other things, 1) Bible study that bears fruit in people's lives, 2) an inward spiritual life that results in good works, and 3) missions; especially to the non-reached peoples.

Franke was a professor at the University of Halle. King Frederick IV of Denmark was encouraged by his Pietist chaplain to support missions. The King could find no one from Denmark who was prepared to go. He turned to Germany and especially the University of Halle for volunteers. He found two. This was the true beginning of Protestant missions in Asia. The Danish – Halle mission would, for many years, make a valuable contribution to the spread of the gospel in Asia.

In 1706, Henrick Plutschau and Bartholomaeus Ziegenbalg arrived with a band of sixty others on the Indian sub-continent in the Danish colony of Tranquebar. Plutschau served until 1711 when he returned to Europe because of poor health. Ziegenbalg served 13 years before dying in 1719. The following is an accurate summary of the problems they faced.

> Like most pioneers, Ziegenbalg and Plutschau were faced with endless difficulties – the hostility of the local Danish community, ceaseless harassment from the surly and unpleasant governor, the ill-will of the Danish clerics sent out to care for the spiritual well-being of the European population, misunderstandings and prejudices in Copenhagen, the dislike of the higher castes, the lack of

interest on the part of the lower castes, the contemptuous hostility of the Roman Catholics. They had the utmost difficulty in finding any place in which to live, and in meeting anyone who would be willing to teach them Tamil.[5]

In spite of such difficulties, within a year the two missionaries had baptized five persons. The first Protestant church building in Asia was erected in 1707. After the opening service, the disgruntled governor had Ziegenbalg imprisoned for 4 months in solitary confinement.

Ziegenbalg was very good in languages and had the whole New Testament translated into Tamil by 1711. Although the Roman Catholics did not do any Bible translation, their work on Tamil religious vocabulary was helpful to him. Before his death in 1719, he had translated portions of the Old Testament which was later finished by other colleagues.

When Ziegenbalg died, the Christian community started and supported by him and other Pietist missionaries, numbered around 350 persons. They also sought to train and ordain pastors for this church from among the harvest. Of Ziegenbalg, Neill lauds: "At point after point, with hardly any precedent to guide him, Ziegenbalg made the right decision, and showed the way that has been followed ever since by the best and most successful among the Protestant missions."[6]

Before leaving the work of these early pietist missionaries in India, mention must be made of their greatest one. His name was Christian Friedrich Schwartz (1726-1798).

Schwartz arrived in India in 1750 as a missionary of the Danish – Halle Mission. The King of Denmark was only willing to support missionary work within his Indian colony, so as Schwartz and others made their way into the larger British ruled areas, they found it necessary to make some changes.

The Anglicans had been impressed with the work of the Lutheran Pietists. Therefore it was not surprising that the Anglican mission organization, the Society for the Propagation of Christian Knowledge (SPCK), was quite

---

[5] Neill, *A History of Christian Missions*, 229.
[6] Neill, 194.

willing to accept Schwartz as one of their missionaries in 1767. The fluidity of this system was such that Schwartz continued to receive support from both German and English churches; plus, his Lutheran ordination was never called into doubt by the Anglicans who allowed him to fulfill all of the roles of an Anglican priest.

Schwartz established a school for children. He was a faithful evangelist, baptizing hundreds of converts. He was a great linguist. In addition to Portuguese, English and Tamil, he also learned Farsi and Hindustani (the languages of the Muslim ruled areas). He was respected by everyone for his integrity. In fact, he was often used as an emissary or mediator between the British and Indian rulers. Upon his death the East India Company, long a thorn in the side of missions, actually erected a monument in his honor. So, too, did the young Hindu *rajah* ("ruler") of Tanjore. Among the epitaphs written by the Rajah on that monument honoring Schwartz were: humble and wise, honest and pure, free from disguise, father of orphans, supporter of widows, and dispenser of light.[7]

Some mention should also be made of Indian co-workers. One of Schwartz's converts was Satyanathan Pillai. He was a Vellalar high caste. He converted in spite of his parent's objections. He was ordained in 1790 and became the first native Tamil missionary of the SPCK. In 1799 he converted a low cast Nadar who was called David Sundaranandam. In spite of persecutions, David was instrumental in a mass movement that saw thousands of Nadar accept baptism. Although, he disappeared around 1806, the mass movement continued.

The faithfulness of the Pietists in this early missionary phase is recounted by Moffett. "Of the fifty-seven missionaries who had served in the Danish mission between 1706 and 1846 when the mission was disbanded, forty-two had died in India, only fifteen returned to Europe."[8]

4.3 William Carey and the Serampore Mission

William Carey (1761-1834) is often called the Father of Modern Missions. He was not the first Protestant missionary as we have already seen. However,

---

[7] Neill, 234.

[8] Moffett, *A History of Christianity in Asia, Vol. II*, 242.

he and his colleagues established the missionary society method of promoting missions which became the predominant pattern for Protestant missions.

Carey was born in Northhampton, England. He was converted as a teenager and became a Baptist. He had little formal education and his vocation was a shoemaker. He began pastoring in 1785, but often had to do secular work to supplement his income. While working, Carey read and studied. He taught himself Hebrew, Italian, French, and Dutch.

In 1792 he published "An Enquiry into the Obligation of Christians to use Means for the Conversion of the Heathen." In this booklet he argued against certain theological positions that had hindered missions (i.e. a hyper-Calvinist understanding of election and the idea that the Great Commission was valid only for the Apostles). He included a historical account of missions from the Apostolic times to the present work of Moravians and Methodists. He presented a statistical survey of the nations that showed most people living in spiritual darkness. Carey compiled the best and most accurate research he could obtain. In doing so it could be said that he laid the foundations for the science of missiology.[9] Biographer, Timothy George, captures the passion behind Carey's research: "Carey's statistics were more than mere numbers on a chart. They represented persons, persons made in the image of God and infinitely precious to Him."[10] He included a practical section that described how foreign missions could be done. Finally he closed by affirming a close relationship between prayer and responsible Christian action. Some years earlier, a prayer movement had started that included prayer for the conversion of "the heathen" (i.e. those people of other non-Christian faiths). Carey wrote, "We must not content ourselves with praying, *without exerting ourselves in the use of means* for the obtaining of those things we pray for."[5]

Finally in October of 1792 a group of 12 Baptist ministers, one lay person, and one ministerial student formed a missionary society. Later it would be named the Baptist Missionary Society. Finances for the society were received through pledges and the proceeds from the sale of Carey's "Enquiry".

---

[9] Timothy George, *Faithful Witness: The Life and Mission of William Carey* (Birmingham, AL: New Hope, 1991), 61.
[10] George, 61.

In June of 1793 the first missionaries supported by the society sailed for India. They were a medical doctor named John Thomas and William Carey, plus his family.

Arriving in Calcutta, John Thomas (brilliant and committed, but unstable) used all of their money in trying to start a medical practice. The next year found them in Mudnabatty working as supervisors in an indigo plantation and factory. Although Carey and others were sometimes criticized for spending "too much" time in secular employment, this was the pattern of missionary work that they had foreseen. The mission society was primarily responsible for recruiting missionaries and providing funds to get them to the mission field. Once on the field the missionaries would largely support themselves.

In 1800, the mission moved to the Danish colony of Serampore, where they were joined by new missionaries including William Ward and Joshua Marshman. With Carey, these three have been called by historians the Serampore Trio.

The Serampore mission had a six-fold strategy.

First, they were active in public witness and preaching. While they could affirm some things good in Muslim and Hindu writings, they regularly denounced Hindu deities and practices. Practices like *sati* (the burning of widows on the funeral pyres of the dead husbands) and the exposure of infants to death colored their views of Hinduism.

Their first convert happened in this way. In Serampore, John Thomas was eating with some other missionaries. Word came that a guru had fallen and dislocated his shoulder. He was asking for the 'doctor-padre'. Thomas, Marshman and Carey rushed to the man and Thomas reset the shoulder. They left him with the words, "A father chastises a child whom he loves."

Krishna Pal was the man's name. He had heard the gospel years before from a European for whom he had done carpentry work. Now, as he went daily to the mission for treatment, he heard the same gospel from Thomas, Ward, and William Carey's son Felix. On December 22nd, Thomas asked Krishna if he understood what he had been learning. He replied that both he and his friend, Gokul, had come to believe that "the Lord Jesus Christ had given His very life for the salvation of sinners." Thomas replied, "Then you are our brother. Come and let us eat together." The invitation to eat was deliberate to indicate that Krishna was breaking caste. He was baptized on December 28th. Gokul was baptized later and both became effective evangelists.[11]

In his journal, William Ward wrote of a sad result. After Krishna's conversion, he noted that Thomas was "almost mad with joy." Three days later Ward reported that Thomas was "quite mad". He had to be tied down to his bed from which he was mouthing profanities. He was released, but died a few months later.

The second strategy involved training national evangelists. In their writings, the Serampore missionaries confirmed that only the means of native preachers was sufficient to spread the gospel throughout India. As already noted, Krishna Pal and Gokul became two of these. The spread of the gospel was slow, but between 1800 and 1821 over 1400 persons were baptized. It is important in comparing statistics to remember that Baptists did not baptize infants, so their baptism numbers only include adult believers. Carey's goal was not just to convert individuals, but to form churches.[12]

Translating scripture was another important strategy. By 1837 when Joshua Marshman, the last of the Serampore trio, died, the scripture had been translated into 40 languages and dialects. William Carey was responsible for 6 translations of the entire scripture and 29 portions into other languages.

The fourth strategy was education. The missionaries believed that a better educated person would be more likely to reject Hinduism and accept Christianity. Marshman and his wife established schools for boys and girls. By 1818 they had 10,000 students in 92 schools. Also, in 1818, Serampore College was founded to give not only a theological education to believers, but a general education to non-Christians.

The fifth strategy involved the establishment of missionary stations radiating outward from Serampore. They wanted to establish preaching points throughout northeastern India.

---

[11] William Ward, *The First Hindoo Convert: A Memoir of Krishna Pal* (Philadelphia: American Baptist Publication Society, 1852), 12.
[12] Chris Sugden, *Seeking the Asian Face of Jesus: The Practice and Theology of Christian Social Witness in Indonesia and India 1974-1996* (Oxford: Regnum Books, 1997), 413.

And finally, they printed newspapers in English and Bengali (the language of Calcutta and the surrounding area). In these papers, they promoted Christianity and denounced evil practices like *sati.*

Although, not a strategy per se, it is worth noting that the Serampore mission structured their mission after the Moravian model. That is, they lived together in a compound and held all things in common. No secular work was done for personal gain, but all moneys earned were put into a common purse for the sake of the gospel. Carey's desire was that Indians would also join the community and be treated the same as European missionaries.[13]

Perhaps to close this section on William Carey and the Serampore mission, it would be helpful to note some of the difficulties that were faced and understand how these in one way or another have been repeatedly found in the history of missions.

William Carey had serious family problems. His wife, Dorothy, was not strong emotionally. One wonders how pleased she was to take her young children to India. At any rate, in 1794 nine-year old Peter, their third son, died. Dorothy's deteriorating mental state collapsed. She never recovered. She spent most of her remaining days confined to her room. She died in 1807.

Problems with other missionaries also surfaced. The situation with John Thomas has already been covered, but in addition to this in later years as newer missionaries arrived on the field they chaffed under the guidelines of the Serampore Mission. The Trio and others had voluntarily agreed to the Moravian model, but some new-comers refused to do so.

Finally, there were problems between the Serampore Mission and the Baptist Missionary Society. The problems were so severe that the relationship between the two was severed for around 10 years, 1827 – 1837. While the problems took various forms and ultimately centered around the college, at issue were different understandings of what a mission society is. For the Trio, the BMS was for the recruitment of missionaries and for the raising of funds required for sending them to the field. They believed the heart of the Society was on the field and that the field personnel should be financially independent of the home Society and able to make unilateral decisions on

---

[13] Sugden, 413.

the field regarding all of their work. Eventually the BMS and some other missionaries came to a different understanding. They believed that the missionary was a servant and employee of the Society that sent the missionary out. Missionaries on the field were responsible to those who provided the funds.

Despite the many trials faced by Carey, his accomplishments are nothing short of remarkable. He started the first printing press in India (which helped support the mission). He then published grammars for seven languages as well as the numerous Bible translations he and others translated. He actively advocated for human rights issues like the treatment of lepers and campaigning against *sati*. He founded Serampore College and sought to establish the church in part of India. Vishal and Ruth Mangalwadi refer to Carey as "the central character in the story of India's modernization."[14]

4.4 Henry Martyn

The last missionary to India that we will consider is the Anglican, Henry Martyn (1781-1812).[15] He was influenced by William Carey's writing and came to India in 1806 as a chaplain of the East India Company.

He apparently fulfilled his responsibilities faithfully as he cared for the employees and families of the company. However, he came to India to witness to the Indians. One of his methods involved preaching in the courtyard of his house in the town of Cawnpore. One day a young man, Shaikh Salih, was visiting his father who lived next door. He heard Martyn preaching and was intrigued. After learning more about Christianity from Martyn, he eventually went with him to Calcutta where he was baptized in 1811 by another Anglican chaplain.

---

[14] Vishal Mangalwadi, *The Legacy of William Carey: A Model for the Transformation of a Culture*, 1st US ed. (Wheaton, IL: Crossway Books, 1999), 25.
[15] Walls points out that Martyn was not technically appointed as a missionary, he was a tentmaker. Yet, "his brief life has become one of the best known and most moving stories in modern missionary hagiography." Walls, *The Missionary Movement in Christian History*, 168.

Upon baptism, Salih took a new name, Abdul Masih. He became the first ordained Indian Anglican minister. He served as a pioneer evangelist and medical missionary in Agra.[16]

Although Martyn did witness to Hindus, he became especially interested in reaching Muslims with the gospel. To that end he worked diligently on Bible translations. (He actually lived in Serampore with William Carey for a time.) He translated the New Testament into Urdu (a Muslim language of India and Pakistan), which is the foundation for the Urdu translation used today.[17]

He also supervised the translation of the New Testament in Arabic. The crowning achievement linguistically was his translation of the New Testament into Farsi.

In order to improve his Farsi language translation, he left India in 1811 to travel to England via Persia, Syria and Arabia. His friends tried to dissuade him from going. He was suffering from tuberculosis. While in Persia, he found he needed to retranslate the New Testament. This he did within a year's time. He stayed in the city of Shiraz and when not at work on the translation, he debated with Muslim scholars in defense of the Christian faith.

Leaving Shiraz, traveling toward Constantinople, he died in the city of Tokat, where he was buried by an Armenian priest. His Persian translation was carried to St. Petersburg and published in 1815. Eventually, the Shah of Iran received a copy and praised it for its "clear and luminous style."[18]

Martyn's journals were edited and published after his death. They became an inspiration to many in the following years. When he first arrived in India, Martyn wrote, "Now let me burn out for God." He died less than 6 years later at the age of 31.

---

[16] Robert Eric Frykenberg, *Christianity in India: From Beginnings to the Present*, Oxford History of the Christian Church (Oxford; New York: Oxford University Press, 2008), 416.
[17] Neill, *A History of Christian Missions*, 267; It should be noted that Moffett claims he translated the
whole Bible, but that is probably a mistake. Moffett, *A History of Christianity in Asia, Vol. II*, 264; He did translate at least the Psalms into Urdu. "Martyn, Henry," *The Oxford Dictionary of the Christian Church*, n.d., 866.
[18] Moffett, *A History of Christianity in Asia, Vol. II*, 377.

4.5 American Baptists in Burma (Myanmar)

Protestant missions came to Burma before American Baptist missionaries Adoniram (1788-1850) and Ann (1789-1826) Judson's arrival, but little or no fruit had resulted. Adoniram and Ann (also called Nancy) were originally appointed as Congregational missionaries by the American Board of Commissioners for Foreign Missions (commonly called, the American Board) in 1811.

They first sailed for India where Adoniram hoped to meet with William Carey and other English Baptists who had influenced his own interest in missions. However, he felt the need to become secure in his own denomination's support for infant baptism as over against the Baptist insistence on believer's baptism. After much study of scripture, he (and later Ann) became convinced the Baptists were correct. Much to the surprise of the Serampore missionaries, they both requested and received baptism as adult believers.

This event made the continuing relationship with the American Board unfeasible. At the urging of William Carey, Joshua Marshman and others, American Baptists formed their own mission board and appointed the Judsons as missionaries.

Unable to stay in India, the Judsons went to serve in Burma. They arrived in Rangoon in 1813 as the first American Baptist missionaries. There they engaged in language study. Adoniram was also a keen student of culture. In 1819 he constructed a traditional *zayat*. This was a bamboo and thatch shelter that was traditionally used as a meeting place for Burmese men.

One month after the *zayat* was constructed and public meetings begun in it, the Judsons had their first convert, a Burmese Buddhist, Maung Naw. Within another year they were able to report a membership of 10 Burmese Christians.

In addition to his evangelistic work, Adoniram was committed to translating the Bible into Burmese. His translation of the Gospel of Matthew was printed in 1817 by George Hough, a newly arrived missionary from America who was a printer. By 1823, he had finished his first draft of the New Testament in Burmese.

In 1824, just after the Judsons moved to the capitol city of Ava, war erupted between Britain and Burma. Adoniram and some other missionaries were taken prisoner by the Burmese as possible English collaborators. His brutal imprisonment has been described thus:

> [The officers] bound him with torture thongs, and dragged him off to the infamous, vermin-ridden 'death prison' of Ava. Twelve agonizing months later he . . . [and others] were marched overland, barefoot and sick, for six more months of misery in a primitive village prison near Mandalay. . . . [During these twenty months he was] half-starved, iron-fettered, sometimes trussed and suspended by his mangled feet with only head and shoulders touching the ground.[19]

He probably owed his life to the ministrations of his faithful wife who, sick herself, travelled far and wide seeking his release. She also was faithful to bring him food since none was provided by his captors. She did all of this carrying their baby girl along with her.

Ann was an effective missionary in her own right. She learned Burmese and spoke it better than Adoniram. She started a school in Rangoon for Burmese girls. She also visited Thai prisoners in the Rangoon jail. She learned Thai, helping to translate the Gospel of Matthew into Thai.[20]

Life in Burma during the best of times was difficult for her and for her husband. Both suffered from fevers. Their young 8 month old son Roger died in Rangoon. She had to return to the States on two occasions because of ill health. Her travails in ministering to her husband destroyed her fragile health. After Adoniram's release from prison, he was asked by the Burmese to serve as a translator to the British in their treaty consultations. He was encouraged by Ann to return to Ava for one of these meetings.[11] Shortly after he left, she was stricken by a fever and died before he could return. The year was 1826. Ann was 37. Six months later, their baby daughter, Maria, died.

---

[19] Moffett, 326.
[20] Moffett, 350. It is possible that the first Thai Protestant convert was due to her work.

After Ann's death, Adoniram suffered periods of deep depression. On one occasion he went out into the jungle. He lived as a recluse in a hut he built himself. There he dug a grave and his mind was filled with thoughts of death. He wrote, "God is to me the Great Unknown. I believe in him, but I find him not."[21]

In spite of his travails, Adoniram did not finally give up his work. He was encouraged by his second wife, Sarah (the widow of missionary George Boardman), who died in 1845, and his third wife, Emily Chubbuck.

Adoniram was a great proponent of evangelistic work among the Karen people of Burma. He made long canoe trips to their jungle villages to share the gospel. He was also indefatigable in working on his Burmese Bible translation which was finally completed in 1834. When he died in 1850, an English-Burmese dictionary which he helped to prepare was readied for publication. Judson's translation of the Burmese Bible is still the most widely used translation in Burmese churches today.

Now it is time to turn to the career of George (1801-1831) and Sarah (1803-1845) Boardman. The Boardmans sailed for Burma in 1825. Their ministry was primarily with the Karen people. Their home base was Tavoy in southern Burma. There they established schools for boys and girls. They also made long grueling trips to mountain and jungle villages to preach to the receptive Karen. George contracted tuberculosis. However, he refused to cease his labors. In early 1831, knowing perhaps that he did not have long to live, he determined to make one more trip to the Karen villages. He was literally carried by Karen believers, for he could no longer walk. One day after witnessing the baptism of 34 persons, George died.[22]

The stories of the Boardmans and Adoniram Judson come together in the story of the Karen man, Ko Tha Byu (c.1778-1840).[23] Ko Tha Byu was the first Karen Christian, though nothing in his earlier life indicated such possibilities. After leaving home in his teen years, he became a robber and

---

[21] Tucker, *From Jerusalem to Irian Jaya: A Biographical History of Christian Missions*, 129.

[22] Robert Torbet, *Venture of Faith: The Story of the American Baptist Foreign Mission Society and the Women's American Baptist Foreign Mission Society* (Valley Forge, PA: Judson Press, 1955), 48–49.

[23] Clifford Kyaw Dwe, "Tha Byu, Ko," ed. Scott W. Sunquist, *A Dictionary of Asian Christianity* (Grand Rapids, MI: Wm. B. Eerdmans, 2001), 829–30.

murderer. Eventually he was sold into slavery, but bought by a Burmese Christian who had hoped to rehabilitate him. It did not work. Eventually Adoniram Judson took him in and taught him to read and write.

After learning about Christianity, Ko Tha Byu applied for membership in the local church. For whatever reason, his baptism was postponed, and he went with the Boardmans to Tavoy. There he was baptized and worked tirelessly as a missionary to his own people until the day he died. His 12 year ministry was a major factor in the beginnings of the strong Karen Baptist work. At his death, 1270 baptized believers were scattered among dozens of villages in southern Burma.

4.6 London Missionary Society Beginnings in China

The London Missionary Society (LMS) was founded in 1795 by Congregationalists, Anglicans, Presbyterians, and Methodists. Robert Morrison (1782-1834) was the first Protestant to work in China. He was a Presbyterian appointed by the LMS.

Morrison arrived in Canton (Guangzhou) in 1807 after a having to travel via the United States because of the opposition from the British East India Company. It was illegal for missionaries to work in China. It was also against the law for Chinese to teach foreigners their language. So, Morrison kept a low profile, but was able to find two Roman Catholic Chinese who were willing to teach him Chinese.

He understood that public evangelism would result in his expulsion. He decided that the best use of his presence in China would be the work of translation. After two years, in a touch of irony, the East India Company hired him as a translator. For the rest of his ministry in China, he was a legal resident working for the East India Company.

The day he was appointed as translator was also his wedding day. He had met Mary Morton in Macao and they were married on February 20, 1809. She bore three children, only one living to adulthood. Mary died in 1821.

Morrison's translation work was remarkable and greatly valued for many years. In 1814 he published a Chinese grammar and a translation of the New Testament. His translation of the New Testament was assisted by the prior work of a Jesuit's partial translation. In 1818, he finished a translation of the

Old Testament. In 1821, he published his Chinese Dictionary in 6 volumes. Finally in 1823, the whole Bible was published in 21 volumes. One historian has noted that none of the earlier translations of the Bible into Asian languages "had the long-term, abiding influence in Asia of Morrison's Chinese Bible".[24] Additionally, he translated the Book of Common Prayer along with many hymns and tracts.

His first Chinese convert was Tsae A-Ko. When Morrison died in 1834 after 25 years of ministry, the LMS could report only 10 baptized Chinese Christians. However, in spite of the slowness of Christian growth, Robert Morrison made an invaluable contribution to the subsequent growth of a Chinese Church.

One final contribution to note is the acceptance by the LMS of Morrison's suggestion to establish a series of missionary bases to the south of China's southern border where Chinese language could more safely be learned and training of future Christian workers could take place. The most important of these stations was in Malacca (a city on the west coast of Malaysia) which had been seized by the British from the Dutch in 1795.

William Milne (1785-1822) was the missionary colleague who helped establish the LMS presence in Malacca. He was from the Congregational Church in Scotland and appointed by the LMS in 1812. At first, he worked with Robert Morrison, helping him with his Old Testament translation and writing tracts. His tract entitled "The Two Friends" was the most effective and widely distributed piece of Christian literature in China during the 19th century.[25]

In 1815 he moved to Malacca where he printed Chinese material and taught. In 1818 he founded the Anglo-Chinese College. (In 1843 the college was moved to Hong Kong.) One of the chief purposes of this college was to prepare missionaries and evangelists for a future when China would be open to Christianity.

In addition to his work at the College, he published two journals; one in English and one in Chinese. It should be noted that he did not limit his work

---

[24] Moffett, *A History of Christianity in Asia, Vol. II*, 288.
[25] Moffett, 290.

to ethnic Chinese, but also ministered to the predominant Malay population as well.

William Milne died of tuberculosis after only 9 years in Asia. However, his legacy lived on. Part of that legacy was a Chinese man he baptized. His name was Liang Fa.[26]

Liang Fa (1787-1855) was a Hakka born near Canton and was, by trade, a printer, i.e. he carved the wooden blocks used for the printing of Chinese characters. He met Milne in Canton and moved with him to Malacca to work on the printing projects.

Liang Fa was a Confucian, but had not been able to achieve the moral life that Confucianism called for. In 1816, he asked for baptism and Milne rejoiced to baptize him.

By 1819, Liang Fa had returned to Canton where he was one of the first to do evangelism in the province outside of the city. In 1823 Robert Morrison ordained him, the first Chinese Protestant to receive ordination.

His work as an evangelist bore fruit, but he did not escape persecution. He even had to return in exile to Malacca for a few years. He came back to China in 1839 and continued his evangelistic labors. In 1848 he began work as a chaplain/evangelist in the LMS Hospital in Canton. Records indicate that in less than four years he had preached to 15,000 people in the hospital – though with little success.

He continued to serve the hospital, but also started a small congregation in a chapel attached to his home. His faithfulness was recognized when, on the day of his funeral, 15 people asked for baptism.

It should also be noted that Liang Fa wrote a 500 page 'tract' entitled "Good Words to Admonish the Age". This became an influential Christian work.

---

[26] A variety of spelling for his name can be found including Leong Kung Fa, Ah Fa and Liang A-Fa.

4.7 Inland China

One of the first names associated with work beyond the coastal cities of China is Karl Gutzlaff (1803-1851). Gutzlaff was a German Lutheran who met Robert Morrison in Europe. He was inspired for missionary service and came to Asia in 1824 with the Netherlands Missionary Society.

He first worked in Indonesia with Chinese refugees. In 1828, he severed connections with the Netherland Missionary Society because they refused to send him to China. He came to Bangkok, Thailand, in that year and worked with Chinese there. He took the Chinese name Guo Shi Li and wore Chinese style-clothing. He also helped to translate the Bible into Thai, but the translation was not adequate for continued use.

He married an English woman in 1829, but she and her new born child died within a year. She left him with a sizeable inheritance which he probably used to help his endeavors to reach China.

From 1831 to 1833 he secured a job of translator for ship captains who traded along the China coast. It must be pointed out that a significant part of that involved opium trading and Gutzlaff was aware it.[27] During this time, he preached the gospel and distributed Christian literature written by him, Robert Morrison, and probably others.

When Robert Morrison died in 1834, Gutzlaff replaced him as the translator and secretary of the East India Company in Canton. As always, Gutzlaff was interested in translating the Bible. During this time, and with the help of some shipwrecked Japanese sailors, he translated the Gospel of John and the Epistles of John into Japanese.

Gutzlaff continued to support himself, in part, by secular employment which included governmental positions. After the first Opium War, he helped the East India Company negotiate the Treaty of Nanjing which, among other things, opened up China to the opium trade. In 1843, forbidden still by China from entering the country, he settled in the British run city of Hong Kong, becoming the Secretary in charge of Chinese affairs for the Hong Kong government.

---

[27] Many other missionaries, like William Milne, spoke out against the opium trade.

During his time in Hong Kong, Gutzlaff established the Christian Union of Native Chinese. These were converts who were trained and then sent into inland China to evangelize and give out Chinese scriptures. His vision was revealed in a letter, "China can only be converted through Chinese. To reach this goal the nation itself has to be stirred and the [gospel] has to be given to it as a graceful gift of God, but not as a present of foreigners or as a teaching of foreign countries." [28] Reporting great success, he was able to raise significant support from the churches in Europe.

Apparently he realized that all was not right, but refused to publicly acknowledge the problems. However, on a money raising trip to Europe, some of his colleagues in Hong Kong reported the facts to Europe.

The facts were bleak indeed. Many, perhaps most, of his 'converts' had lied. The majority of his 'converts' were opium addicts who saw Gutzlaff as a source of easy money. They falsified reports of travel and conversions. They took the Scriptures given to them for distribution, sold them back to the printers, who in turn sold them back to Gutzlaff.

Gutzlaff returned to Hong Kong in great embarrassment and shame. He died shortly after in 1851. However, his vision of bringing the gospel to inland China did not die with him.

One of the converts who had cheated him repented and became a great Hakka evangelist. His name was Jiang Jioran (Kong Jin). The Hakka Church grew in Guangdong Province and today is found in Hong Kong and Taiwan. It is also worth noting that Jiang's wife, Ye Huansha, promoted Christian education for females and translated Chinese Christian tracts into the Hakka language.

Hudson Taylor (1832-1905), the founder of China Inland Mission (later renamed Overseas Missionary Fellowship), called Gutzlaff the grandfather of the China Inland Mission.[29] It is to Taylor's work that we now turn.

James Hudson Taylor was born to devout Methodist parents. His health was not good, but as a young person he felt called to missionary service in China.

---

[28] Moffett, *A History of Christianity in Asia, Vol. II*, 296.

[29] A. J. Broomhall, *The Shaping of Modern China: Hudson Taylor's Life and Legacy: Volume One* (Carlisle: Piquant Editions, 2005), 5.

He received some medical training in anticipation of his missionary work. He was sent to China by the Chinese Evangelization Society (CES), which owed its formation to Gutzlaff. He arrived in 1854. He quickly adopted Chinese dress, dyed his hair black, and wore it in Chinese pig-tail style – much to the ridicule of other missionaries.

In 1856 he resigned from the CES and moved to Ningpo. He married Maria Dyer whose parents had died as missionaries in China. In 1860, because of his ill health, Taylor and his wife had to return to England.

One Sunday morning in 1865, Taylor went for a walk, alone on a beach. There he was confronted by the fact that millions of Chinese were dying without knowledge of the gospel, while English Christians were enjoying the comforts of their churches in morning worship without giving any thought to the lost of China. He determined that ill health or no, he had to return to China.

He began praying for others who would join him. He deposited 10 pounds in a bank for the China Inland Mission – though it as yet only existed in his imagination. In 1866, he, his wife, a married couple, 5 single men, and 9 single women sailed for China and the China Inland Mission became a reality. Again, he was criticized by other missionaries; this time for coming out without a supporting denomination and bringing too many women.

The China Inland Mission (CIM) was a great success, at least in terms of personnel and area covered. By 1882, every province in China had CIM missionaries. By 1895 over 640 missionaries were serving in China with CIM. However, the lasting contribution of the CIM in China has been questioned. Their primary emphasis was on pioneer evangelism. They were not as concerned about starting churches or training local ministers. The weakness of this strategy came to light when the Boxer Rebellion began in 1900. This rebellion began in northern China and launched a purge of foreigners and those influenced by the foreigners.[30] The Boxer Rebellion and, later, the Communist takeover of China both "illustrate the inherent

---

[30] For more on the Boxer Rebellion and the aftermath, see Diana Preston, *The Boxer Rebellion: The Dramatic Story of China's War on Foreigners That Shook the World in the Summer of 1900.* (New York: Walker Books, 2000).

weakness of a policy that did not make the building of a strong local ministry and church its number one priority."[31]

Ill health and organizational needs did not allow Taylor to remain in China for all of his remaining years. However, he returned in 1905. He died that year in China after addressing a gathering of Chinese Christians. Remarkably, the Taylor family continues their work among Chinese, with several generations devoted to reaching the Chinese with the gospel.

4.8 Church Growth in Korea

The first Protestant missionary to reach the islands off the coast of Korea was Karl Gutzlaff. He was the interpreter on a trading ship that landed on an island in 1833. During the week there, he translated the Lord's Prayer into Korean by using the Chinese characters found in the Chinese Bible.

The second missionary was more intentional. He was R. J. Thomas (1840-1866). He came to China as a missionary with the LMS in 1864. He met some Korean Catholics who had fled from persecution in Korea (Catholicism was banned since 1791 after a number of Korean Catholics were martyred). He wanted to leave Shanghai and do pioneer evangelism, so he determined to go to Korea. In August of 1865, he managed to spend over two months on Korea's west coast. He dressed in Korean clothes and was taught Korean by Roman Catholics in the area. In 1866 he sailed again for Korea. He was on a trading vessel that penetrated the country via the Taitong River south of Pyongyang. Eventually a fight erupted between those on the ship and the Koreans. The ship was set on fire and all died. Two accounts surfaced about Thomas' death. One stated that he died in the fires on the boat. The other said he was on the shore where he was killed by a soldier to whom he had offered a Chinese Bible just before the soldier struck him.[32]

Horace Allen (1858-1932) is credited as the first Protestant missionary to live in Korea. He was a Presbyterian medical doctor. The Presbyterian Church in America sent him out in 1884. He worked first as the physician for the American Consulate. Since missionaries were at that time banned from Korea, this gave him a legal reason for being in the country.

---

[31] Tucker, *From Jerusalem to Irian Jaya: A Biographical History of Christian Missions*, 185.

[32] Moffett, *A History of Christianity in Asia, Vol. II*, 529–30.

Just months after his arrival in the country, a nephew of the queen was injured in a failed attempt by rebels seeking to overthrow the current monarchy. Allen was called for and with his help, the nephew recovered. The king was grateful and allowed Allen to open a clinic. This clinic became a focal point for early missionary work in Korea.

In 1885, the first ordained Presbyterian minister entered Korea. He was Horace Underwood (1859-1916). At first, he attached himself to Allen's hospital. He taught chemistry and physics to medical classes. Allen urged caution in terms of evangelism. A government edict forbidding the propagation of foreign religions was still in effect.

Nevertheless, Underwood secretly baptized the first Korean Protestant in Korea. His name was No Tosha. He was Allen's interpreter. Soon there were more Korean Christians, and they took the responsibility to share the gospel among their own people.

In the same year Underwood arrived, the first Methodist missionary came as well. He was Henry Appenzeller (1858-1902). He and his wife, Ella, actually travelled on the same ship as Underwood, but returned to Japan for a few days before coming permanently to Seoul. He worked cooperatively with the Presbyterians, especially in Bible translation.

He was very interested in education. He started the first western-style school in the country in 1885. Today it is called Paichai University. When he discovered that all of the literature in Korea was printed in Chinese, he opened a book store that specialized in English books and Korean language books. Eventually this became the Methodist Printing and Publishing House.

Appenzeller drowned in boating accident as he was traveling to a Bible Translation Committee meeting. He was 44 years old.

In 1887, Horace Underwood started the first Protestant church in Korea. It was a Presbyterian Church in Seoul. In the same year, just months later, Appenzeller opened the first Methodist Church in Korea, also in Seoul. According to Moffett, "For the next hundred years and more the

Presbyterians and the Methodists formed the foundational infrastructure for a Protestant advance in Korea that had no equal anywhere else in Asia."[33]

One of the reasons often advanced for the growth of the Presbyterian Church in Korea was their adoption of the Nevius Method for doing missions.

John L. Nevius (1829-1893) was a Presbyterian missionary to China. In China, he began to question the missionary methods of his colleagues. He developed methods that had been influenced by Henry Venn, the honorary secretary of the Church Missionary Society in England and Rufus Anderson, a leader in the American Board of Commissioners for Foreign Missions.[34] Both of these men were early users of the term "indigenous church".[35]

Nevius' methods were not embraced by his colleagues in China, but in 1890 he was invited to visit Korea and addressed the Federal Council of Protestant Evangelical Missionaries. After his visit, the Presbyterian mission adopted the Nevius Method and required all missionaries to adhere to it.

The Nevius Method has often been summarized under the three headings of self-propagation, self-government, and self-support – or the Three Self Movement. However for clarity's sake a more detailed look at this method will be helpful.[26]

1. Missionaries were to be responsible for widespread itinerant personal evangelism.

2. Every believer was involved in learning from a more advanced believer and at the same time teaching a younger believer. This was called "self-propagation".

3. Each group would choose its own unpaid leaders. Groups would form a circuit and contribute to the salary of circuit helpers who would act as 'elders' traveling from group to group. These circuit helpers were also chosen by the groups themselves. This pattern was called "self-government".

---

[33] Moffett, 533.

[34] Wilbert R. Shenk, "Rufus Anderson and Henry Venn: A Special Relationship?," *International Bulletin of Missionary Research* 5, no. 4 (October 1981): 168.

[35] John Nevius, *The Planting and Development of Missionary Churches*, Reprint of the 4th ed. (Nutley, N.J: P & R Pub., 1973).

4. "Self-support" was encouraged by having each group pay for the salary of the circuit helpers and once the church could afford it, a paid pastor would replace the circuit helpers. Church buildings would only be constructed when the local groups or churches could pay for them.

5. Systematic Bible studies were led by group leaders and circuit helpers. The missionaries in Korea used a series of Bible Training Classes (BTS) along with periodic conferences to equip as many believers as possible.[36]

6. The groups were to practice strict discipline after the biblical pattern.

7. Cooperation with other groups and churches was encouraged.

8. The groups were also to show concern for the economic life of the people.

Before leaving this brief survey of the beginning of Protestant work in Korea, it might be helpful to consider reasons why the Church has grown so remarkably in Korea, especially when compared to other Asian countries.

At least five reasons have been suggested; the use of Nevius Methods, cooperation between Protestant missions, an emphasis on prayer and the fact that the abusive colonial power was Japan and not a western 'Christian' country. [37] Another possible reason is that Buddhism and the Chinese religions were not dominant before Christianity entered the country. According to William Barrett over 81% of Koreans practiced a local shamanistic form of religion in 1900.[38] These reasons give us a human perspective on the Korean movement, but we must recognize the work of God in the midst of the Korean church. In particular, there was a great revival that swept through the Korean church beginning in Pyongyang in January of

---

[36] Sung-deuk Oak, "Presbyterian Mission Methods and Policies in Korea, 1876-1910," in *Korean Church, God's Mission, Global Christianity*, Regnum Edinburgh Centenary Series 26 (Oxford: Regnum Books International, 2015), 42.
[37] G. Thompson Brown, "Korea," ed. Scott W. Sunquist, *A Dictionary of Asian Christianity* (Grand Rapids, MI: Wm. B. Eerdmans, 2001), 448.
[38] Moffett, *A History of Christianity in Asia, Vol. II*, 553.

1907. The revival, occurring over a span of two years impacted the whole Korean peninsula even spreading into Manchuria and China. It was during this time that the practice of early morning prayer became normative in the Korean church.[39] The church grew exponentially in the first decade of the 20th century and experienced significant growth again after the Korean War in the 1950s.[40]

4.9 Pietistic Missionaries in Indonesia

The Indonesian archipelago represents diverse ethnic groups, each with their own language, culture, and history. The story of Christianity in Indonesia is best told in fragments. The story begins on the eastern end of the Indonesian islands. There was a stronger Portuguese presence on the eastern side of Indonesia and, thus, the Catholic church was established there in the 16th century, but it was often at the hands of colonizers, rather than missionaries. This meant that coercive and even violent tactics were used in the conversions.[41] Nevertheless, the Catholic church was established among some of the ethnic groups in Eastern Indonesia.

The Protestant effort begins with Joseph Kam (1769-1833), who was a member of the Dutch Reformed Church in the Netherlands. He was influenced by Pietism and British Evangelicalism. In 1814 he arrived in Indonesia as a missionary of the London Missionary Society. During this brief period, England controlled Indonesia, but when the Dutch regained control, Kam transferred to the Netherlands Missionary Society (NZG).

He worked in several places but his primary base of operations was on Ambon, the principle island in the Moluccas. Although he was not the first to bring the gospel to this area of Indonesia, he is called "the Apostle to the Moluccas". The title is not without merit. When he arrived in Indonesia, he found only one Dutch pastor left in the northern islands and a general malaise throughout the Church.[42]

---

[39] Oak, "Presbyterian Mission Methods and Policies in Korea, 1876-1910," 42–43.
[40] Oak, 47.
[41] Robert Day McAmis, *Malay Muslims: The History and Challenge of Resurgent Islam in Southeast Asia* (Grand Rapids, MI: Wm. B. Eerdmans Publishing Co., 2002), 32.
[42] Moffett, *A History of Christianity in Asia, Vol. II*, 370–71.

In addition to extensive evangelism, Kam performed a variety of ministries for the local churches. He preached, exercised church discipline, provided the sacraments, made Christian literature available, and encouraged the churches to be more evangelistic. He also called for more missionaries to join him in the work. Never returning to the Netherlands, he worked until he died some 19 years after arriving in Indonesia.

The final result was a rejuvenated Christianity that today is represented in three different denominations. The Protestant Church in the Moluccas, the Christian Evangelical Church in Minahasa, and the Christian Evangelical Church in Timor are all indebted to his years of faithful service.

Shifting to the western side of the archipelago, Ludwig I. Nommensen was another missionary influenced by pietism. He was German and appointed to serve in Indonesia by the German Rhenish Mission (RGM).[43]

Nommensen was committed to work with the feared Batak on the island of Sumatra. In the year of his birth, the first two missionaries had entered the Batak area. They were quickly martyred and eaten by the cannibalistic head-hunters.

After learning the Batak language from Batak traders along the coast, he began to travel inland. The following story is delightfully told by Nellie DeWaard and illustrates the courage and patience that would be hallmarks of Nommensen's 56 years of service to the Batak.[44]

> Straight to the courtyard of the Radja the stranger went, followed by the curious villagers. The King, turning contemptuously to his unwelcome visitor, rudely asked him, 'and what are you doing here in Silindoeng? Why have you come?'
>
> 'I would like very much to come and live with you here in order to teach all who wish to, how to become clever and happy,' was the reply.

---

[43] The RGM was formed as an interdenominational mission by Lutherans and Calvinists.

[44] Nellie DeWaard, *Pioneer in Sumatra: The Story of Ludwig Nommensen* (London: OMF International, 1962), 10–12.

This astonishing announcement caused an uproar, and it was a long time before it was quiet enough to hear what anyone was saying. Live here! Thus far these people had isolated themselves from the rest of the world and, according to ancient custom, anyone who came uninvited to their valley was declared outlaw, the legitimate prey of anyone who wished to kill him. Those of the men who had travelled to the coast had begun to realize they could not live cut off from the rest of the world for ever, and they were in favour of the missionary coming to live among them, but many of the others were not. The debate raged back and forth. Then evening came on and still there was no decision.

The stranger listened patiently as the matter was discussed. At last one of the opposers turned fiercely to him saying, 'Now an end to your jokes. When are you leaving?'

'Never,' was the calm reply. 'Did I not say I wanted to build a house and live here?'

'Then we will burn it down.'
'And I will build it again,' answered the white man firmly.

'We will cut off your legs and throw you into the river,' threatened another one of the opposition.

'Friend, you know you do not mean that,' answered the missionary with a disarming smile.

The men just could not come to a decision. The next day the Radjas from the nearby villages came to confer about the matter. The white man persisted calmly in his request as the Kings deliberated pro and con. It went on for five days. Gradually the personality of the stranger won the confidence of the Radjas and they seemed about to consent to the proposition.

But suddenly the situation became tense again. One of the Radjas brought up the question of the responsibility for the missionary's life. Using figurative language which nevertheless revealed the real threat of danger, he said, 'If a man throws one kernel of rice on the street will not the chickens pick it up and eat it.'

The man stood up. Even the opposing party felt the strength of his faith when these words came emphatically from his lips, 'If the man who threw the kernel of rice in the street drives away the chickens, then they will not be able to eat up the kernel.'

Hearing these words, it was clear to all that this stranger had a strong Ompoe Semangat, a grandfather-spirit who was very powerful and able to protect. So he was to be allowed to live in the valley.

Though the way to remain and live among the Bataks had apparently opened, yet when it came to the actual building of the house some of the Radjas again had objections and doubts. Once again the conferences were resumed and no headway could be made toward a decision because of the obstinacy of the contending parties. In the end the white man, tiring of the constant delay, one day took the thickest book he had to the meeting and told the Radjas he was going to write down in it the names of the men who still wished to prevent him from building the house. Because of their superstitious fear of books and writing, no one had the courage to continue the opposition openly. They were quite sure that by writing their names in a book he would gain power over them, so the matter was dropped.

This is how it came about that on a certain day a beginning could be made with the building of the first missionary home among the Bataks of Sumatra, Indonesia. Beams, a few boards, bamboo mats, and rattan ropes were all that were needed, and soon the building was completed. This is how Ludwig Nommensen, the first white missionary to live among the Bataks, gained a foothold.

Nommensen was true to his word. He came to live among the Batak and he did. He lived like them in terms of 'conveniences' and food. He lived among them for 56 years returning for short visits to Germany only four times; 1880-81, 1892, 1905, and 1912. The personal cost was great. During his years on the field his two wives and four of his nine children passed away.[45] Nevertheless, in faith he persevered.

Nommensen won the appreciation of the Batak as he lovingly doctored their physical ailments. He and missionaries who joined him opposed slavery, war between the villages, and cannibalism. Seeing the need for vocational training, he opened a trade school for the Batak.

However, Nommensen's primary goal was the spread of the gospel and the growth of the Church. His first converts were expelled from their villages and came to live near Nommensen's house. Their Christian village was called *Huta Dame* (Village of Peace).[46] However, this situation was short-lived since mass conversions began within a few years of his appearance. As village leaders were won to Christ whole villages began turning to the Church. Nommensen was rarely content to remain in one place, but as churches were planted and nourished in one area, he and other missionaries would travel to more distant Batak tribes. He was driven by a vision of the Batak coming to faith. In his own words:

> In spirit I see scattered everywhere Christian congregations, schools and churches, groups of Bataks old and young, making their way to these churches: on every side I hear the sound of church bells calling the believers to the house of God. I see everywhere cultivated fields and gardens, green pastures and forests, tidy villages and dwellings in which are found the properly dressed descendants of this people. Still more I see preachers and teachers, natives of Sumatra, standing on the platforms and behind the pulpits, pointing out the way of the Christian life to both. You will say that I am a dreamer, but I say, No! I am not dreaming. My faith

---

[45] Lothar Schreiner, "The Legacy of Ingwer Ludwig Nommensen," *International Bulletin of Missionary Research* 24, no. 2 (April 2000): 83.

[46] J. Raplan Hutauruk, "Nommensen, Ludwig Ingwer," in *A Dictionary of Asian Christianity*, ed. Scott W. Sunquist (Grand Rapids, MI: Wm. B. Eerdmans, 2001), 608.

> visions all this; it shall come to pass for all kingdoms shall
> be his and every tongue shall confess that Christ is Lord.[47]

Some of his missionary colleagues questioned the validity of mass conversions followed by mass baptisms. His response was that missionaries needed to learn to fish with nets, not hooks.[48] Nevertheless, Nommensen understood the need for Christian growth in faith and knowledge. To that end he translated Luther's Small Catechism and the New Testament.

He encouraged churches to be self-sufficient. Each congregation should be led by a teacher-preacher. This leader would not be paid by foreign missionaries or foreign boards. He encouraged converted village leaders to take on some responsibilities in the churches. This gave more status to Christianity as the native evangelists from these churches went to other villages.

Local congregations were organized into a 'resort' which was led by a pastor. Several 'resorts' formed a district presided over by a superintendent. The completed denominational structure was led by a bishop. When Nommensen died in 1918, the Batak church counted 180,000 members, 788 teacher-preachers, and 34 ordained Batak pastors.[49] Today the Batak Protestant Christian Church is the largest church in Indonesia and one of the largest in Asia with a membership of over 3,000,000.

The third and last missionary to Indonesia that we will mention is Albert C. Kruyt (1869-1949). Kruyt was not directly influenced by Pietism, but the mission board that sent him to Indonesia was inspired, at least partly by the earlier Pietist movement. Kruyt was appointed to Indonesia by the Netherlands Missionary Society. (His parents had been missionaries to Indonesia with the same Board.)

---

[47] As quoted in Paul B. Pedersen, *Batak Blood and Protestant Soul: The Development of National Batak Churches in North Sumatra.* (Grand Rapids, MI: Eerdmans, 1970), 64.

[48] Moffett, *A History of Christianity in Asia, Vol. II*, 624.

[49] E. Nyhus, "An Indonesian Church in the Midst of Social Change: The Batak Protestant Church 1945-1957" (Dissertation, University of Wisconsin-Madison, 1987), 25; Hutauruk, "Nommensen, Ludwig Ingwer," 608.

Kruyt, Nicolaus Adriani and their wives were the first missionaries appointed to work in Central Celebes.[50] Kruyt arrived in Central Celebes in 1892. He did itinerant preaching and opened mission schools for the next 7 years though with little success. In 1905 and 1906, the Dutch colonial government established greater control over the region and forbade a number of native religious practices. It was after this time that the local people began to respond more positively to Kruyt and the other missionaries. In 1913 he added to his duties by accepting the directorship of a training college for the local Christian leaders. He retired back to the Netherlands in 1932 after 40 years of work in Central Celebes. However, he continued to work on a New Testament translation started by his colleague Adriani, but left unfinished at his death. Kruyt finished it and it was printed in 1935.

The significance of Albert Kruyt's missionary work rests in part on the development of a way of doing missions which came to be called the Sociological Missionary Method.[51]

This method can be summarized as follows.

1. The missionary should learn the local language and study the local culture and religion.

2. The missionary should proclaim the gospel within the culture, not against it.

3. The missionary should seek to preserve local customs that are not contrary to Christianity.

4. The missionary should approach communities, not individuals. Kruyt recognized the importance of community decision-making and wanted to wait until a community was ready before offering baptism.

---

[50] The following historical summary is based on the English abstract of a doctoral dissertation by Gert Noort, "The Road from Magic to Faith: Life and Work of Alb. C. Kruyt (1869-1949), Missionary in Central Celebes Indonesia" (Dissertation, Utrecht University, 2006).

[51] Christian G. F. de Jonge, "Kruyt, Albertus Christian," in *A Dictionary of Asian Christianity*, ed. Scott W. Sunquist (Grand Rapids, MI: Wm. B. Eerdmans, 2001), 458.

5. The missionary should seek positions of leadership within the church for the village leaders. Kruyt believed that it was best if the community social structure could be paralleled in the local church.

Kruyt believed a kind of evolutionary continuity was possible as tribal religions became Christian. This understanding had great influence in Europe until Karl Barth and others began to affirm an absolute discontinuity between the gospel and human religions.[52]

4.10 Malaysia and Singapore

Francis Thomas McDougall (1817-1886) was a pioneer missionary to Sarawak on the island of Borneo. He was born into a military family and spent many of his early formative years around the Mediterranean. He studied for a surgical degree which he received and then later received an M.A. degree from Oxford University. He married Harriette Bunyon in 1843 and she encouraged him to receive ordination as an Anglican priest.

McDougall was invited by Rajah (Ruler) James Brooke (an Indian-born Englishman)[53] to come to his independent country of Sarawak. He arrived in Kuching in 1848 to support the Rajah by bringing Christianity and "civilization" to the indigenous Dayak. He and his wife were missionaries for almost 20 years – returning to England in 1867. Five of their children died in Sarawak. They were eventually supported by the Society for the Propagation of the Gospel (SPG).

McDougall's accomplishments included evangelistic fruit. In 1851, the first five converts received Holy Communion.

He also started a day school for Malay boys, which, however, failed within a few years. Around the same time, he started a more intentionally Christian

---

[52] Noort, "The Road from Magic to Faith: Life and Work of Alb. C. Kruyt (1869-1949), Missionary in Central Celebes Indonesia."

[53] The so-called "white rajahs" in Sarawak were three generations of British rulers who ruled with complicated ties to the British Empire. James Brooke was an "anti-colonial colonialist" who sought civilization, Christianity, and commerce on Borneo. Jin Huat Tan, *Brookes, the British, and Christianity: Christian Missions and the State in Sarawak, 1841-1963*, STM Series (Seremban: Seminari Theoloji Malaysia, 2012), 5–9.

school in his home. The school attracted Dayak and Chinese students. It was a residential school. The students who were given to him by relatives were immediately baptized and educated in the Christian faith. "This school, which has educated the leaders of Sarawak society over the past 150 years, was to become probably his most enduring legacy."[54]

In addition to the work mentioned above, he also had an active medical practice by which he hoped to attract people to Christ. He was honored as the first medical missionary of the Church of England. He translated the Book of Common Prayer into Malay and wrote a Malay catechism. McDougall also worked on translations into the indigenous languages.

In 1853, McDougall was consecrated as Bishop of Labuan, a tiny island and British colony off the coast of Sarawak. The next year Rajah Brooke added Sarawak to McDougall's title. McDougall was consecrated Bishop in the city of Calcutta and was, thus, the first Anglican bishop consecrated in Asia.

Two additional notes will close this brief account of McDougall's career.

First, McDougall was in some ways the antithesis of what many considered appropriate for a missionary. He had "a combative nature that rendered dialogue irksome, an intolerant streak that made him a difficult colleague, and a melancholic hypochondria that resulted in his being . . . galvanized by physical danger."[55] His adventuresome spirit was not always appreciated by the home office. Stephen Neill recounted,

> In 1862, when he was sailing with Captain Brooke, the Rajah's nephew, the ship was attacked by pirates, who greatly outnumbered the crew. McDougall incautiously mentioned in a letter to *The Times* that "my double-barrelled Terry's breach-loader proved a most deadly weapon for its true shooting and certainty and rapidity of firing"; on which Bishop Tate of London remarked: "When you next get into a similar encounter, you must get your wife to write about it."[56]

---

[54] David A. Edwards, "The Legacy of Francis Thomas McDougall," *International Bulletin of Missionary Research* 31, no. 4 (October 2007): 205.
[55] Edwards, 204.
[56] Neill, *A History of Christian Missions*, 290.

Second, McDougall came later in his career to believe that the indigenous religion of the Dayak was touched by the Spirit of God. After visits to Dayak longhouses, McDougall realized that the Dayak were aware of a supreme creative power. In a sermon in 1851, McDougall, making reference to Paul in Athens, noted that the Dayak cultures had elements of goodness and truth by which God's image could still be discerned in those people. The Christian missionary should build on that foundation rather than seek to destroy it. It is interesting that when he sent the sermon to the SPG for possible publication, they refused it as too radical.

In 1884, two years before his death, he preached another sermon. In that sermon to SPG supporters, he noted,

> 'There is one looking upon us all, Christian and Heathen alike, who is the life and light of men and who lightened every man that cometh into the world' The perceptive missionary would therefore notice that there are movements and thoughts within "the poor heathen's heart" that can arise from no other source than 'the gracious working of the Spirit of God'

> McDougall therefore believed that the message of the missionary should be dominated not by words of terror about hell and damnation but by a gentle whisper "of Him who has been with them all along," whose voice they have heard already, though they knew it not. Besides hearing the voice of God's power in storm and thunder, 'the heathen have heard another and softer voice in the inner movements of their being, in the very thought which stirred them to brave and manly and righteous deeds, in fulfilling the duties of family affection and acts of compassion and tenderness for the sick and suffering, the stranger and the orphan.'[57]

---

[57] Neill, 207.

Another missionary to be discussed here is the Methodist, William Oldham (1854-1937). He has been called the Founder of Methodism in Singapore and Malaysia.[58]

Oldham was born in Bangalore, India. His father was a British military officer. When he was a teenager, Oldham was converted during a Methodist crusade in Pune. Eventually, he went to study in Methodist schools in America. He and his wife, Mary, were going to India to serve as missionaries, but a surprise awaited them at their arrival. James Thoburn, missionary visionary in India, challenged them to consider a new field that was opening up in Malaysia in the new British colony of Singapore.

Thoburn and the Oldhams sailed to Singapore in 1885. The decision to do this was entirely the decision of the Methodist missionaries in India. Two years later at a debate on the irregularity of this move, a Board member ended the debate by stating, "I believe we have established a mission [in Singapore] and did not know it."[59] Two years later in 1889, official recognition and financial support was granted to the work in Singapore.

Because of ill health, Oldham had to return to the States in 1889 after only four years of service. However, in those few short years, he laid a foundation for a Methodist Church that was to grow into the largest church in Singapore and in Malaysia.

Following is a list of some of his work and accomplishments.

1. In 1885, he helped found the first Methodist Church in Singapore (today Wesley Methodist Church). He served as their first pastor. Within their first year, sufficient funds were raised to erect their first building.[60]

2. His weekly pattern was to preach 5 times; sometimes in Tamil, sometimes in English.

---

[58] Chee Sin Ho, "Oldham, William Fitzjames," in *A Dictionary of Asian Christianity*, ed. Scott W. Sunquist (Grand Rapids, MI: Wm. B. Eerdmans, 2001), 616.

[59] Moffett, *A History of Christianity in Asia, Vol. II*, 609.

[60] Bobby E. K. Sng, *In His Good Time: The Story of the Church in Singapore 1819-2002*, 3rd edition (Singapore: Singapore Bible Society, 2003), 113–14.

3. Although he spoke Tamil, he recognized the importance of having ethnic Tamil evangelists and appointed Benjamin Pillai as missionary to the Tamils in Singapore.

4. Chinese business men were impressed with him and wanted their sons to study with him, especially to learn English. This led in 1886 to the beginning of the Anglo-Chinese school. The first year began with 13 students. The next year student enrollment jumped to 104 and continued to climb even after Oldham had to return to the States. Twenty years after its founding the school had 1400 students. During his time in Singapore, Oldham taught 5 to 8 hours a day at the school.

5. He opposed the opium trade. He returned in 1904 to Asia as the Missionary Bishop for Southern Asia. He was immediately asked to serve on a government opium commission.

6. He advocated for women's work and called on Methodists to appoint female missionaries. Sophie Blackmore was the eventual answer to his urging. She served effectively for 40 years.

Oldham served in other capacities for Methodist missions that fall outside the scope of this book, but one last anecdote is worth noting. Oldham met a group of Chinese business men early in his career in Singapore. The men had formed a club called "Celestial Reasoning Association". They had regular meetings to improve their English. It was this group of Chinese business men who were the stimulus for the Anglo-Chinese school mentioned earlier.

In 1936 at the age of 81, Oldham returned to Singapore for the last time. He was there to participate in a weeklong celebration of the founding work he had established.

> An elderly Chinese man watching the historical pageant which was part of the festivities was the sole surviving member of that group of 30 whom Oldham had addressed 50 years earlier at the Celestial Reasoning Association. As the Chinese sage watched the drama unfold, his soul was deeply stirred, and two days later his old friend, the aged

bishop, baptized him into the fold in a moving ceremony at Wesley Church.[61]

The Malaysian Peninsula was ethnically diverse with Chinese, Malays, and Indians. In a previous chapter, we talked about the impact of Robert Morrison on the Chinese in Malaysia. The British restricted evangelistic efforts among the Muslim Malay population in an effort to maintain harmony in the colony. William Shellabear (1862-1948) stands out as one who made strides toward the Malay community. Shellabear began in the military, including a tour in Singapore. He began to experience a tension between his military vocation and his Christian life. He came back to Malaysia and Singapore with the Methodist Mission, under Oldham's direction. Shellabear established the Methodist printing press and produced hymns, tracts, and catechisms in Chinese and Malay. His burden was for the Malay and he spent time learning the language and culture of the Malay. He also focused heavily on changing the minds of the British toward the Malay. He believed the Malay community would be more open to evangelism if Christians spent more time learning their language and culture. His greatest legacy was as a linguist. He produced a Malay grammar that is still in circulation and translated the whole Bible in the Malay language using terminology that Malay Muslims could understand.[62]

4.11 Baptists and Presbyterians in Thailand

American Baptist work began in Thailand in 1833 with the arrival of John Taylor Jones and his wife, Eliza Grew. They had been missionaries in Burma especially among the Peguan (Mon) people. Gutzlaff and his colleague Jacob Tomlin had requested help from the Baptist mission in Burma to come to Thailand. The Joneses were the result of that request.

Translation work was the primary focus of Jones. He completed the New Testament translation into Thai in 1843. His wife was also interested in language and prepared a Thai dictionary building on Gutzlaff's earlier work.

---

[61] Ho, "Oldham, William Fitzjames," 616.
[62] Robert A. Hunt, "The Legacy of William Shellabear," *International Bulletin of Missionary Research* 26, no. 1 (January 2002): 28–31.

Although Jones' work was focused on ethnic Thai, he found the Chinese more responsive. In 1833 he baptized four Chinese.[63] Before turning to the expansion of that Chinese work, it is appropriate to remember that death was often a real threat to these early missionaries. Eliza died of cholera in 1838. Jones' second wife also died in Thailand. Then finally Jones, himself, died in 1851 of dysentery.

William Dean (1807-1895) is the name most associated with the Chinese work of Baptists in Thailand. William Dean spoke of his first encounter with John Jones.

> "My acquaintance with Mr. Jones," said Mr. Dean, "commenced at Singapore in 1835. There I encountered with him an attack from Malayan pirates, by whom he was thrown into the sea; and there as the mark of the deadly piratical spears, and in the last stage of exhaustion, I succeeded in drawing him into our boat."[64]

Dean had also been wounded by spears, but a fishing boat passed by and they were brought back into Singapore.

Dean arrived in Bangkok in 1835. The work of the mission was gradually divided into two divisions; one for Thai and one for Chinese. Jones took charge of the Thai division, with Dean over the Chinese work.

In 1837 Dean organized the first Protestant Church in eastern Asia. Dean was the pastor. There were 11 members, three of whom were Asian (Chinese). From this small beginning, Maitrichit Baptist Church evolved.[65] He also encouraged theological education and native leadership. He ordained Thailand's first indigenous pastors. Additionally, he wrote a number of biblical commentaries in Chinese.

The Presbyterian work in Thailand has been more extensive than any other Protestant denomination. Thus, it is with some reservation that we only look

---

[63] Kenneth Elmer Wells, *History of Protestant Work in Thailand, 1828-1958* (Bangkok: Church of Christ in Thailand, 1958), 18.

[64] Wells, 16.

[65] In the 20th century Maitrichit grew from 200 members in 1948 to almost 1200 members in 1984. It was also responsible for starting most of the 28 churches associated with the 12th district of the Church of Christ in Thailand.

briefly at the work of one of these missionaries. His name is Daniel McGilvary (1828-1911).

Daniel McGilvary arrived in Bangkok in 1858 as a missionary of the Presbyterian Church, USA. In 1860 he married Sophie Bradley who was the daughter of pioneer missionary doctor, Dan Bradley. Together they served in Petchaburi, a city south of Bangkok and the first Presbyterian work outside of the capital city.

McGilvary had an early interest in northern Thailand, then a semi-autonomous kingdom ruled by a prince but under the sovereignty of the Monarch of Siam (Thailand). After having made a survey trip to the north, he, his wife and two children moved to the northern city of Chiang Mai in 1868. This new Presbyterian work was called the Lao Mission.
The following is a description of what they faced.

> It was indeed launching out on an adventure in faith; no friends or home awaited them at their journey's end and in that jungle city there would be no mail or telegraph service connecting them with the outside world; houses for rent or hotels did not exist; their box of medicines with Moore's book, 'Family Medicine for India', their only material help in illness; their reception friendly or otherwise depended entirely on the whim of a temperamental ruler . . .

> Before them lay the long tiresome river journey with its more than forty rapids. It was not until 3rd April three months after leaving Bangkok that their boats finally crawled into Chiengmai, their desired haven. They found a public rest house twelve by twenty feet in size, partially enclosed, with a tile roof, and a teak floor. In this and other temporary buildings they lived for more than eight years and received the throngs that pressed about them. Privacy was a thing that did not exist.[66]

---

[66] Laura McKean, "The Narrative of Chiengmai," in *Historial Sketch of Protestant Missions in Siam 1828-1928*, ed. George Bradley McFarland, reprint (Bangkok: White Lotus Press, 1999), 116.

He worked in northern Thailand until his death in 1911. The work began with great promise – six men converted in the first year, though two of them (Nan Chai and Noe Sunya) were later martyred. He was an indefatigable evangelist and church planter. He helped to start several rural Christian communities. His exploratory tours took him all over northern Thailand and into Burma, Laos, and China. The result of these tours was, as other missionaries joined him, the establishment of mission stations in many of the principle towns of the north.

In addition to the above, he introduced western medical practices to northern Thailand, supported the training of indigenous workers, and encouraged the establishment of mission boarding schools. Today the primary theological training school in northern Thailand is named after him – McGilvary College of Divinity.

The work in northern Thailand always progressed faster than elsewhere. By the time of McGilvary's death, 20 churches had been founded with a membership of over 4,000.[67] These numbers are small for a period stretching over 40 years, but they point to a commitment to northern Thailand that would not be swayed.

---

[67] Herbert R. Swanson, *Khrischak Muang Nua* (Bangkok: Chuan Printing Press, 1984), 169–70.

Part Two: The Church in Asia: Modern, Indigenous and Global

"The Christian story is serial, its center moves from place to place. No one church or place or culture owns it."

–Andrew Walls[1]

The Christian faith is a pilgrim faith. When the gospel is translated into the local language, idiom, and culture, it no longer appears foreign. The New Testament, written in Greek and using terms and ideas from the Hellenistic world is an early example of what would happen every time Christianity takes root in a new place.

Throughout the world there are expressions of Christianity that look and feel foreign and expressions that look and feel local. However, in most cases, Christianity ends up with a mix of foreign and local. This is due to the fact that Christianity is constantly moving from one culture to the next. We are at once a people in a certain cultural location and a part of the trans-global family of Christ.

Some Asian Christian intellectuals have constructed Asian theologies that tap into philosophical ideas of Asian worldview issues. While these play with Asian ideas, they end up being theoretical abstractions fit primarily for the halls of academia. Simon Chan recognizes another stream of indigeneity worth exploring: "Much of what the West knows as Asian theology consists largely of …accounts of what Asian theologians are saying, and…theologians seldom take grassroots Christianity seriously. Yet it is at the grassroots level that we encounter a vibrant, albeit implicit, theology."[2] What we explore in this section is birthed out of Christians living out their faith in their context in a way that further localized its expression.

---

[1] Andrew Walls, "The Mission of the Church Today in the Light of Global History," *Word & World* XX, no. 1 (Winter 2000): 18.
[2] Simon Chan, *Grassroots Asian Theology: Thinking the Faith from the Ground Up by Simon Chan* (Downers Grove, IL: IVP Academic, 2014), 7.

As Christianity has put down roots in places all over Asia, expressions of Christianity emerged that helped Christians in that place feel at home in their faith. These expressions of Christianity are intensely local and yet remain thoroughly Christian.

Chapter 5: The Three-Self Movement Illustrated in China and Korea

"Seventy-five years ago when the first Protestant missionaries landed in Korea they walked for miles through valley after valley in which the name of Christ had never been heard. Today the visitor driving along Korea's highways is rarely out of sight of a Christian church."

–Samuel H. Moffett[1]

"If we come to a place to found a church, then it must be local, intensely local, without anything extraneous to rob it in the slightest of its local character."

–Watchan Nee[2]

5.1 Beginning and Implementation in Korea

The Three-Self Movement was conceptualized by two men: Henry Venn (1798-1873) and Rufus Anderson (1797-1880). However, in one sense they were simply affirming the mission understanding current in their day.

> The objective of planting indigenous churches that would be capable of sustaining their own life, growing their own pastoral ministry and initiating mission on their own account was shared by almost all missions in this period [mid-19th century]. Posterity has paid most attention to the statements of "Three-Self" principles produced by Henry Venn and Rufus Anderson, but the fact that two mission strategists on either side of the Atlantic arrived independently at similar conclusions is less surprising if one regards them as seeking to elucidate the principles

---

[1] Samuel Hugh Moffett, *The Christians of Korea* (Friendship Press, 1962), 15.
[2] Watchman Nee, *The Normal Christian Church Life*, 2nd ed. (Living Stream Ministry, 1980), 136.

which would guarantee the achievement of a generally accepted goal.[3]

Henry Venn was an Englishman. From 1841 to 1872 he was the honorary secretary for the Church Mission Society (CMS). He functioned in reality as the chief executive. He was instrumental in getting recognition by the Anglican episcopacy for this voluntary mission organization.

Venn believed in the importance of planting indigenous churches. He advocated a strategy that would begin with small cells that would join together to form a larger grouping which would become a "Native Pastorate Church". These churches were to be self-governing, self-supporting, and self-extending". He ultimately wanted to see "the euthanasia of the mission" by which he meant that indigenous leadership would take charge of the churches and the missionaries would move on to a new field to begin again with an evangelistic emphasis.[4]

Anderson was an American. He wanted to be a missionary to India, but was instead employed in the home office of the American Board of Commissioners for Foreign Missions (ABCFM). He served as an Assistant Secretary and then from 1832 to retirement in 1866 as the Foreign Secretary. He has been called "the most influential American mission statesman, both theoretician and administrator."[5]

In 1855, he visited the mission work in India. The results of that visit were the dispersing of central mission stations, the organization of village churches, and the ordaining of native pastors. Like Venn, Anderson promoted the establishment of indigenous congregations that would be self-supporting, self-governing, and self-propagating. Missionaries were to be evangelists, not pastors. The newly planted churches must become the responsibility of the local membership. Perhaps his most influential disciple

---

[3] Brian Stanley, "Christian Missions, Antislavery and the Claims of Humanity, c. 1813-1873," in *World Christianities c. 1815-c. 1914*, ed. Sheridan Gilley and Brian Stanley, vol. 8, The Cambridge History of Christianity (Cambridge: Cambridge University Press, 2006), 489.
[4] Timothy Yates, "Venn, Henry," in *A Dictionary of Asian Christianity*, ed. Scott W. Sunquist (Grand Rapids, MI: Wm. B. Eerdmans, 2001), 872.
[5] R. Pierce Beaver, "Anderson, Rufus," in *Concise Dictionary of the Christian World Mission*, ed. Stephen Neill, Gerald H. Anderson, and John Goodman (London: Lutterworth Press, 1971), 21.

was the Presbyterian missionary John Nevius whose methods were adopted by the Korean Presbyterian Mission.[6]

5.2 The Three-Self Movement Illustrated in China

It is to China that we turn to see a uniting of the Three-Self idea with indigenous movements.[7] Three such movements will be surveyed: the Jesus Family of Jing Dianying, the Little Flock of Watchman Nee, and the Three-Self Patriotic Movement.

Jing Dianying was born in 1890 in the town of Mazhuang in Shandong Province.[8] He was born into a strong Confucian family, but at the time of his conversion was considered a Buddhist. He attended a Methodist school and was converted by a Methodist missionary, Nora Dillenbeck. She eventually left the Methodist board and worked with Jing for two year prior to her death. Jing, his wife, Dillenbeck, and others established a Christian cooperative store in 1921. Eventually a silk weaving industry was added. It all was renamed in 1930 as the Jesus Family (*Yesu Jiating*).

The Jesus Family was "a unique Pentecostal communitarian Church."[9] The Pentecostal nature of the movement was connected to the Assemblies of God influence in Jing's life. In 1924 an Assemblies church in a nearby town began experiencing revival. In that revival Jing had charismatic experiences. One writer reported that

> Jing was around thirty-five years old at the time. He sought very hard to have union with God in love and to apply Chinese mysticism into western theology. Together with the author of the book [Ma Honggang, a disciple of Jing is the likely source of this information], they received the baptism of the Spirit in an Assemblies of God meeting in 1925. Henceforth he sought after speaking in tongues,

---

[6] See chapter 4.

[7] No attempt in this book has been made to define "indigenous", but one aspect that I believe is present in genuine indigenous expressions is that the driving force behind an 'indigenous' church or movement is always native or national persons.

[8] It is not clear when he died. Those who list death dates do so with a question mark. Two dates have been suggested: 1953 and 1973. We know that he was imprisoned in 1952 and sentenced to 20 years.

[9] Tiedemann, "China and Its Neighbors," 396.

prophecy, singing and dancing in the Spirit, seeking inspirations from the Holy Spirit and living a Spirit-filled lifestyle.[10]

The charismatic or Pentecostal element of the Jesus Family was prominent in that every morning the various communes would gather for prayer and worship before going out to work. And they would meet again in the evenings. These meetings included speaking in tongues, prophecies, and the interpretation of dreams. At times, some people would fall on the ground where they would roll and scream, or simply lie there silently.

Jing is reported to have advised a recent convert,

> My beloved brother, you must kneel down in a secret place, and pray with all your heart, 'Dear Lord Jesus, forgive all my sins since birth. Dear Lord, send Your Holy Spirit moving in my heart, helping me to confess all my sins.' No matter how sick you are, how terrible your situation is, you can pray to Him and He will show you His way, even whatever you may ask of Him. You will be comforted and helped. It is even best if there is crying in your prayer, having a tingle feeling, quivering, losing control of your tongue. Then you will know that Lord Jesus is God indeed. You will have Joy Unspeakable. . . He dwells in hearts of those who confessed their sins with delight. He can speak to you through dreams and manifests Himself in visions when you are praying. However, the most valuable is you are being changed and His presence seen. You feel that you are His and He is yours.[11]

The communal nature of the Jesus Family is also clear. All who joined were required to leave their earthly families. They must sell their possessions and give the proceeds to the Family. In the various communes, each member had work to do. Each commune was considered self-sufficient with its own industry and farming. They also ran their own schools. A chapel was the center of each commune.

---

[10] Timothy Yeung, "The Chinese Expression of Pentecostalism," *Cypberjournal for Pentecostal Charismatic Research*, no. 16 (2007), http://www.pctii.org/cyberj/cyberj16/yeung.html.

[11] Yeung.

Jing and others were active in evangelism throughout north and northwestern China. By 1949 there were well over 100 communes with over 10,000 members. The largest was in Mazhuang. Each commune was led by a *Jiachang* (family head).

Interestingly enough, many of the Jesus Family members supported the Communist movement because of its egalitarian philosophy. Wu Yaozong had been a YMCA official and was responsible for drafting a document entitled "the Path and Endeavors of Chinese Christianity in New China" which affirmed a positive relationship between the Chinese Church and the Communist party. This was in 1950. A quarter of the signers of that document were reportedly members of the Jesus Family. At first, good relationships with the government were maintained.

However, in 1952 or 53, Jing's nephew accused him of collaborating with the imperialists. Jing was sentenced to 20 years in prison. The Jesus Family movement was officially disbanded. Eventually in 1958 those churches still functioning were absorbed into the unification program of the Communist government.

However, it has been noted that the influence of the Jesus Family continues to be felt in certain parts of country. One commentator observed,

> Most Christian groups in central Shandong are of Family background and their influence remains in the provinces. . . . [One of several characteristics that remain] are early morning emotional prayer meetings with loud crying, simultaneous prayers and manifestations of the Spirit like speaking in tongues, trances, [etc.].[12]

The second movement is Little Flock. Watchman Nee (Nee To-sheng) was born into a Christian family in Swatow, China in 1903. In 1916 he enrolled in a junior high school run by the Church Mission Society at the Anglican Trinity College. He was converted at a gospel meeting led by a Methodist evangelist, Dora Yu.[13] This was in 1920. For the next few years he was

---

[12] Allan Anderson, *An Introduction to Pentecostalism: Global Charismatic Christianity* (Cambridge, UK: Cambridge University Press, 2004), 135.
[13] Scott Sunquist considers Dora Yu one of the most significant Chinese evangelists in the twentieth century. Sunquist, *Explorations in Asian Christianity*, 65.

influenced by Holiness literature, the Keswick Movement, [14] and the Brethren Church. He was apparently an avid reader and read biographies of many great Christian persons.

In 1923 he began a publishing ministry that started with devotional magazines. In 1928, he wrote the first of many books. This one was entitled *The Spiritual Man*.[15] Ten years later, he wrote his most popular book, *The Normal Christian Life*.[16] These writings and others extended his influence far beyond the land of China.

In 1927, Nee began a house church in Shanghai. This church quickly grew. He affirmed that it should be self-propagating, self-governing, and self-supporting. However, it may be noted that the latter did not happen overnight. The Brethren Church in England provided some financial help for around 20 years. The name for this new Chinese church was Little Flock (*Xiaoqun*) or Christian Assembly (*Jidutu Juhuichu*).

One of the important principles affirmed by Nee was that only one true church should exist in each city.[17] New churches were started in other cities in China. Nee had a team of fellow workers; Witness Lee, Simon Meek, and Faithful Luke. The Little Flock was anti-denominational and they asked Christians from other churches to leave theirs to join Little Flock. Therefore, at least part (certainly not all) of their growth was attracting persons who were already Christian from other churches.

In 1947, Nee and the Little Flock adopted a mission strategy that had already been practiced by Witness Lee for several years. It was called the Jerusalem

---

[14] The Keswick movement was a holiness spirituality emphasis arising from regular Evangelical conventions held at Keswick in the Lake District of England. The roots of this convention were in the earlier Evangelical group referred to as the Clapham Sect. The Clapham Sect became known for combined Evangelical convictions mixed with active concern for social issues. The Keswick movement was less focused on social issues and more focused on inward spiritual growth. Gordon Mursell, *English Spirituality: From 1700 to the Present Day* (London: Westminster John Knox Press, 2001), 223.

[15] Watchman Nee, *The Spiritual Man* (New York: Christian Fellowship Publishers, 1968).

[16] Watchman Nee, *The Normal Christian Life*, Reprinted edition (Wheaton, IL.; Fort Washington, PA: Tyndale House Publishers, Inc., 1977).

[17] Nee, *The Spiritual Man*, 75.

Principle. In the Book of Acts it was reported that the Church grew when families fled from persecution in Jerusalem. They went to other towns and cities, establishing churches in many places. The Little Flock decided that this was a strategy that could be intentionally implemented. Several families would move to a new place and begin a church. This strategy was very successful. By 1949 there were over 700 local churches with a combined membership of 70,000.

In 1950, Nee was in Hong Kong. As he prepared to return to China, his colleague, Witness Lee begged him not to go because of the new Communist government. He is reported to have responded, "I do not care for my life. If the house is crashing down, I have children inside and must support it, if need be with my head."[18]

In 1952, Nee was arrested at least in part because he opposed the confiscation of some of the church's property. He was sentenced to jail in a work camp and died a few months after his release in 1972.[19] A few other leaders of the Little Flock were also imprisoned, but the movement as a whole was not regarded as imperialistic. In 1958 most of the Little Flock supported the Three-Self Patriotic Movement and joined the government sponsored organization. A few congregations went underground.[20]

However, this did not end the Little Flock or Christian Assembly movement. It has spread to Taiwan, Hong Kong, the Philippines, Singapore, and almost any other place with a significant Chinese population. This continued growth was partly due to Nee's emphasis on training lay people. This meant that church members were not waiting on clergy to lead them. It also meant that many people had undergone training to help lead the churches.

In addition to its anti-denominationalism and insistence on one church per city, the Little Flock of Watchman Nee had no ordained clergy. Anyone could technically have a part in preaching and in leading church ceremonies. No symbols, including crosses, were allowed in their simple church buildings. They also refused to observe Christmas and Easter.

---

[18] Sie Kwan Tung, "The Waves of the 'Local Church': Watchman Nee's 'Little Flock' in China," *Bridge* 56 (2-23): 12.
[19] Tung, 20.
[20] Angus I. Kinnear, *Against the Tide, the Story of Watchman Nee* (Wheaton, IL: Tyndale House Publishers, 1973), 266–67.

It is worth noting that Witness Lee continued to work outside of China. He became the primary leader of Christian Assembly churches in Taiwan and Southeast Asia. However, the nature of the "Little Flock" changed under Witness Lee's leadership and is regarded by many Chinese Christians as cult-like. In 1967 he introduced "a form of public, emotional repentance of sin by loud confession". Thus, his followers are also called "Yellers".[21]

By way of comparison it has been noted that the Yellers and the earlier Jesus Family had similar emotional experiences. The following quote does not mention the Jesus Family by name, but these revivals were a part of its historical lineage.

> A sympathetic account of a revival movement in the early 1900s, calling it "the greatest spiritual movement in the history of missions in China", described how people would confess "with sobs, shrieks, and groans," falling on their faces, until 'their separate cries were merged and lost in the swelling tide of general weeping'. The same account noted that "strange thrills coursed up and down one's body', and that everywhere could be heard 'the agony of the penitent, his groans and cries and voice shaken with sobs." This account, written eighty years [incorrect dating if the Yellers began in the 1960s] before the Yellers, could very well be a present-day description of their yelling expressions.[22]

In Communist China, the Three-Self movement took a political face. As already alluded to, many of the Chinese Christians were not opposed to the Communist takeover and at least some actively promoted it. All in these two groups desired a truly indigenous Church, a Church built along the Three-Self pattern.

The architect of what was to evolve was Wu Yaozong (1893-1979). Wu was a Chinese Christian who worked with the Young Men's Christian Association (YMCA) for over 20 years. During that time, he became increasingly discontented with western Protestantism, accusing it of nurturing capitalism. He criticized missionaries, and affirmed his belief that

---

[21] Allan Anderson and Edmond Tang, "Independency in Africa and Asia," in *A World History of Christianity*, ed. Adrian Hastings (Grand Rapids, MI: Wm. B. Eerdmans, 2011), 121.

[22] Anderson and Tang, 122–23.

the British and Americans were using the Chinese church to further their own imperialistic designs.

He became a supporter of Marxism and believed that the Protestant Church would have to divorce itself from capitalism in order to survive the victory of the socialist movement. In 1950, Wu started the Three-Self Reform Movement which sought to encourage the cooperation of the churches with the Communist government in the establishment of national self-sufficiency.

In 1954, the movement was officially established as the Three-Self Patriotic Movement. At this meeting, Wu emphasized love for country and love for the Church. At this point, the TSPM came under the direct influence of the communist government. Additionally, a national council was resurrected and called the China Christian Council (CCC). One historian noted that at that time:

> The TSPM/CCC assumed the position it still holds as a semi-autonomous agency that regulates the affairs of China's Protestants in accordance with the principles of self-support, self-government, and self-propagation. . . . Such principles encapsulate the patriotism the TSPM/CCC was designed to engender among Christians whose Euro-American denominational identity had become a liability. [23]

The Christian leaders of the TSPM saw it as the only realistic way for Chinese Protestants to demonstrate patriotism to the new China. In the 1950s, those indigenous sects and conservative Protestant churches that resisted unification became the target of denunciation campaigns sponsored by the TSPM. Among those who suffered the consequences were Jing Dianying and Watchman Nee.

During the Cultural Revolution (1966-1979) the TSPM/CCC was almost incapacitated and Wu himself was humiliated by the Red Guards. However, with the end of the Cold War, the TSPM/CCC was revitalized and as noted above continues to function today. In 2007, the TSPM/CCC claimed 16,000,000 members. [24]

---

[23] Richard Fox Young, "East Asia," in *World Christianities*, vol. 9, The Cambridge History of Christianity (Cambridge: Cambridge University Press, 2014), 460.

[24] Also, it should be noted that the Catholics have their own officially recognized organization with perhaps 4,500,000 members. Protestants and Catholics who have

These figures played a significant role in preparing the Church in China for the difficult times of the Cultural Revolution. We will likely never know how many people were imprisoned and/or martyred during this dark era.[25] As we've seen, this was not the first attempt to purge the Church from China (cf. the rise of the Ming Dynasty in the 14th century and the Boxer Rebellion in 1900). For several decades little was known about the state of the Church in China. Some assumed that it was all but completely decimated once more. When the so-called "bamboo curtain" lifted in the early 1980s, the world was surprised to find that not only had the church survived such sustained persecution but had thrived. In addition to TSPM/CCC, and the Catholic Church, there were large networks of underground churches.[26] There is not room in this volume to record the many accounts of Christian perseverance

---

refused to join either organization probably number more than double those Christians who are registered.

[25] Lawrence gives two sources on the extent of persecution during the "cultural revolution": "This figure is even more difficult to ascertain with certainty. We will probably never know how many Christians were killed in this modern holocaust. According to Judith Banister, Chief of the Chinese Branch of the U.S. Bureau of the Census, 'More people died in China during the period of the Great Leap forward than in all the battles of First World War, or the holocaust of Europe's Jews, or the Soviet Collectivization and Stalin's terror.' Ansley of The National Academy of Sciences and Princeton University says that "about 27 million" died. Both quoted in Carl Lawrence, *The Church in China: How It Survives and Prospers Under Communism* (Minneapolis, MN: Bethany House Publishers, 1985); Dennis McCallum, "Watchman Nee and the House Church Movement in China: Unpublished Paper," 1986, https://www.xenos.org/essays/watchman-nee-and-house-church-movement-china.

[26] Adeney estimates 113,000 Christians were in China in 1900. There was then considerable growth and the devastating persecution. The numbers of the church in China are difficult to verify with certainty, but Barrett estimated 81 million Christians in 2000. More recent estimates exceed 100 million Christians in China. David H. Adeney, *China: The Church's Long March* (Ventura, CA: Baker Publishing Group, 1985), 41; Barrett, Kurian, and Johnson, *World Christian Encyclopedia*; Tom Phillips, "China on Course to Become 'world's Most Christian Nation' within 15 Years," *The Telegraph*, April 19, 2014, http://www.telegraph.co.uk/news/worldnews/asia/china/10776023/China-on-course-to-become-worlds-most-Christian-nation-within-15-years.html.

and conviction during these decades under persecution. Moreover, Chinese Christians have begun sending missionaries to the rest of the world.[27]

---

[27] Paul Hattaway, *Back to Jerusalem: Three Chinese House Church Leaders Share Their Vision to Complete the Great Commission* (Carlisle; Waynesboro, GA: Piquant; Gabriel Resources, 2003).

Chapter 6: Three East and Southeast Asian Indigenous Movements

> *"Any authentic indigenous theology—indeed, any theology for that matter—must be missiological and pastoral in its fundamental conception."*

–Hwa Yung[1]

6.1 Sadrach Surapranata

Sadrach Surapranata (c.1835-1924) was the focal point of a significant indigenous movement which began in the 19th century on the Indonesian island of Java.

Indonesia was at that time and remains today a predominantly Islamic country. However, during Sadrach's time there was a scattered Christian presence. It can be described under three categories. The *Indische Kerk* in central Java was composed primarily of Europeans and of Christian communities that were established by various missionary organizations.[2] These two categories, united as one, tended to demand a break from indigenous culture (at the urging of the Dutch East India Company) and emphasized pure doctrine. Additionally, there were communities started by lay people (Dutch and Eurasian) and Javanese evangelists.[3] Normally, these Javanese converts were baptized by ordained ministers belonging to other

---

[1] Yung, *Mangoes or Bananas?*, 19.

[2] This was a union Church created by King William I in 1835 by uniting all of the existing denominations in Indonesia into one denomination.

[3] "The gospel was effectively introduced to the Javanese through laymen and laywomen, particularly Eurasians who had contact with both cultures. They were followed by Javanese who presented the gospel in indigenous forms. Most important of these was Coenraad Laurens Coolen, son of a Dutch father and Javanese mother from the Solo nobility. In 1829 he got permission to clear the jungle and establish a village at Ngoro, East Java. This became the first place of contact between the gospel and Javanese village life. It provided a laboratory for experimentation in penetrating Javanese culture with the gospel." Willis, *Indonesian Revival Why Two Million Came to Christ*, 29.

groups. They were more likely to form separate communities with ties to local culture and society.

Sadrach (whose given name was Radin) was born into a poor family along the coastal region of North Central Java. He was later adopted by a well-to-do Muslim family. This was a fairly common practice among 19th century Javanese and was done for the purpose of education.

From the ages of 6 to 10, he attended the equivalent of a public school where he learned to read the Qur'an. Upon graduation, he studied under a traditional Javanese religious teacher. This teaching is called *ngelmu* which means knowledge. However, that word can be used for various kinds of knowledge from Islamic teaching to knowledge of magic.

At the age of 17, Sadrach went to East Java where he studied in several *pesantrens* (Muslim religious boarding school). Sutarman Partonadi describes this educational system.

> The *pesantren* was basically a continuation of the Koran school. Its "curriculum," however, was broader and more profound. Stress was placed not only on memorizing and reciting the Koran, but also on exegesis of and commentary on the Koran and other Moslem books. Islamic obligations and teachings were also studied. The *santris* [a Muslim student or graduate from a *pesantren*] were trained to become intellectually independent.

> The most significant element of the *pesantren* was not one of intellectual formation, but one of spiritual formation. Here students were equipped and prepared to enter into real society and life.[4]

During this time he met a Dutch missionary named J. E. Jellesma and perhaps other Christians, but was not led to conversion.[5] Instead he returned to Central Java, where he chose to live in an exclusive Muslim area.

---

[4] Sutarman Soediman Partonadi, *Sadrach's Community And Its Contextual Roots. A Nineteenth-Century Javanese Expression of Christianity.* (Amsterdam: Rodopi Bv Editions, 1988), 57.

[5] Jellesma was among the first to see the importance of an indigenous church among the Javanese and began a church intended to be a model for others. Th. Sumartana,

At this time he met his former teacher who had become a Christian. An important aspect of 19ᵗʰ century Javanese culture was the relationship between *guru* (teacher) and *murid* (disciple) and the increasing of one's discipleship following through debate. In its simplest terms, two *gurus* would hold a public debate. The loser then became the disciple of the winner. Normally the loser's disciples would follow their teacher into the new relationship.

Sadrach's former teacher had lost a debate to a Javanese Christian evangelist named Tunggul Wulung. At this point, Sadrach became interested in Christianity. His interest was further peaked when Tunggul Wulung affirmed that becoming a Christian did not necessarily mean abandoning traditional Javanese customs.

Following contacts with Dutch missionaries and lay Christians, Sadrach finally decided to be baptized. After receiving religious instruction from a missionary, he was baptized by a minister of the *Indische Kerk* on April 14, 1867. At this point he adopted a new 'Christian' name – Sadrach from the story of Shadrach, Meshach and Abednego in the Book of Daniel.

For the next few years, Sadrach was involved in a number of activities. He distributed Christian literature, helped other evangelists start Christian villages, and used the traditional public debate method of evangelism. He was a Christian *guru.* In this later activity, around 1869, Sadrach worked in conjunction with Christina Petronella Stevens-Philips who was a Euro-Indonesian. She had started a house church which eventually grew to over 300 members. Sadrach's converts were given further instruction by Stevens-Philips.
After about a year of working with Stevens-Philips, Sadrach moved 25 kilometers south to the village of Karangjasa which was to become the headquarters for Sadrach's community. Working now as a fully independent evangelist and using the public debate method, he won other *gurus* (also called *kyais*). At this point each *kyai* began to be taught be Sadrach himself.

However, as would be the case throughout his career, Sadrach was not entirely separated from the earlier Christian community.

Mission at the Crossroads: Indigenous Churches, European Missionaries, Islamic Association and Socio-Religious Change in Java 1812-1936 (Jakarta: Pt BPK Gunnung Mulia, 1991), 28.

> Sadrach considered Stevens-Philips his formal "protector", the "bridging figure" with the Dutch authorities, including the *Indische Kerk* and the Dutch missionaries. All of Sadrach's Javanese converts were baptized by the minister of the *Indische Kerk* in Purwareja as a result of Stevens-Philips' mediation.[6]

For many years, Sadrach would depend on ministers and missionaries to perform baptism and to provide Holy Communion. He felt that only ordained persons had the right to conduct these sacraments. This means that when relationships were broken with the western dominated Church, several years passed during which the sacraments were not administered.

However, before the break, baptism statistics were impressive. Within three years, the membership of Sadrach's community had increased to almost 2500 persons with 5 churches having been erected in 5 villages.

Sadrach's community grew for many reasons. He was obviously an effective communicator as his victories in public debates illustrated. He was also considered to have the ability to control evil spirits. For example, he rented rice fields that were considered haunted by deadly spirits and cultivated them without harm. He was considered to have the ability to do miracles, including healing. His services were conducted in the local Javanese language. His converts, especially the converted *kyais* (gurus), were effective in bearing witness as well.

After the death of Stevens-Philips, Sadrach became the near undisputed leader of the community. Following Javanese tradition he added to his name to indicate his new position. The addition was Surapranata which means "he who has the courage to minister"[7] or "he who makes the regulations".[8] Either way, Sadrach clearly saw himself as the new leader.

Sadrach's relationships with the Dutch missionaries and the *Indische Kerk* were rarely smooth. On various occasions attempts were made to entice him

---

[6] Partonadi, *Sadrach's Community And Its Contextual Roots. A Nineteenth-Century Javanese Expression of Christianity.*, 66.

[7] Partonadi, 71.

[8] Sumartana, *Mission at the Crossroads: Indigenous Churches, European Missionaries, Islamic Association and Socio-Religious Change in Java 1812-1936*, 69.

to join his community to the western Church. He rejected these overtures. There were also attempts at removing him from leadership so that the westerners could take control. On one occasion he was jailed for refusing to take a government ordered vaccination for small pox. This was at the instigation of those missionaries and other westerners who opposed his leadership.

However, there was one missionary who consistently sought to understand Sadrach and work with him. His name was Jacob Wilhelm. In recognition of his sympathies and in need of an ordained minister, Sadrach asked him to become the minister of the community. In 1883, Wilhelm became the official minister of the community that included 26 elders, 22 *mesjid* (mosques or local communities), and 3,039 members. At this meeting of Sadrach, Wilhelm, and the elders, a name was chosen. The community was to be called *Wong Kristen Kang Mardika* (the Group of Free Christians).

It is possible that Wilhelm had recommended the word *mardika* since he was a firm believer in the need for the community to maintain its Javaness – without compromising Biblical norms. However, this was not a new idea to Sadrach or his community.

> The inclusion of the word *mardika* (free, independent) indicated that the independence of the community, which since the very beginning had been a prevailing characteristic, was to be maintained. All interference from the outside was to be rejected, whether from the government or from the *Indische Kerk* in Purwareja. Positively, the word *mardika* implied that the community had the right to express its faith freely, and to manage and organize itself in a way that was relevant to the context of which it operated.[9]

The relationship between Wilhelm and Sadrach was practically unique among missionaries and nationals at that time. Wilhelm did not see himself as the supervisor of Sadrach. Indeed, he saw them as equals. In a picture that

---

[9] Partonadi, *Sadrach's Community And Its Contextual Roots. A Nineteenth-Century Javanese Expression of Christianity.*, 76–78.

startled many westerners, a photograph was taken in which both Wilhelm and Sadrach were sitting in chairs next to each other.[10]

There was a clear division of duties. Sadrach spent most of his time in working with the Javanese evangelists, going from village to village, often engaging in public debates with influential *gurus or kyai.* Wilhelm concentrated on teaching, preaching, pastoring, and administering the sacraments. He also reorganized the community to be more in line with the Reformed tradition. This was accomplished in part by translating various Reformed texts.

1892-93 proved a pivotal and difficult year for Sadrach and his community. Suspicions about Sadrach's orthodoxy and the true Christian nature were raised – not for the first time. The upshot was that the primary mission organization in the area that supported Wilhelm's work voted to remove Sadrach from his position of evangelist. To that end they appealed to the government to revoke his permit to work as an evangelist. The government rejected the request, but the break between Sadrach's community and the missionary community was now complete. Perhaps due to the stress of the events surrounding him, Wilhelm became ill and died during this time. Considering the importance of Sadrach as the *guru* of the community, it is not surprising that the vast majority of the membership remained with him. Of the 6,374 converts, only around 150 sided with the missionaries.

In the years that followed, Sadrach hoped to reunite with the missionaries if sympathetic ones like Wilhelm could be found. One or two were promising, but nothing materialized. The work of the church continued well, with remarkable growth happening in new villages with amazing frequency. However, the administration of the sacraments was missing.

Eventually, and for a variety of reasons we can only guess at, Sadrach brought his community into the *Apostolische Kerk* (Apostolic Church). This was a Pentecostal type denomination that traced its roots back to Edward Irving (1792-1834). There were congregations in the Netherlands and it was this Dutch connection that was present in Indonesia. The first missionaries arrived in the 1880s.

---

[10] Partonadi, 77.

By the 1890's Sadrach had become familiar with the Apostolic Church and had worshipped in one of their congregations in Magalang which was led by a Chinese "apostle." Finally, in 1899, Sadrach went to Batavia where one of the Apostolic Church missionaries ordained him as "the apostle of Java."[11] One of the first things he did on returning to Karangjase was to serve the Lord's Supper to his community. Finally, he was ordained.

Sadrach continued to lead his community until his death in 1924. Within 10 years after his death, Sadrach's community divided. Fully half would eventually unite with the Dutch missionary organization. Another group remained with the Apostolic Church. The smallest group called itself *Pasamuwan Kristen Jawi Netral* (the Neutral Javanese Christian Church). Additionally some members eventually joined the Roman Catholic Church.

It is time now to examine some of the unique features of this indigenous movement and understand the general Dutch missionary opposition to them.

In terms of organization, the most important feature is the significance of the relationship between *guru* and *murid*. The typical Javanese community of *guru* and *murid* has been described thus: "Stress was placed on the idea of brotherhood. The bond between guru and *murid* was marked by a vow of faithfulness and obedience on the part of the *murids*. The community which resulted emphasized loving one another and encouraging solidarity among the members."[12]

As the number of communities arose in various places, Sadrach was not able to look after each of them on a regular basis. Therefore he began to appoint leaders for each community. Various titles were used, all from the Javanese Muslim community, e.g. *susipuh*, *guru igama*, or *imam*. It is perhaps because of the Muslim flavor that the local Muslim communities tolerated them. Additionally Sadrach appointed three of his most trusted evangelists to act in his stead in relationship to the various communities.

For historical purposes, it may be noted that Wilhelm did lead the broader community to adopt a more institutional church structure build along Reformed lines. Technically, Wilhelm was listed as the Minister and Sadrach as Evangelist; however, Sadrach's influence as chief *guru* was never really

---

[11] Partonadi, 92.
[12] Partonadi, 109.

lessened. Therefore, when the break occurred with the Dutch missionaries, the community returned to its more indigenous model. It was a model that it was able to keep as a member of the Apostolic Church since Sadrach was ordained as their Apostle.

The indigenous nature of Sadrach's community can also be seen in their worship and the rituals they adopted. However, it should be noted that each community was free to conduct its own services as it saw fit, so there was no single pattern.

As has already been noted, the church buildings were called *mesjid* (mosque). In addition to a church bell, some of them used a drum as a call to worship. This was a local Muslim custom. The structure of Sadrach's church in Karangjasa is interesting. It has a three-tiered roof and, in place of a cross or a crescent, it had a *cakra* (a disk with several protruding arrows). The three tiers were interpreted as symbol of the Trinity. The *chakra* was a weapon used by Sri Kresna in Javanese folklore. However, the understood symbolism was that the gospel is able to penetrate the hardest heart.

Worship services generally included prayers, songs, Scripture reading, a sermon or testimony, and an offering. Traditional Javanese poetry forms (tempang) were used during these services. Sadrach, himself, "set the Ten Commandments, the Apostles' Creed, the Lord's Prayer and some other special prayers to various types of *tempang*."[13]

The Creed used by Sadrach has been translated as follows:

> I believe that God (*Allah*) is One.
> There is no God but God.
> Jesus Christ is the Spirit of God,
> Whose power is power is over everything.
> There is no God but God.

---

[13] Lukas Vischer, ed., *Christian Worship in Reformed Churches Past and Present* (Grand Rapids, MI: Wm. B. Eerdmans Publishing Company, 2002), 184; Roger L. Dixon, "The Major Model of Muslim Ministry," *Missiology: An International Review* 30, no. 4 (October 2002): 446. However, it is possible that Sadrach did not do all of this composing. He may have used some composed by another indigenous evangelist who he admired. His name was C.L.Coolen. He worked in East Java and Sadrach did visit him on occasion.

Jesus Christ is the Spirit of God.[14]

Another illustration of indigenous expression was found in the Thursday evening gatherings.

> The phrases "lha illah lha illolah, Yesus Kristus ya Roh Allah" [There is no God but God. Jesus Christ is the Spirit of God] were repeated, beginning in a soft voice. The volume gradually grew *louder*, accompanied by hand-clapping and head movements from side to side and up and down, alternately. The emotion grew more and more intense until finally a state of trance or mystical union was induced.[15]

Sadrach's community adapted many local customs (*adat*) to make them more Christian, e.g. rituals related to pregnancy, childbirth, marriage, death, farming, and harvest. Most of Sadrach's converts lived in rural Muslim communities so the similarities between Sadrach's rituals and those of the Muslim's would be appreciated. Much to the distress of the missionaries, circumcision was never abolished in the life of the community.

Only one example will be given of a Christian *adat*. The 40th day after the birth of a child was considered important in Javanese culture and had a ceremony associated with it. Therefore, Sadrach developed a liturgy based on Luke 2:22-23. During the ceremony, the *imam* would use flower petals to sprinkle water on the child's head in the name of the Father, Son, and Holy Spirit. Incense was burned during the ceremony and the congregation would chant a *tembang*. Afterward they joined together for a traditional ceremonial meal.

It should also be pointed out that Sadrach did not accept all of the Javanese Muslim rituals for his community. He rejected rituals that were used to honor the spirits of the dead. He also rejected the public rituals associated with historic Islam, i.e. celebrating events in the life of Mohammed.

---

[14] Partonadi, *Sadrach's Community And Its Contextual Roots. A Nineteenth-Century Javanese Expression of Christianity.*, 135.
[15] Partonadi, 136.

Lukas Vischer noted that when Sadrach's community joined the Dutch church, these indigenous practices died away.[16]

It is now time to look at the main objections raised by the Dutch missionaries to Sadrach.[17]

First, he was accused of having too much authority. This they believed was contrary to Calvinism. He acted, they believed, more like a Pope than a minister among equal ministers. There can be no doubt that in this fact, Sadrach was acting within the Javanese context. Whether it was unCalvinistic or unbiblical is another question.

Second, they believed the continued use of Javanese *adat* was contrary to the Pauline emphasis that in Christ old things have passed away. Rebirth and new life in Christ meant, for the missionaries, an abandonment of the old life including *adat*. It has become clear to many Christians, both missionaries and local, that these earlier missionaries were often blind to their own wedding of Christianity to Western cultural forms and practices. They also seemed unwilling to acknowledge another Pauline emphasis, i.e. "I have become all things to all people, that I might be all means save some" (1 Cor. 9:22b).

Third, they reacted negatively to his proclamation that Jesus was the prophesied *ratu adil* (Just King) and our *panutan* (example to follow and obey). The missionaries believed that these titles did not stress the deity of Christ.

The *ratu adil* was an eschatological figure in Javanese folklore that had been influenced successively by Hinduism and Islam. The *ratu adil*, at the end of the age, would establish a kingdom where suffering and injustice would be eliminated.[18] One commentator has suggested that the Christ found in Luke resonates with the *ratu adil* imagery of Javanese folklore.

> What can be learnt from the Javanese expectation of *Ratu Adil*? First, it opens our eyes toward the deepest need of the

---

[16] Vischer, *Christian Worship in Reformed Churches Past and Present*, 184.

[17] In addition to the four enumerated above, Sadrach was also accused of unproven actions, i.e. lying, greed for money, etc.

[18] Philip van Akkeren, *Sri and Christ: A Study of the Indigenous Church in East Java* (London: Lutterworth P, 1970), 40–41.

Javanese. They are longing not only for the spiritual liberation – freedom from sin and the power of darkness, but also, for the social liberation – freedom from poverty, suffering, social injustice, and backwardness which are still prevalent in their everyday life experience.

What does Jesus say about himself? At the momentous event in Nazareth which marked the beginning of his public ministry, Jesus revealed himself by proclaiming his messianic mission:

> The Spirit of the Lord is upon me,
> because he has anointed me
> to preach good news to the poor.
> He has sent me to proclaim freedom for prisoners
> and recovery of sight for the blind,
> to release the oppressed,
> to proclaim the year of the Lord's favor (Luke 4:18-19, NIV).

. . . It seems that the messianic mission of Jesus announced here embraces both the spiritual and earthly dimension. In other words, Jesus pictured himself as both the spiritual and social liberator.[19]

Fourth, they believed Sadrach's emphasis on the gospel as *ngelmu* was insufficient. As we will see in a moment, Sadrach did call for obedience to the law of God revealed in the *ngelmu* of Christ. The missionaries believed that Sadrach had lost the Biblical emphasis of salvation by grace through faith.

This fourth emphasis connects to the idea that Jesus is our *panutan*. In order to understand Sadrach at this point it is important to remember that his cultural background emphasized the absolute importance of *ngelmu* (esoteric

---

[19] Gani Wiyono, "Ratu Adil: A Javanese Face of Jesus?," *Journal of Asian Mission* 1, no. 1 (1999): 74–75.

knowledge) for understanding the essence and meaning of life, and for achieving perfection.[20]

No one is able to achieve this perfection on his or her own. A mediator is needed. A *guru* is needed to teach the right way. This *guru* had to be a true *panutan.* His perfect truth would be evident from his perfect moral conduct.

Partonadi summarized this aspect of Sadrach's teaching as it applied to his understanding of Christ.

> It is clear that Sadrach understood the Gospel as a type of *ngelmu*, but he viewed it as a *"ngelmu* plus," the highest, noblest, and true *ngelmu* . . . distinct from and superior to the other *ngelmus* he had learned. This was the *ngelmu* from the guru and *panutan* Jesus, who died and was risen, as Sadrach stressed in his debates. . . . Emphasis was placed on Christian ethics and the obedient fulfillment of the divine law taught by [Jesus]. Jesus was the exemplary figure whose entire life . . . consistently proved the truth and triumph of his Christian *ngelmu* through obedience to the law even unto death. His resurrection proves the triumph of his *ngelmu*, . . . Salvation, then, stressed following the example of Jesus. Focus was upon the *Imitatio Christi* (the imitation of Christ) as the most perfect man.[21]

Finally, in this first section on indigenous expressions of Christianity, it is appropriate to raise an issue that will follow us throughout. It is the issue of "modernization."

> Sadrach was the last of the great nineteenth century evangelists who preached in an indigenous way. Rapid economic development at the turn of the century and the national awakening from 1908 onward – which emphasized the pivotal importance of formal education – sidelined the

---

[20] Sumartana, *Mission at the Crossroads: Indigenous Churches, European Missionaries, Islamic Association and Socio-Religious Change in Java 1812-1936*, 69.

[21] Partonadi, *Sadrach's Community And Its Contextual Roots. A Nineteenth-Century Javanese Expression of Christianity.*, 220–21.

> lifestyle and evangelical methods of these mystics. Ironically enough, when much later European evangelists finally began to speak of indigenization, Indonesian evangelists had already become modern (western). The modernization and later independence of Indonesia entailed leaving aside the "burden of tradition."[22]

The correctness of the above observation is evident in that many of the churches who chose, after Sadrach's death, to join with the Dutch mission churches did so with the promise that their children would receive education at the popular mission schools.

6.2 Kanzo Uchimura and Mukyokai

Kanzo Uchimura has been called "one of the most influential and original Christian thinkers in Asia"[23] and "the greatest Japanese evangelist".[24] He left writings that have been collected in 50 volumes of biblical studies, theological works, diaries, and correspondence. His movement is estimated to number 35,000 persons, mostly in Japan, but also in Taiwan and Korea.

Uchimura was born on March 23, 1861 to a samurai family.[25] However, in 1868 the Tokugawa shogunate fell and the samurai system came to an end. At the age of 12, his father sent him to a private western-modeled school in Tokyo. The following year he entered Tokyo School of Foreign Language. As a child, Uchimura was a fairly typical Japanese in terms of religious sentiments mostly containing Confucian, Shinto, and folk religion elements. In 1873, the government began allowing Christianity to return officially to Japan. Shortly thereafter, Uchimura came into contact with the Christian faith.

---

[22] John C. England et al., eds., *Asian Christian Theologies: A Research Guide to Authors, Movements, Sources, Vol. 2: Southeast Asia* (Delhi: ISPCK, 2003), 148.

[23] Suzuki Norihisa, "Uchimura Kanzo," in *A Dictionary of Asian Christianity*, ed. Scott W. Sunquist (Grand Rapids, MI: Wm. B. Eerdmans, 2001), 858.

[24] Emil Brunner, "A Unique Christian Mission: The Mukyokai (Non-Church) Movement in Japan," in *Religion and Culture: Essays in Honor of Paul Tillich*, ed. Walter Leibrecht (New York: Arno Press, 1979), 858.

[25] Hiroshi Miura, *The Life and Thought of Kanzo Uchimura, 1861-1930* (Grand Rapids, MI: Wm. B. Eerdmans Publishing Co., 1997), 15–51.

In 1876, at the age of 16, Uchimura entered the Sapporo Agricultural College in Sapporo, Hokkaido. One of the advisors to the school was William S. Clark, the president of Massachusetts Agricultural College in Amherst. He served less than one year in Japan, but had a remarkable influence. He came hoping to promote Christianity. All of his first-year students became Christian.

Uchimura joined the school the following year. The zealous seniors put great pressure on the juniors to become Christian. Uchimura apparently led the opposition, but in the end was persuaded, almost against his will, to sign a statement of Christian faith. In his autobiography he wrote,

> The public opinion of the college was too strong against me, which it was beyond my power to withstand. . . . I finally yielded and signed it. I often ask myself whether I ought to have refrained from submitting myself to such a coercion. I was but a mere lad of sixteen then, and the boys who thus forced me 'to come in' were all much bigger than I. So, you see, my first step toward Christianity was a forced one, against my will, and I must confess, somewhat against my conscience too. [26]

In spite of the less than ideal beginning, Christianity took root in Uchimura's soul. He noted, "Christian monotheism laid its axe at the root of all my superstitions. . . . One God, and not many, was indeed a glad tiding to my little soul." [27] Uchimura and his six Christian classmates began regular services in their dorm rooms on Sundays. The pattern of his later movement can be observed in embryo in these early experiences.

> The little church was entirely democratic, and every one of us stood on the same ecclesiastical footing as the rest of the members. This we found to be thoroughly Biblical and Apostolic. The leadership of the meeting therefore devolved upon each one of us in turn. He was to be our pastor, priest, and teacher,—even servant – for the day. He was responsible for calling us together at the appointed time, his room was to be our church, and he must look [*sic*]

---

[26] As quoted in Miura, 19.
[27] Miura, 21.

how we were to be seated there. He alone could sit upon a stool, and his people sat before him in the true Oriental fashion, upon blankets spread upon the floor. For our pulpit, the mechanical Hugh [a practical member of the church] fitted up a flour-barrel which we covered with a blue-blanket. Thus dignified, the pastor opened the service with a prayer, which was followed by reading from the Bible. He then gave a little talk of his own, and called up each of his sheep to give a talk of his own in turn.[28]

After graduating and securing jobs, Uchimura and other graduates from the school determined to begin their own church in Sapporo. Without going into the details, Uchimura and his friends became disillusioned with the denominationalism of the local Methodist and Anglican churches. Uchimura and some others had been baptized by the Methodist missionary. Other graduates had been baptized by an Anglican. They sensed a kind of competition between the churches that they found abhorrent. Additionally, they wanted a church that was free from restrictions of creeds and complicated rituals. And they wanted the preaching to be done by Japanese.

The Sapporo church was begun. Four graduates, including Uchimura took turns preaching. Within months, the church attendance began to reach sixty. Perhaps in 1883, Uchimura left the city. He returned 13 years later to find that the church had grown to around 250 and one of his original friends was still serving as the unpaid pastor.

As noted, Uchimura's experience of denominational conflict soured him more and more to the idea of the institutional church. Another experience followed. In 1883, Uchimura married a Japanese Christian lady. Within six months, he divorced her apparently over accusations of her unfaithfulness. The Christian churches blamed Uchimura for the breakup because he refused to allow his wife to return to him though she had expressed regret for her defects and because she had not committed adultery which was the only valid reason for divorce.

Shortly afterwards, in 1884, Uchimura went to the U.S.A. where he expected to find a truly Christian nation. He was very disappointed. Through an acquaintance, Uchimura made contact with a Quaker family in Philadelphia.

---

[28] Miura, 21–22.

They helped him secure a job as an attendant at a home for intellectually challenged children. He worked there for about 8 months. He was impacted by two Quakers, Wister and Mary Morris. Years later, upon her death, he wrote,

> And, all these years, I was conscious that she was my partner in my Christian works. She often told me that 'thee is almost a Quaker theeself'; and I was always sorry that I was 'almost' and not 'entirely'. Still all my critics recognized in me 'a strong Quaker influence,' and that 'influence' was Mary Morris.[29]

Uchimura had some problems with mental instability at this time and moved to New England where he rested, wrote, and observed American fisheries. (His emphasis at the Agricultural College had been in the area of fish science.) In 1885, he committed himself to Christian mission work and enrolled at Amherst College. He was greatly influenced by the president of the college, Julius Seelye. On March 8, 1886 he wrote in his diary,

> Very important day in my life. Never was the atoning power of Christ more clearly revealed to me than it is to-day. In the crucifixion of the Son of God lies the solution of all the difficulties that buffeted my mind thus far. Christ paying my debts, can bring me back to the purity and innocence of the first man after the Fall. Now I am God's child, and my duty is to believe Jesus. For His sake, God will give me all I want. He will use me for His glory, and will save me in Heaven at last.[30]

Uchimura graduated from Amherst College in 1887 and enrolled in the Hartford Theological Seminary in Connecticut. At least in part because of ill health, he only studied there for four months before returning to Japan.

A debatable question is whether or not Uchimura ever wanted to become ordained. The issue is dealt with in Miura, pages 33-34. At any rate, he did not graduate and receive ordination. Some years later, he noted his satisfaction at not being ordained, in spite of the fact that some letters were

---

[29] Miura, 31.
[30] Miura, 32–33.

written to him addressing him as "reverend." He preferred to be addressed as Mr. He noted that the *samurai* detested the *bozu* (priest).

> *Bozu* is a rice-consumer, a good for nothing, a dispenser of vanities – that is, in the eyes of the *Samurai*. . . . Japanese do not honor salaried ministry. . . . To have confidence in matters of religion, a man must be strictly independent in his way of living. . . . If Paul were now living in Japan, he would have said, . . . 'It is better for me to die than that I should become a salaried minister.'[31]

Uchimura returned to Japan in 1888. He first secured a job as principal of a new school 250 miles north of Tokyo. He had understood it was run by local people, but in fact all of the foreign teachers were paid by an American mission board. Eventually, Uchimura had to resign because of differences of opinion with the missionaries.

He returned to Tokyo in 1889 and married a childhood friend. He also acquired a job as a teacher at another school in Tokyo. In January of 1891 an event occurred which secured Uchimura's place in Japanese history. A month earlier an imperial directive concerning education was published. It was called the Imperial Rescript on Education. On the 9th of January, the school held a special ceremony in which all of the students and faculty were to bow their heads one after another to the rescript which contained the Emperor's name. Uchimura, believing the ceremony was too similar to the way bowing before relics was performed in Shinto and Buddhist ceremonies, refused to bow. He was declared a traitor to Japan and lost his job. This event is still mentioned in Japanese textbooks today.

Shortly after this event and the subsequent uproar, Uchimura became ill. His wife nursed him back to health, but she died within the year.

Uchimura was able to secure other teaching jobs, but never for very long. Finally, in 1893 in Kyoto, with a new wife, he decided to abandon his teaching career and focus on writing. In the years to come, he wrote books, served as newspaper editor, and published magazines.

---

[31] Uchimura, *The Japan Christian Intelligencer*, II, No. 3, May 5, 1927, quoted in Raymond P. Jennings, *Jesus, Japan, and Kanzo Uchimura: A Study of the View of the Church of Kanzo Uchimura and Its Significance for Japanese Christianity* (Tokyo: Kyo Bun Kwan, Christian Literature Society, 1958), 27.

In 1897, Japan declared war on China over Korea. At first, Uchimura supported the Japanese position, believing they were justified and the end result would benefit both Korea and China. However, when the Japanese were victorious, Uchimura was appalled at the final result. Later in 1903 he wrote against the Russo-Japanese War and indeed against all wars.

Shortly after this he moved to a suburb of Tokyo where he would remain for most of the next 23 years until his death in 1930. During these years he devoted himself to Bible study, publishing a monthly magazine entitled *Seisho no Kenkyu* (Biblical Studies), and giving lectures every Sunday on the Bible. He earned his living through subscriptions to his magazine and by charging attendance fees for his teaching.

The *Mukyokai* (No Church or Non-Church) movement started by Uchimura continues today. Its features have changed very little from those advocated by its founder. They have been enumerated as seven.[32]

1. It is a Bible centered form of Christianity which emphasizes the New Testament.
2. The Japanese relationship between master and disciple is important in the work of evangelism.
3. There are no ordained clergy or paid ministers. Uchimura believed that 'ministers' should have another job so they would not be controlled by a church that paid their salaries. Independence was always a key for him.
4. The congregation's expenses are defrayed in part by the fact that everyone attending a service pays an admission fee.
5. Apart from their Bible studies, *Mukyokai* has no formal organization.
6. Each congregation publishes its own monthly magazine.
7. All services and meetings are held in private homes or rented buildings.

Uchimura was Japanese and Christian. In his own life, these two realities could not be separated. He wrote,

---

[32] Miura, *The Life and Thought of Kanzo Uchimura, 1861-1930*, 113.

> I love two J's and no third; one is Jesus, and the other is
> Japan. I do not know which I love more, Jesus or Japan. I
> am hated by my countrymen for Jesus' sake as Yaso [a
> name used for Christians by the Japanese] and I am disliked
> by foreign missionaries for Japan's sake as national and
> narrow. No matter; I may lose all my friends, but I cannot
> lose Jesus and Japan. For Jesus' sake, I cannot own any
> other God than His Father as my God and Father; and for
> Japan's sake, I cannot accept any faith which comes in the
> name of foreigners. Come starvation; come death; I cannot
> disown Jesus and Japan.[33]

Uchimura believed that the Christianity that could save Japan must come
directly from God and be cultivated in Japanese hearts. He recognized that
Japan had received germs of truth by way of missionaries, but this was not
enough to save Japan.

Christianity needed to be grafted onto *Bushido*. Uchimura's early education
had been based on the *Samurai* code of *Bushido.* This included an emphasis
on honesty, bravery, and honor. Uchimura wrote,

> Bushido is the finest product of Japan. But Bushido by
> itself cannot save Japan. Christianity grafted upon Bushido
> will be the finest product of the world. It will save, not only
> Japan, but the whole world. Now that Christianity is dying
> in Europe, and America by its materialism cannot revive it,
> God is calling upon Japan to contribute its best to His
> service. There was a meaning in the history of Japan. For
> twenty centuries God has been perfecting Bushido with this
> very moment in view. Christianity grafted upon Bushido
> will yet save the world.[34]

A fourth emphasis in *Bushido* was on independence. This was such an
important part of Uchimura's self-understanding that the following quote is
given.

---

[33] Miura, 52.
[34] Miura, 66.

From the very beginning of my religious life, I made up my mind to be independent. That is to say I believe in Christianity, but will not fall under the command of foreign missionaries. I also made up my mind not to engage in missionary work using money from the foreigners. I have practiced this resolution by and large for fifty years ever since I took up my faith. In fact, there was no other way except to rely on myself because there were very few Japanese who would help in Christian missionary work at that time. I have been on the verge of starvation many times. I have prepared to die of hunger three times. I always thought that if I could not engage in mission work without asking other men for help, then I would stop it. I am extremely grateful that I have been able to come to this day with my (Christian) faith without starving to death or by having to ask other men for help. Independence is surely the foundation of my faith. By being independent, I found more interests in life, understood the blessings of God, and experienced that God was really living and miraculously rescues those who rely on him.[35]

It is clear throughout his writings that Uchimura believed in Christianity but not the institutional church. Below is one of the clearest expressions of his belief in what Christianity is and is not.

Christianity is essentially the religion of the Cross. It is not simply the religion of Christ but the religion of Christ *crucified*. It teaches us not that we are to be crucified like him, but that he was crucified for us. The Cross is not merely a symbol of Christianity; it is its centre, the corner-stone upon which the whole structure rests. Sins forgiven and annihilated on the Cross, blessings promised and bestowed upon the Cross – indeed, no Cross, no Christianity. . . . Christianity is not an institution, a church, or churches; neither is it creed, nor dogma, not theology; neither is it a book, the Bible, nor even the words of Christ. Christianity is a person, a living person, Lord Jesus Christ, 'the same yesterday, today, and forever.' If Christianity is

---

[35] Miura, 72.

156

> not this, the ever-present HE, it is nothing. I go directly to
> Him, and not through churches and popes and bishops and
> other useful and useless officers. 'I in them and they in Me.'
> – so says He of His disciples.[36]

As one commentator has noted *Mukyokai* is the church for those who have no church.[37] It is like a dormitory or an orphanage for those who are homeless. *Mukyokai* is for the many Christians in the world who have no church. Looking into the Book of Revelation, Uchimura saw that in heaven, there is no organized church with bishops and teachers or baptism and Communion. Therefore, the true form of the church is in fact *Mukyokai*.

In the West, the sacraments, or ordinances, are considered very important in the life of the Church. Some exceptions, like the Quakers, exist, but they are very few. Therefore, it is significant that Uchimura found little positive to say about the sacraments. Miura notes that Uchimura believed that when the early church "broke bread in their homes and ate together" (Acts 2:42, 46) this was not the Sacrament of Holy Communion. "It was not the Sacrament, but a banquet. . . . The Sacrament practiced in churches today was originally the holy feast of the believers, but this pleasant banquet was changed into the formal Sacrament when the heart's love cooled."[38]

In spite of his harsh words for the institution of the Church and its rituals, he had a moderate side. One of his followers noted, "The Teacher disliked the Lord's Supper, Baptism, and church organization, but when it was necessary for the spirit of his followers he has on occasion even administered baptism."[39]

Uchimura's moderate side could also be seen in his continuing concern for the Sappora Independent Church that he and his fellow graduates had begun years earlier. In 1928, for two or three months Uchimura stayed in Sapporo and helped the church. He preached every Sunday and helped the church to find a minister, for at that time it had none. After one of Uchimura's disciples

---

[36] Jennings, *Jesus, Japan, and Kanzo Uchimura: A Study of the View of the Church of Kanzo Uchimura and Its Significance for Japanese Christianity*, 49.

[37] Miura, *The Life and Thought of Kanzo Uchimura, 1861-1930*, 107.

[38] Miura, 88.

[39] Jennings, *Jesus, Japan, and Kanzo Uchimura: A Study of the View of the Church of Kanzo Uchimura and Its Significance for Japanese Christianity*, 50.

became the pastor ('teacher in charge of the church'), Uchimura wrote to a former classmate who was a member of the church.

> I cannot think that the institutional church is the spirit of Christ, therefore supporting of continuity of it prevents the progress of the Gospel. In this point, you and I are of a different opinion beforehand. However, because of the long-time friendship, we saw only each other's virtues, not faults. I have been doing something self-contradictory both to you and to the Sapporo Independent Church. It is inexcusable as a principle, but I excuse it as an affection. Now, at the time of bringing my life work to a conclusion, I must thrust personal considerations aside, then hand down impartial, firm belief to posterity. Thus, I would like to end my life as a genuine Mukyokai-shugisha [a non-churchist], cutting off all connection with all institutions which have the name church.[40]

In the following year, Uchimura died. Just prior to his death in 1930, he ordered that his magazine be stopped and his Sunday meetings be discontinued. He wanted to ensure that no church would be built on his memory.

Because the *Mukyokai* movement has no membership rolls, statistics are debatable. In 1951, some estimated that 100,000 were attending various *Mukyokai* meetings. Today the number of *Mukyokai* followers is estimated between 20,000 and 50,000.[41]

Whatever the actual numbers may be, it is true that *Mukyokai* followers have been influential. The intellectual thrust of the movement has resulted in influential *Mukyokai* scholars and administrators in various Universities. The present United Nations General Secretary, Ban-Ki Moon, is a follower of the Korean branch of *Mukyokai*.

---

[40] Miura, *The Life and Thought of Kanzo Uchimura, 1861-1930*, 104.

[41] It should be noted that according to David Barrett in 1995 there were only 2,383 followers in Japan and 1,000 in South Korea. Barrett, Kurian, and Johnson, *World Christian Encyclopedia*, 418, 686.

6.3 The Philippine Independent Church or Iglesia Filipina Independiente (IFI)

The Philippine Independent Church (hereafter designated as IFI) arose in the context of the desire for freedom by the Filipino people. An understanding of that context is significant for understanding the IFI.

In the 15th century, Spanish forces came to the Philippine islands with the goals of colonization and Christianizing. In 1572, Manila was captured. By 1597, 134 missionaries from various orders were working on the islands. In 1611, the first Christian University in the Philippines was established. By 1650, almost 50% of the population affirmed their Christian (Roman Catholic) faith.

This startling growth may reflect a number of reasons:

1. Local chiefs were targeted for conversion. Often when a chief converted, the people living under him followed him into the Church.

2. Some Roman Catholic practices could take the place of local customs. Two examples can illustrate this. Praying to the saints could take the place of spirit worship. New believers could use rosaries and wear crucifixes in the place of popular talismans.

3. It would have been impossible, whether intended or not, that the people would not feel intimidated by the Spanish military forces. Conversion would have appeared to be the safest course of action.

Spain was to rule the Philippines for over 300 years. However, opposition was never entirely suppressed. Until the mid 17th century the opposition and revolts tended to be anti-Christian. By around 1650, the revolutionaries in their opposition to Spanish rule tended to hold onto their Christian faith.

Two of the festering issues in the 19th century were the low number of Filipinos who had been ordained as priests by the Catholic friars and the amount of property and power that these friars held. In 1872, three Filipino priests were accused of fomenting rebellion because they were known to be sympathetic to those who were critical of the Spanish friars. They were executed and became hero martyrs for the rebellion that would follow.

It is in this context that two men would arise who would give birth to a new church – the Philippine Independent Church. They were Isabelo de los Reyes, Sr. (1864-1938) and Gregorio Aglipay (1860-1940).

De los Reyes' interests and influences have been summarized as follows,

> [He] was an ardent nationalist and Filipinologist, and has been termed 'father of Philippine folklore.' He was also a vigorous labor leader and the founder and/or editor of six papers and journals . . . He founded Union Obrera Democratica, an early labor union, was a prominent leader in movements of workers and was jailed for labor agitating. He campaigned for the rights of Filipino clergy, was firmly anti-American and a close associate of Aglipay and Mabini [another important person in the early years of the IFI]. He became the key organizer, liturgist and theologian for the IFI. In later years he co-founded the Republican Party of the Philippines.[42]

Before looking at the actual formation of the IFI, a similar summary for Aglipay is appropriate.

> He became active in supporting the campaigns for the Filipino clergy and, as a priest in Manila, and later in Cavite he remained in contact with nationalist groups and leaders in the later revolution. In May 1898 he was appointed military vicar general by Aguinaldo [the leader of the revolution], and worked closely with Mabini to establish schools, seminaries, and adequate administration for local government. As Vicar General Aglipay issued 'semi-schismatic' manifestos (Oct. 1898), and was excommunicated in 1899. Following attempts to form a national (Roman) Catholic Church, he joined Isabelo de los Reyes in the establishment of the Iglesia Filipina Independiente (1902) – which quickly became a mass

---

[42] "Isabelo do los Reyes y Florentino Sr. (1864-1938)" in England et al., *Asian Christian Theologies: A Research Guide to Authors, Movements, Sources, Vol. 2: Southeast Asia*, 352.

movement representing especially laborers, share-croppers and the poor. . ... He came to believe that only by revolution would the friars be forced to relinquish lands and controlling power, and the Spanish hierarchy be replaced by Filipino bishops.[43]

Additionally, it may be noted that when the Americans defeated the Spanish in 1899 but did not grant the Philippines the independence it desired, Aglipay (and also Reyes) joined guerrilla forces in fighting against the Americans until 1901 when he and others surrendered.

A sketch of some important dates will be given by way of outlining the establishment of the IFI.

As has already been noted, in 1898 the leader of the revolution appointed Aglipay as the military chaplain or military priest of his movement. A day after his appointment he published a manifesto:

My beloved brethren: Inasmuch as the Revolution tends to liberate the Filipino people from Spain, it is also necessary that we also work to throw off the yoke with which the Spanish clergy pretends to subjugate us so that we may be worthy successors of the Filipino priests who sacrificed themselves in defense of our unquestionable rights which were usurped with the greatest arrogance by the [Spanish] friars who made themselves Lords of our beloved country. The Revolutionary Government of the Philippines is supporting us in our aims because it cannot recognize as head of the Filipino clergy any Spanish bishop, for the powerful political influence of the [Spanish] clergy in the Spanish government is proverbial.[44]

Although Aglipay opposed the authority of the Spanish clergy, he assisted in the release of some who had been imprisoned by the revolutionaries. However, he assumed the right to appoint Filipino priests to positions of authority. It was this action, coupled with his support of the revolutionaries,

---

[43] "Gregorio Aglipay (1860-1940)" in England et al., 350–51.
[44] Klaus Koschorke, Frieder Ludwig, and Marian Delgado, eds., *A History of Christianity in Asia, Africa, and Latin America, 1450-1990: A Documentary Sourcebook* (Grand Rapids, MI: Wm. B. Eerdmans, 2007).

which led to his excommunication from the Roman Catholic Church in 1899. It seems that Aglipay had hoped to rid the Philippines of the Spanish friars and have the church in the Philippines function directly under the authority of the Papacy. However, with his excommunication this became an impossibility.

In 1901, Isabelo de los Reyes, Sr. returned to the Philippines from which he had earlier been exiled for his opposition to Spanish friars. He returned planning to help establish an independent church. In 1902 this became a reality.

On August 3, 1902 at a meeting of the General Council of the Union Obrera Democratica (the labor union he had started), de los Reyes proclaimed the establishment of the IFI. He nominated several persons (who were not present) to assume positions of leadership in the new church. For *Obispo Maximo* (Supreme Bishop) he proposed Gregorio Aglipay.

Aglipay was initially reluctant to take the position, but was persuaded in September of 1902. The growth of the new church was striking. In the very first year, Aglipay claimed that 3,000,000 out of a Filipino population of 7,000,000 had joined the IFI. More reliable estimates suggest maybe 25% of the population. In some cases where a local priest joined the IFI, he brought congregation, church buildings, and church lands into the movement. However, the courts ruled in 1907 that all such buildings and properties belonged to the Roman Catholic Church. This caused growth not only to slow, but in some areas, actually decline.

Although the IFI has sometimes been identified by the terms Aglipayanism or the Aglipayan Church, such designations are incorrect. Aglipay affirmed,

> The Filipino people are my witness that I am not the author of the Philippine Independent Church; neither did I intervene in its preparation. I was sleeping in Ezpeleta Street when I was awakened and told that in a meeting at the Centro de Bella Artes in Manila, August 3, 1902, the Filipino people proclaimed the new church . . . .
> The Philippine Independent Church was founded by the people of our country. It was a product of their desire for

> liberty – religiously, politically and socially. I was only one
> of the instruments of its expression.[45]

Eventually Aglipay and other leaders in the church tried to make connections with Protestant churches. In fact, he even met with some Protestant missionaries prior to the official establishment of the church. However, they were less than enthusiastic since Aglipay, in meeting with them, did not affirm Scripture as "the rule and guide in doctrine and life."[46]

As early as 1905, the IFI became Unitarian. Its statement of faith in that year denied the doctrines of the Trinity and original sin. The IFI is probably the only church in history that had a 'catholic' polity and liturgy, but was Unitarian in theology.

However, this Unitarian emphasis did not sit well with the rank and file priests and membership who remained more traditional. With the death of the original leadership, the IFI rejected Unitarianism and became more mainstream.[47]

After Aglipay's death in 1940, a struggle over leadership ensued. The majority followed Isabelo de los Reyes, Jr. who was *Obispo Maximos* from 1946 to 1971. In 1955, the courts ruled in favor of his supporters, and it maintained the largest part of the original membership.

In 1946 Reyes, Jr. made an agreement with the Episcopal Church of the U.S.A. This allowed persons studying for the priesthood of the IFI churches to be trained at St. Andrew's Theological Seminary in Quezon City. A year later, the IFI adopted a new declaration of faith that moved it away from Unitarianism and back into traditional orthodoxy. In 1961 a Condordat of Full Communion was signed between IFI and the Episcopal Church. This introduced IFI to the Anglican Communion and agreements have been

---

[45] Apolonio Ranche, "An Introduction to the Iglesia Filipina Endependiente (Philippine Independent Church)," *Iglesia Filipina Indepentiente* (blog), accessed July 10, 2008, http://www.ifi.ph/history.htm.

[46] Koschorke, Ludwig, and Delgado, *A History of Christianity in Asia, Africa, and Latin America, 1450-1990: A Documentary Sourcebook*, 106.

[47] It is interesting to note that Reyes, who seemed more adamantly anti-Catholic than Aglipay, returned to the Roman Catholic Church in 1936 – recanting those affirmations early made that contradicted Roman Catholic teaching. He died with a papal benediction in 1938.

signed with many other of the Anglican denominations. Additionally, agreements have been signed with the Old Catholic Churches (a denomination that broke away from the Roman Catholic Church) and the Evangelical Lutheran Church of Sweden. In 1963, Reyes, Jr. became the first chairman of the National Council of Churches in the Philippines.

The desire for orthodox theology and ecumenical relations with other Christian denominations are affirmed in IFI articles of religion, numbers 17 and 18.[48]

> When this church withdrew from the Roman Catholic Church, it repudiated the authority of the pope and such doctrines, customs, and practices as were inconsistent with the word of God, sound learning and good conscience. It did not intend to depart from catholic doctrines, practices and disciplines as set by the council of the undivided church. Departures that occurred were due to exigencies of the times, and are to be corrected by the official action so that this Church may be brought to the stream of historic Christianity and universally acknowledged as a true branch of the Catholic church (IFI article on religion no. 17).

> Opportunity is to be sought for closer cooperation with other branches of the Catholic church and cordial relations shall be maintained with all who acknowledge Jesus Christ as Lord and Savior (IFI article on religion no. 18).

It is worth noting that the present day IFI has retained its interest in social concerns.

> The Supreme Council of the IFI . . . and IFI leaders of lay movements . . . have continued the earlier Independiente traditions of social witness and reflection. The bishops have issued occasional statements and open letters on major social or political issues and also acted to support protest movements or to provide sanctuary for striking workers.

---

[48] Dionito M Cabillas, "The Distinctive Contribution of the Church [IFI] on Church Unity and Mission," *Iglesia Filipina Indepentiente* (blog), accessed October 29, 2018, http://ifi.ph/?page_id=106.

Their statements have, for example, included Open Letters to the President of the Philippines and to other national leaders and movements calling for agrarian reform, for the end of foreign domination and for nationalist industrialization, for basic social services, human rights for all ethnic groups, and for peace and dialogue in southern Philippines.[49]

---

[49] "Supreme Council of Bishops, Philippine Independent Church (Iglesia Filipinas Independiente – IFI" England et al., *Asian Christian Theologies: A Research Guide to Authors, Movements, Sources, Vol. 2: Southeast Asia*, 485.

Chapter 7: Three Indian Indigenous Movements

*"No one single human culture has ever been, in and of itself, sacred. Yet,
all cultures have been capable of becoming sacred, to a greater or lesser
degree, depending on how much their essentials could be transformed so as
to reflect everlasting verities that are truly sacred."*

–Robert Frykenberg[1]

7.1 Pandita Ramabai

Women have played a significant role in the indigenization of Christainity
in different places. Pandita Ramabai has been called "A Maker of Modern
India". Elaborating on that title, Roger Hedlund wrote that she "was a social
activist and radical advocate of women's rights and egalitarianism. . . An
articulate spokesperson on behalf of suppressed Hindu women, her advocacy
has earned her a place of honour in modern Indian history."[2] Before her
death, she was given the Kaiser-i-Hind award by the king of England. This
was one of the highest awards that an Indian could receive during the period
of British rule. Then in 1989, the Indian government issued a
commemorative stamp honoring her as a builder of modern India.[3]

Ramabai was born in 1858 into a Brahman family. Although her father was
orthodox by nature, he was supportive of the education of women. This was
contrary to the current culture. Much to the consternation of others, he taught
his wife the holy language, Sanskrit, as well as religious philosophy. Six
children were born to the couple, with Ramabai being the youngest. Ramabai
was taught by her father as a child and then later by her mother. Her early
years were spent in a forest-ashram.

Her parents were Hindus and true seekers, going on pilgrimage from place
to place, making offerings, and practicing asceticism. Although, her father

---

[1] Frykenberg, *Christianity in India*, 241.
[2] Roger E. Hedlund, ed., *Quest for Identity: India's Churches of Indigenous Origin*
(Delhi: ISPCK, 2000), 157.
[3] Keith J. White, "Jesus Was Her Guru," *Christian History | Learn the History of
Christianity & the Church* 87 (2005): 16–21.

had been a wealthy man, poverty eventually overcame the family. Both he and his wife died during a famine in 1874. On his death bed her father said to Ramabai, "Remember my child, you are my youngest child, my most beloved child. I have given you into the hand of the one God; you are His, and to Him alone you must belong and serve Him all your life."[4]

With an older brother, Ramabai continued the life-style of her parents. She went on pilgrimage to many sacred places and was consistent in encouraging the education and uplifting of women. She came to Calcutta in 1880 and already had made a name for herself. At that time Calcutta was the capital of India and the seat of learning. The Senate of Calcutta University summoned her before them. There she was granted the title of "Pandita."[5] At that time she was the only woman in all of India who was officially recognized as "learned".

During this time, Ramabai's brother died. She accepted a marriage proposal from a young Bengali man. He was of the Shudra caste, which meant that Ramabai broke caste restrictions by marrying him. He was a member of the new religion, Brahmo Samaj. She too joined this religion that affirmed only one God, thus rejecting the polytheism of Hinduism. It denounced caste distinctions and dependence on Hindu scriptures. Jesus Christ was also held in high regard by Brahmo Samaj, though they rejected the claims of Christianity.

A daughter was born in 1881. She was named Manorama. Less than a year later, Ramabai's husband died. She and her daughter moved back to her home area in Maharastra where she began living as a 24 year old widow.

As already noted, Ramabai had been an exponent of the needs and rights of women. Now the plight of child widows in Indian society was brought home to her. In traditional society, widows were either burned on the funeral pyres of their husbands, or they were forbidden to remarry and often forced to live in humiliating circumstances. In order to ease the plight of these widows, Ramabai began to lecture all over the state of Maharashtra on their needs. To alleviate the suffering of these child widows, she also started institutions in many of the large cities, like Poona and Bombay.

---

[4] Shamsundar Manohar Adhav, *Pandita Ramabai* (Madras: Christian Literature Society, 1979), 5.
[5] The word is in the feminine form. Pandit is Hindi and refers to a learned person.

While in Calcutta, Ramabai had come into contact with Christians. There she had been given a Sanskrit version of the Bible and had been taught by a missionary about the gospel. Ramabai wrote, "I eagerly learnt everything which I could about the Christian religion, and declared my intention to become a Christian."[6] However, her husband had opposed this, so she had not followed through.

In Poona (now Pune), she met another missionary who encouraged her and then helped her and her daughter Manorama to travel to England. In England they stayed in the Community House of an Anglican religious community called The Community of St. Mary the Virgin. It was there, five months after arriving, that Ramabai and her daughter were baptized. This was in 1883.

It should be noted that one of the most important persons in her pilgrimage into the Christian faith was the Marathi Indian, Father Nehemiah Goreh, who was both a Sanskrit scholar and a Brahmin convert to Christianity. She had met with him occasionally in Poona before setting off for England. While in England the correspondence between Ramabai and Fr. Goreh was of great significance for her spiritual life. On one occasion after her baptism, she wrote,

> I was indeed impressed with the holy life of the Sisters, and their sublime unselfishness, and am so impressed to this moment, but I must say for the sake of truth that their life was not the cause of my accepting faith in Christ. It was Father Goreh's letter that proved that the faith which I professed (I mean the Brahmo faith) was not taught by our Vedas as I had thought, but it was the Christian faith, which was brought before me by my friends disguised under the name of Brahmo religion. Well, I thought if Christ is the source of this sublime faith, why should not I confess Him openly to be my Lord and my Divine teacher? And so I did, and do confess Him my Saviour. I believe Him to be the Son of the Most High and His Messiah. But this confession does not mean that I believe also all the doctrines taught by

---

[6] Hedlund, *Quest for Identity: India's Churches of Indigenous Origin*, 158.

other people, unless they be proved to be true from Christ's own words.[7]

It is also worth noting that Ramabai had some doubts about the deity of Christ and the doctrine of the Trinity. It was, again, her correspondence that Fr. Goreh that aided her in accepting the traditional orthodox beliefs concerning the person of Christ and the doctrine of the Trinity.

After her conversion she lectured on Sanskrit and did some studies at a women's college. In 1886, she went to America where she published an English language book, *The High-Caste Hindu Woman*, which detailed the plight of women in India and made her even more of a celebrity. The American Ramabai Association was founded which assisted her in starting a ministry for needy women and children. This was in 1889.

The institution was called Sharada Sadan (Home of Learning) and opened first in Bombay. Later in 1890 it was moved to Poona (now Pune). Initially, the ministry was designed to be entirely secular, but gradually conversions took place. Because of these conversions, the Hindu members of the advisory board resigned. However, the American Association agreed to continue support of the ministry as it became an avowedly Christian institution. Thus Ramabai "became the pioneer-founder of an indigenous national evangelistic mission in India – probably the first of its kind."[8]

Eventually a more extensive institution called Mukti (that is, 'deliverance') Mission was inaugurated at Kedgaon, near Poona. This was in 1898. The following is a description of this remarkable place.

> It was difficult to find any institution in the whole of India that was run or administered on the lines of the Ramabai Mukti Mission at Kedgaon. Mukti was and is, in fact, an Ashram.[9] Ramabai was the first Indian to be in charge of an institution in which foreign women worked, a phenomenon unknown in those days when India was under British rule. Every aspect of this Mukti Mission Ashram

---

[7] Adhav, *Pandita Ramabai*, 136.

[8] Adhav, 18.

[9] "Ashram is a settlement of Christians devoted to simplicity of life and fellowship in service." G. P. V. Somaratna, "Ashram Movement," in *A Dictionary of Asian Christianity*, ed. Scott W. Sunquist (Grand Rapids, MI: Wm. B. Eerdmans, 2001).

was Indian: the Indian method of worship in the church; the Indian food served to both Indians and foreigners alike seated on low wooden stools in the dining hall; the Indian dress made of lowly cotton woven mostly on the handlooms worked by the women inmates [members, not prisoners!] of Mukti.[10]

At some point in her spiritual pilgrimage, Ramabai came into contact with a form of Christianity that emphasized the work of the Holy Spirit. According to one of her biographers, Ramabai had some type of spiritual experience in 1895 in which "she felt that through the blessing of the Holy Spirit thirteen years after her baptism she had come to know Jesus Christ as her personal Saviour."[11]

In 1897 Ramabai invited Minnie Adams, an early Pentecostal missionary from America, to work at the Mukti Mission. Ramabai visited her American Association in 1898 and on her return journey to India went to England and attended a Keswick Convention. She had an opportunity to speak to the Convention and asked them to pray for evangelism and revival to India. Returning to India, she established prayer bands of her girls and sent them into the surrounding villages to pray and evangelize. In 1903 she sent her daughter to enlist prayer support from a prayer movement in Australia. In 1904 she heard of the great revival occurring in Wales. Then in 1905 revival came to India. Ramabai wrote,

> I was led by the Lord to start a special prayer circle at the beginning of 1905. There were about seventy of us who met together each morning and prayed for the true conversion of all the Indian Christians, including ourselves, and for special outpouring of the Holy Spirit on all Christians of every land. In six months from the time we began to pray in this manner, the Lord graciously sent a glorious Holy Ghost Revival among us, and also in many schools and churches in this country.[12]

---

[10] Adhav, *Pandita Ramabai*, 44.

[11] Hedlund, *Quest for Identity: India's Churches of Indigenous Origin*, 159.

[12] Adhav, *Pandita Ramabai*, 19.

Preaching bands from Mukti carried the message of revival into the villages and as noted above there was great response. Healings, speaking in tongues, prophecy and other 'gifts' of the Spirit became manifest.

Earlier in 1897 a church had been organized at Mukti. A description of that beginning is found in a periodical published by Mukti.

> In 1897, as an outcome of special services by Rev. W.W. Bruere, many trusted Jesus. On November 15, 116 women and child-widows were baptized. On Christmas day, Pandita Ramabai, Miss Abrams, and Rev. Bruere, the first pastor, organized the Mukti Church, taking the Bible as its only creed. [13]

In addition to the work already mentioned, Ramabai wrote books, composed hymns (some of which are still in use), and translated the Bible into the Marathi language.

One of her Marathi hymns has been translated into English. It is entitled "Dear Friend Jesus". Part is presented below.

> Without support, where shall I go and lie down?
>   And seek rest, after the heavy burden of sin;
> Wandered in the hope of seeking a redeemer
>   And searched and searched everywhere;
> But met none who could make me happy;
>   Longed to abandon the world,
> And prayed in my mind that this boon be granted;
>   Lo! There came Christ to meet me.
> *Lord Jesus Christ, Dearer than Life,*
>   *Sacrificing Himself redeemed me,*
> *And brought me to everlasting life.*
>   *He is dearer than the dearest to me.* [chorus]
>
> I will always adore and worship my Beloved
>   Trusting always in Him;
> Going near Him, will I serve Him
>   And at His feet, for the sake of love;

---

[13] Hedlund, *Quest for Identity: India's Churches of Indigenous Origin*, 163.

> Lo, how dearly He holds my hand in His!
> May the Lord always rule over me
> And He abide in me for ever
> I have embraced the invaluable love of Jesus.[14]

Ramabai died in 1922. She had made arrangements for the Christian and Missionary Alliance to serve in an advisory capacity and to assume certain administrative responsibilities with the caveat that Mukti continue "as a distinct Indian organization on the basis of faith in God to meet all its needs."[15]

Mukti continues today. On their website they list the following institutions and activities that are presently a part of Ramabai's legacy.[16]

An orphanage takes care of hundreds of neglected and poverty-stricken children. At Mukti they live in multiple families of 12 to 20 girls. They are also provided with an education.

This education is given in Mukti's schools – primary and high schools. Over 1000 students attend, many from nearby villages. Additionally, there is a school for the blind.

Mukti also provides medical services both through a large hospital and teams of medical personnel who travel to villages.

Homes and vocational training are provided for widows, outcasts, unwed mothers and special needs children.

And finally, the Mukti church which can seat 2000 persons continues to provide opportunities for worship and Bible study.

7.2 Sahdu Sundar Singh

> Sundar Singh was the first to show the world how the
> Gospel of Jesus Christ is reflected in unchanged purity on
> the Indian soil. He represents a simple, childlike, and yet

---

[14] Adhav, *Pandita Ramabai*, 190–91.

[15] Hedlund, *Quest for Identity: India's Churches of Indigenous Origin*, 163.

[16] "Mukti Mission US | About," *Mukti Mission* (blog), 2018, http://muktimission.us/.

clear and spiritual religious faith based entirely upon the
New Testament, expressed in an Indian spirituality.[17]

Whether, Sundar Singh was 'first' or not is debatable and, as we shall see,
his faith was not based "entirely" on the New Testament. Nevertheless, he is
certainly a striking example of what an indigenous form of Christianity could
look like in India.

Sundar was born on September 3, 1889. He was born in the Punjab to a
wealthy Sikh family. They seemed to have been a fairly tolerant family. His
mother may have been more Hindu than Sikh. She held up before him the
model of the Hindu *sadhu*. She desired that eventually he would "abandon
the things of the world and strive to obtain that inner Peace, alone permanent
and permanently satisfying, the quest for which has been immemorial in
Indian religion." [18] His mother died when he was 14. This may have
accentuated his spiritual quest in the ensuing years of his youth.

He studied the writings of Hinduism including the *Bhagavad Gita* and
several of the *Upanishads*. He also read the *Granth* of Sikhism and the
Qur'an of Islam. He practiced a form of yoga which he learned from a Hindu
sadhu. Still the peace he sought eluded him.

He attended a Presbyterian mission school in his home town. There he was
introduced to the Bible. At first, he was repelled by Christianity.

What follows is a first-person account of his conversion on December 18,
1904 at the age of 15.

> Preachers and Christians in general had often come to me
> and I used to resist them and persecute them. When I was
> out in any town I got people to throw stones at Christian
> preachers. I would tear up the Bible and burn it when I had
> a chance. In the presence of my father I cut up the Bible
> and other Christian books and put kerosene oil upon them
> and burnt them. I thought this was a false religion and tried
> all I could to destroy it. I was faithful to my own religion,

---

[17] Samuel Matthew, "Sundar Singh," in *A Dictionary of Asian Christianity*, ed. Scott
W. Sunquist (Grand Rapids, MI: Wm. B. Eerdmans, 2001).
[18] B H Streeter and A. J. Appasamy, *The Sadhu: A Study in Mysticism and Practical
Religion* (London: Macmillan Co, 1921), 4.

but I could not get any satisfaction or peace, though I
performed all the ceremonies and rites of that religion. So I
thought of leaving it all and committing suicide. Three days
after I had burnt the Bible, I woke up about three o'clock in
the morning, had my usual bath, and prayed, 'O God, if
there is a God will you show me the right way or I will kill
myself.' My intention was that, if I got no satisfaction, I
would place my head upon the railway line when the 5
o'clock train passed by and kill myself. If I got no
satisfaction in this life, I thought I would get it in the next.
I was praying and praying but got no answer; and I prayed
for half-an-hour longer hoping to get an answer. At 4:30
A.M. I saw something of which I had no idea at all
previously. In the room where I was praying I saw a great
light. I thought the place was on fire. I looked round, but
could find nothing. Then the thought came to me that this
might be an answer that God had sent me. Then as I prayed
and looked into the light, I saw the form of the Lord Jesus
Christ. It had such an appearance of glory and love. If it had
been some Hindu incarnation I would have prostrated
myself before it. But it was the Lord Jesus Christ whom I
had been insulting a few days before. I felt that a vision like
this could not come out of my imagination. I heard a voice
saying in Hindustani [Urdu], 'How long will you persecute
me? I have come to save you; you were praying to know
the right way. Why do you not take it?' The thought came
to me, 'Jesus Christ is not dead but living and it must be He
Himself.' So I fell at His feet and got this wonderful Peace
which I could not get anywhere else. This is the joy I was
wishing to get. This was heaven itself. When I got up, the
vision had all disappeared; but although the vision
disappeared the Peace and Joy have remained with me ever
since.[19]

Sundar's family was unhappy with his announcement that he had become a
Christian. They tried every enticement and even resorted to various kinds of
humiliation. Finally, he was disowned and banished from his home.
Apparently, poison was mingled in his last meal, but he survived.

---

[19] Streeter and Appasamy, 5–7.

Sundar was baptized on September 3, 1905 in the Church of England. He decided that he would live the life of a Christian *sadhu*. As such he wore a saffron robe and turban.[20] He carried no money with him, but everywhere he went he depended on the good-will of the people. Sometimes he was given food and shelter. Other times he ate only what he could find in the wilds and slept under trees.

He travelled throughout northern India and the Himalayan Mountains into Afghanistan. In 1908 he made his first trip to Tibet. Afterwards, he planned to spend some time in Tibet each year. Between 1908 and 1929 it is said that he made at least 20 trips to that country which was closed to missionary workers.[21]

He did work with others, like S. E. Stokes, an American who was committed to founding a brotherhood in India based on the principles of St. Francis of Assisi. Sundar and Stokes worked together for a couple of years preaching in villages and ministering in a leper colony. Although, Sunday spoke well of St. Francis, he was never interested in starting a movement of Christian *sadhus*. He viewed religious institutions with some suspicion.

He did study for a few months at St. John's Divinity College in Lahore. He had been granted a license to preach and was moving towards being ordained a deacon. However, he realized that by taking Holy Orders in the Church of England, his freedom to work with all manner of Christians and to go wherever he might be led would be limited. Therefore, he returned the license and refused to be ordained.

An important event took place around 1914. Sundar felt impelled to follow Jesus by undertaking a 40 day fast. Apparently, he was unable to complete the fast, but it nevertheless had a remarkable effect on his life. Any doubts

---

[20] "He knew, true son of India that he was, that in the saffron robe of the *sadhu* doors would be open to him that would otherwise be closed. He would not be qualified to preach in the churches but, clad in the robe of one who was known to have taken the path of renunciation, he could reach the villagers, the common people, even the high-caste women secluded in their zenanas." Phyllis Thompson, *Sadhu Sundar Singh: A Biography of the Remarkable Indian Disciple of Jesus Christ* (Singapore: Genesis Books, 1994), 42.

[21] Charles E. Moore, "Introduction," in *Sadhu Sundar Singh: Essential Writings*, Modern Spiritual Masters Series (Maryknoll, NY: Orbis Books, 2005), 21.

that he had that his peace and joy came from God and not his own particular personality were erased as his peace increased even as his bodily powers weakened. Also, after the fast, certain temptations that had afflicted him were lessened or done away with entirely.

In 1918, Sundar visited the south Indian city of Madras (now Chennai). His fame preceded him, and thousands turned out to hear him wherever he spoke. His preaching tours took him to other places, including Sri Lanka, Myanmar, Malaysia, China and Japan. In 1920, he made the first to two trips to Europe. He also visited the United States and Australia.

When Sundar returned to India from his second trip to Europe his health began to fail him. This was in 1922. It is little wonder, due to his rugged life as a traveling *sadhu* and the pressures of international fame. One illustration of the kind of life he lived as a *sadhu* will suffice as an example of the kinds of experiences that happened over and over again.

> Traveling by way of Khaibar Pass, I went to Afghanistan. Here the people troubled me very much, first believing me to be a spy and then because I preached the Gospel. In one place the villagers had made complete arrangements for my murder, when one person secretly informed me about the intention of the people. . .. Rising by night, I fled in another direction.
>
> As I went, there were perfect torrents of rain, and I was drenched through. On the evening of the next day I arrived at another village, dead tired, hungry and thirsty and wet through. Besides, it was hilly country, with the cold of the month of February, no place to stay for the night except a ruined hut, full of mud and cow-dung. Here I shivered throughout the night. The people were so hard-hearted as not to offer me either fuel or bread. I was sure that before morning I would contract either pneumonia or rheumatism, but thank the Lord, in spite of all this exposure, I took no harm.[22]

---

[22] As quoted in A. J. Appasamy, "A Biographical Introduction," in *The Real Life* (Madras: Christian Literature Society, 1968), ix.

He "took no harm" and the people were amazed so that they welcomed him into their community and he stayed some days with them sharing the gospel. He 'took no harm', but perhaps in the long run the harm was done by this and many other deprivations during his journeys.

From 1922 to 1929 he devoted himself to writing because his health no longer allowed him to travel. He had eye problems which required surgery. He had heart attacks, ulcers and other physical problems.

Fortunately, his father had, around 1918, become a Christian and had left Sundar some money. This he used, per his father's wish, to purchase a small house in Sabathu, below Simla on the Himalayas. There he wrote 8 devotional works, all of which have been translated into English. The titles include: *At the Master's Feet, With and Without Christ, The Real Life, Reality and Religion, The Search after Reality, Various Aspects of the Spiritual Life, Visions of the Spiritual World, and The Real Pearl.* The popularity of his work is seen in that at least portions have been translated into 40 languages.

Finally, in 1929, much to the consternation of his friends, Sundar decided he should return again to Tibet. He left on that journey but never returned to his home, apparently dying in the mountains while taking the Good News of Jesus to those who had never heard.

As we think of Sundar's contribution to an indigenous Christianity in India, it may be helpful to consider the following topics: The sources of his 'authority', his understanding of Church, and the ideal of the Christian *sadhu.*

The sources of his life and thought as a Christian were three: the Bible (a copy of the New Testament was the only book he carried with him everywhere), nature, and visions.

Concerning the first two Sundar said,

> The Bible and the Book of Nature are both written in spiritual language by the Holy Spirit. The Holy Spirit being the author of life, all Nature, instinct with life, is the work of the Holy Spirit, and the language in which it is written is spiritual language. Those who are born again have the Holy

Spirit for their mother. So to them the language of the Bible and of Nature is their mother tongue, which they easily and naturally understand.[23]

In light of the pantheism found in Hinduism, it is important to note that Sundar was not a pantheist. In fact, he repudiated the pantheism found in the Hindu religion.

He was asked, 'Is there any difference between your study and the Hindu's study of the Book of Nature? Did not the Hindu seers, the poets of the Vedic hymns, also read the pages of the Book of Nature?' 'Yes, they did,' he replied, 'but they lost God in Nature. The Christian mystic finds God in nature. The Hindu mystic thinks that God and Nature are the same. The Christian mystic knows that there must be a Creator who has created the creation.[24]

One illustration of how Sundar "read" the book of nature relates to some doubts he had concerning the value of intercessory prayer offered by us sinners. However, in reading the Book of Nature, his doubts were overcome. This is how he read it:

I saw clouds being formed from the vapour which arose from sea-water. I thought that as the vapour came from salt water that the rain which descended would be salt water too. So I stretched out my hand and catching a few drops tasted them, and, behold, they were fresh and sweet. The sun having shone, the salt had been left behind in the sea. So when we pray, thoughts arise up from our hearts like vapour. The Sun of Righteousness shines on them and anything that is evil is left behind. From the clouds thus formed, showers of blessing fall upon the world.[25]

A bit more must be said about Sundar's visions or ecstasies. According to Streeter and Appasamy, the ecstasies of Sundar were frequent occurrences

---

[23] As quoted in Streeter and Appasamy, *The Sadhu: A Study in Mysticism and Practical Religion*, 193–94.
[24] Streeter and Appasamy, 194–95.
[25] Streeter and Appasamy, 97.

that always left him refreshed. Four other characteristics are mentioned. The "place" in the vision is always the same, i.e. the Third Heaven. The visions were ineffable, i.e. they could never be adequately described by human language. The ecstasies were not a dream state, but a state of clearer and more continuous thought than he was normally capable of. Finally, Jesus Christ was always at the center of the picture.[26]

What follows is a firsthand account from Sundar:

> At one point I was a good deal perplexed about the doctrine of the Trinity. I had thought of three separate Persons sitting as it were on three thrones; but it was all made plain to me in a Vision. I entered in an Ecstasy into the third heaven. I was told that it was the same to which St. Paul was caught up. And there I saw Christ in a glorious spiritual body sitting on a throne. Whenever I go there it is the same. Christ is always in the centre, a figure ineffable and indescribable. His face shining like the sun, but in no way dazzling, and so sweet that without any difficulty I can gaze at it – always smiling a loving glorious smile. I felt when first I saw Him as if there were some old and forgotten connexion between us, as though He had said, but not in words, 'I am He, through whom you were created.' . . .
>
> The first time I entered Heaven I looked round about and I asked, 'But where is God?' And they told me, 'God is not to be seen here any more than on earth, for God is Infinite. But there is Christ, He is God, He is the Image of the Invisible God, and it is only in Him that we can see God, in Heaven as on earth.' And streaming out from Christ I saw, as it were, waves shining and peace-giving, and going through and among the Saints and Angels, and everywhere bringing refreshment, just as in hot weather water refreshes the trees. And this I understood to be the Holy Spirit.[27]

---

[26] Streeter and Appasamy, 139–42.
[27] Streeter and Appasamy, 54–55; Sundar experienced a variety of mystical sensations. There were times of seeing visions of Jesus or experiencing sensational joy that seemed to be from God. Other times he experienced visions of light or pricking of needles or strange warmth that had no joy in it. He considered these sensations not from God, but from Satan. Thompson, *Sadhu Sundar Singh*, 96.

Sundar was baptized into a church fellowship. He also spoke in churches both in the East and the West. When able, he felt blessed to receive Holy Communion. Nevertheless, he was not interested in starting churches or in promoting church growth per se.

He never baptized anyone, refusing to baptize even his father. He led converts to others for baptism. We do not know how many persons were converted by his witness. On one occasion he mentioned having "two or three hundred god-children" for whom he regularly prayed by name.[28] It is possible that these were people whom Sundar personally led to Christ.

He was critical of the church in the West because of its materialism. He was also critical of the church in India. The strongest churches were in the South, but as a whole they were not worthy of great praise because of the remaining problems of caste divisions, lack of love, and lack of zeal for evangelism.

Concerning an indigenized Indian church, Sundar believed, "the people should sit down on the floor. . . They should take off their shoes instead of their turbans. Indian music should be sung. Long, informal addresses should take the place of sermons."[29]

While always affirming that the fullest revelation is from Jesus Christ, Sundar recognized that the Spirit had also been at work in Hinduism. He believed the *Bhagavad Gita* was compatible with the Gospel of John. So, it is not unreasonable that he would have understood that some of the 'higher' elements of Hinduism might be recognized by the Church. He believed that Christianity was the fulfillment of Hinduism.

The final issue is the ideal of the *sadhu*. Sundar saw himself as a Christian *sadhu*. Unlike Hindu *sadhus*, Sundar he did not stress in his personal life a world-denouncing asceticism. He was not seeking to accumulate merit or achieve perfection.

> In general, Sundar's motives for adopting the sadhu life are clear. He has done this because it gives him complete

---

[28] Streeter and Appasamy, *The Sadhu: A Study in Mysticism and Practical Religion*, 96.
[29] Streeter and Appasamy, 231.

freedom, it releases him from the distractions of earthly business, it enables him to practice virtue, so extolled in Indian books, of regarding in the same spirit fortune as well as misfortune; because principally, it seems to him the best way to commend the Gospel to the multitudes of India; perhaps, too – though he never says this – because that life more than any other makes possible the literal imitation of the life of Jesus, and, finally, because he has the unanalysable but imperative conviction that he has been called by God to do so.[30]

Sundar was asked to start a school to train men for being Christian *sadhus*. However, he always declined. He feared the disintegrating pressures that appeared inherent in organizational structures. These pressures would more normally appear after the founder has died, but he did not want to leave any organization that had such a bleak future.

Others have sought to imitate Sadhu Sundar Singh. But as one scholar noted, "Although many minor figures have followed his example, of wandering *sannyasa*, this has not as yet found much favour in the life of the main Protestant Churches in India."[31]

Although Sundar himself did not initiate new movements or churches, others who encountered him did. As a young high school student, N. Daniel met Sundar. Although they never met again, Sundar had a great influence in his life. N. Daniel eventually started the indigenous movement called The Laymen's Evangelical Fellowship.[32] Another person influence by him was Bakht Singh. According to one historian, "Bakht Singh knew and was greatly influenced by Sadhu Sundar Singh, and taught a mystical union with and intimate devotion to Christ."[33] More will be said about Bakht Singh and his Assemblies later in this chapter. And, finally, mention can be made that

---

[30] Streeter and Appasamy, 245.

[31] Robin Boyd, *An Introduction to Indian Christian Theology* (Madras: Christian Literature Society, 1977), 253.

[32] The note of Sundar Singh's influence on N. Daniel and Daniel's subsequent movement is found in Hedlund, *Quest for Identity: India's Churches of Indigenous Origin*, 167–71.

[33] Allan Anderson and Edmond Tang, "Independency in Africa and Asia," in *The Cambridge History of Christianity, Vol. 9: World Christianities c. 1914-c. 2000*, ed. Hugh McLeod (Cambridge: Cambridge University Press, 2006), 116.

Sundar's influence is also felt in the Christian Ashram movement in India that has had both Protestant and Catholic manifestations.[34]

Sundar's life continues to raise questions about what Christianity can or should look like in India. Samuel Mathew has affirmed, "His life and ministry are a challenge to rethink and reorganize patterns of Christian spirituality for southern and central Asia."[35]

7.3 Bakht Singh

Bakht Singh, as his name indicates, was born into a Sikh family in 1902. He was born in an area of the Punjab which today is found in Pakistan.

Bakht Singh attended a local Christian school for seven years. By his own words he "was very bitter against the Gospel of Christ."[36] When he passed his intermediate examination he received a leather bound Bible. He promptly tore the contents out, tossing them, and kept the cover because it was attractive.

As a young person, he was an orthodox Sikh. He was faithful to observe the religious rituals in the Sikh temples. He also participated, as a Sikh, in various social services. However, he did not have any real joy from these activities.

After graduation, he wanted to go to England for further studies. His father opposed this because Bakht was the oldest son, and he wanted him to be involved in the family business. His mother also opposed his leaving for she feared he would abandon his Sikh religion. He assured her that he would not. She then convinced the father to allow him to go and to support him while he was there.

---

[34] Neill, *A History of Christian Missions*, 483. Neill, in the same place, describes the movement thusly: "The term Ashram is rather loosely used of any group of men and women who, living together in community, observe the rules of simplicity of life and of devoted service to their neighbors."
[35] Matthew, "Sundar Singh," 806.
[36] Bakht Singh, "How I Got Joy Unspeakable and Full of Glory," Brother Bakht Singh: A Servant of God, 2007, http://www.brotherbakhtsingh.org/webtestimony.html.

His promise to his mother went by the wayside after only a few months in England where he studied in an Engineering school in London. He cut his hair and shaved his beard off. He began to smoke, drink alcohol, and wear expensive clothes, all the while lying to his father about how he was spending the family money.

Still, happiness was not his, nor did it seem to be truly present among those people he encountered throughout Europe.

In 1928, he travelled with some students to Canada on a holiday. While on the ship he read a notice that a worship service would be held in the first-class dining room. He was disinterested in the service, but wanted to see this fine dining room, so he attended. Following is his own account of what happened.

> I went and occupied one of the back seats. When they all stood up to sing hymns I stood up too, and when they sat down I sat down too, and when the preacher began to preach, I went to sleep as I did not want to listen. When the sermon was over they all knelt down to pray and I was the only person who kept sitting in the chair. I said, 'These people do not know anything about religion. They have exploited my country and I have seen them eating and drinking. What do they know? After all my religion is the best religion.' So my national, intellectual and religious pride prevented me from kneeling and I wanted to go out. But I found one man kneeling on the right and another kneeling on the left and I said to myself it would not be right for me to disturb them. Still I could not kneel. Then I began to say, 'I have been to Mohammedan mosques and Hindu temples. I have taken off my shoes and washed my feet to show respect for those places. I must honour this place too out of courtesy.' So breaking my national pride, I knelt down.

> Please note that this was the first time I was attending a Christian service. I had never read the Bible before nor had anyone spoken to me about salvation. When I knelt down I felt a great change coming over me. My whole body was trembling. I could feel divine power entering me and lifting

> me up. The first change that I noticed in me was that a great
> joy was flooding my soul. The second change was that I
> was repeating the name of Jesus. I began to say, 'Oh, Lord
> Jesus, blessed be Thy name, blessed be Thy name.' The
> name of Jesus became very sweet to me.[37]

Neither then, nor on his return to England, did he share this experience with anyone. He gave up smoking and drinking. And he would go to church buildings during the week and sit alone in peace and quiet.

Returning to Canada to complete some requirement for his agricultural engineering course, he came to the city of Winnipeg. There he asked a friend to borrow a Bible. The friend gave him his pocket New Testament. He began reading through the New Testament and felt Christ speaking to him. He was convicted of his sins and confessed. He was then assured of his salvation. Later he would write,

> I did not know how, but knew that the blood of Jesus only
> could save me. I could not explain the fact, but joy and
> peace came into my soul; I had the assurance that all my
> sins were washed away; I know that the Lord Jesus was
> reigning in my heart. I just kept on praising Him.[38]

Later, after further reading in the New Testament, he prayed that God would heal his nasal problems and his faltering eyesight. He reported that the next morning, he was healed.

Finally, in February, 1932, he was baptized. Later he experienced a call to serve God. He stayed in Canada and America for about a year, preaching and sharing his testimony in various places.

In 1933, he returned to his home. At first, his parents and family refused to welcome him. But eventually both his father and mother converted.

In the following years, Bakht Singh preached all over India with great success. However, he became disillusioned with the denominational churches and began his first church. It was started in Madras and called

---

[37] Singh.

[38] Singh.

Jehovah Shammah. This was in 1941. Many other similar churches were started in the province of Andra Pradesh, in other parts of India, and in other countries.

In 1951, Bakht moved to Hyderabad and called the new establishment Hebron. According to one account, from the 1950s to the 1970s, "the local churches established by Brother Bakht Singh and his coworkers were the fastest growing local churches in India."[39]

Bakht also travelled abroad, helping to start churches from America to Australia. In 2000, he died after battling Parkinson's disease for 10 years.

The movement begun by Bakht Singh is called Bakht Singh Assemblies.[40] The importance of this movement is affirmed by Roger Hedlum, who calls it "a remarkable indigenous Christian witness" that seemed "to meet a need not met by existing traditional churches." Although the movement is largely south Indian in membership, many north Indian cultural patterns and Punjabi Sikh worship patterns have been adapted for use.[41]

The Bakht Singh Assemblies have no hierarchical structure or paid clergy. Elders are chosen who give guidance in the spiritual life of the church. The Assemblies are considered a spiritual dwelling place for God. Only 'born again' persons are members.

> The biblical understanding of the Church, states Bakht Singh, means, "only those men and women who have been redeemed by the Lord Jesus Christ." Such a Church is a "spiritual" entity with no need for earthly organizational rules. "No man-made constitution whatever can truly bind together the Church of God."[42]

On a typical Sunday morning, people would begin to gather at the church around 10:00. Singing and praying commence as more and more people arrived, kneeling down and praying as they entered the place of worship.

---

[39] T. E. Koshy, "Brother Bakht Singh--A Saint of God: An Overview of His Life and Ministry," Brother Bakht Singh: A Servant of God, 2007, http://www.brotherbakhtsingh.org/briefbio.html.
[40] Hedlund, *Quest for Identity: India's Churches of Indigenous Origin*, 175.
[41] Hedlund, 178–79.
[42] Hedlund, 176.

A Brief History of Christianity in Asia

Then they would join in with singing. Each service could have three sermons (of unequal length). The first sermon was an exhortation by one of the leaders to worship, typically followed by an extensive time of singing and prayer. The second sermon, centering around the Lord's Supper which follows. The Lord's Supper represented the highest point of the service. Next is the longest of the three sermons. Finally, an offering was taken; then all would kneel for a benediction before closing with a short chorus.[43] These services often lasted three or more hours.

Usually, the members then join together for a simple meal called the love feast. Afterwards, the Assemblies follow Bakht Singh's emphasizes on scripture, prayer, evangelism, concern for the poor, Christian fellowship, and a conservative life-style.

This life-style is in part a reflection of Indian patterns and in part Bakht's own understanding of scripture. Women are subordinate to men and wear a veil in public settings. Drinking, smoking and going to the movies are not permitted.

However, one important feature of the Assemblies that is not typically Indian is that they have always ignored caste distinctions. Economic divisions are also discouraged. As all sit together on mats, caste and economic status become irrelevant. Another uniting function is the use of various languages simultaneously in the singing of songs. Sermons are often translated into two or more languages.

Another unique feature of Bakht Singh Assemblies is the annual "Holy Convocation". These are 8 – 10 day meetings that thousands may attend. During Bakht's life time, these annual Convocations would end with 200 to 300 persons being baptized.

The Assemblies of Brother Bakht Singh have been one of the fastest growing Christian movements in India, 120,000 members were numbered in 1970. In

[43] This description depends on Kuchipudi Clement, "Bakht Singh" in Dictionary of Asian Christianity, edited by Scott W. Sundquist, 53. The following is a simpler account given by Hedlund. "Devotional singing, testimonials, shared experiences, the congregation seated on mats on the floor with participation by all as moved by the Holy Spirit, and the central prominence of the Bible which is carefully expounded for about an hour (with translation as required) – these are regular features of the assemblies gathered for Sunday worship", Hedlund, 154.

1995 the count reached 216,000.[44] In spite of this growth, doubts exist about the future of the movement. It has been noted that the India of the 1940s when Bakht Singh began his ministry is far different from the India of today. The Assemblies may have problems reaching out to groups that represent vastly different world views and life expectations.

Additionally, the movement may suffer from divisions since the death of its founder in 2000. Already it is reported that divisions are occurring. One group wants to preserve the memory and connection to Bakht Singh. They are the conservatives. The progressives, on the other hand, include elders from "open" assemblies. In some cases two assemblies now exist in the same locality.[45]

Whatever the future may hold, it can be affirmed that Bakht Singh was faithful to his understanding of the Christian faith. With that understanding, he became one of India's greatest indigenous church planters.

---

[44] Barrett, Kurian, and Johnson, *World Christian Encyclopedia*, 368.
[45] Hedlund, *Quest for Identity: India's Churches of Indigenous Origin*, 156.

Part Three: The Church in Asia: Advance and Movement in 20th and 21st Century

"Christianity began in Asia, but Asia has been the least hospitable region for Jesus and his followers."

–Scott Sunquist[1]

Much of the first half of this book tells the stories of pioneers who boldly took the gospel to places where no one yet had taken the gospel. Then we tell the stories of those who helped indigenize the gospel in cultures across Asia. The gospel has never and should never be captive to one particular culture. This final section of the book looks at the continued growth and maturation of the church throughout Asia. While there are a few volumes that seek to capture the breadth of Asian church history,[2] there is a need for an updated comprehensive account of the last 120 years of Christian growth and expansion in Asia. There is increasing interest in the history of Asian Christianity, and more volumes devoted to Asian church history are finally giving much needed depth, detail, and nuance to this important topic.[3]

---

[1] Sunquist, *Explorations in Asian Christianity*, 1.

[2] Perhaps the best known histories of Christianity Asia are by Moffet and Latourette, but both of them conclude their coverage prior to World War I. Moffett, *A History of Christianity in Asia, Vol. II*; Kenneth Scott Latourette, *A History of the Expansion of Christianity: Vol. 6: The Great Century: North Africa and Asia: 1800 A.D. to 1914 A.D.* (Grand Rapids, MI: Zondervan Publishing Company, 1944).

[3] A few noteworthy volumes that have been published in recent years: Daniel H. Bays, *A New History of Christianity in China* (Chichester, West Sussex ; Malden, MA: Wiley-Blackwell, 2011); Frykenberg, *Christianity in India*; Sunquist, *Explorations in Asian Christianity*; Robbie B. H. Goh, *Christianity in Southeast Asia*, Southeast Asia Background Series 7 (Singapore: Institute of Southeast Asian Studies, 2005); Brian Stanley, "Twentieth-Century World Christianity: A Perspective from the History of Missions," in *Christianity Reborn: The Gloabl Expansion of Evangelicalism in the Twentieth Century*, ed. Donald M. Lewis, Studies in the History of Christian Missions (Grand Rapids, MI: Wm. B. Eerdmans, 2004), 52–86; Alvyn Austin, *China's Millions* (Grand Rapids, MI: Wm. B. Eerdmans Publishing, 2007); England et al., *Asian Christian Theologies: A Research Guide to Authors, Movements, Sources, Vol. 2: Southeast Asia*; John C. England, John M. Prior, and Jose Kuttianimattathil, eds., *Asian Christian Theologies: A*

The twentieth century saw rapid changes in transportation, and communication technologies made the world more interconnected. Even violent conflicts became global affairs (WWI and WWII). The Church of Asia was greatly impacted by these globalizing developments. Denominations grew in their global reach, and Christian movements spread from one corner of the globe to the other three corners with great rapidity. Paul Pierson suggests three major changes impacting the Asian church in the last century.

First, Christian missions became increasingly conservative and inter-denominational, which had direct consequences on the church. Second, theological liberalism became a strong influence in many mainline churches, particularly through the World Council of Churches. These first two changes meant an increase in disunity and conflict among Christians around the world. The third significant change came with the emergence of the Pentecostal movement, which soon became a significant part of the global church. By the end of the twentieth century, two-thirds of Evangelical Christians were found in Asia, Africa and Latin America.[4]

Scott Sunquist says "In 1910 Christianity was like a roller coaster at the top of a great incline: filled with great hope, but on the cusp of a wild ride. The twentieth century was that wild ride."[5] In these final three chapters, we will see the influence of these various developments on the Asian Church.

Research Guide Authors, Movements, Sources: Volume 3: Northeast Asia (Delhi; Quezon City; Maryknoll, N.Y: Orbis Books, 2004); John C. England et al., eds., *Asian Christian Theologies: A Research Guide to Authors, Movements, Sources: Volume 1: Asia Region, South Asia, Austral Asia.* (Delhi; Quezon City; Maryknoll, N.Y: Orbis Books, 2005).
[4] Paul E. Pierson, "The New Context of Christian Mission: Challenges and Opportunities for the Asian Church," in *Asian Church and God's Mission*, ed. Wonsuk Ma and Julie C. Ma (Manila: OMF Publishers, 2003), 13.
[5] Sunquist, *Explorations in Asian Christianity*, 108.

Chapter 8: Movements of Revival and Growth

"Every major advance of the kingdom of God on earth is signaled and brought about by a general outpouring o the Holy Spirit."

–Richard Lovelace[1]

By the turn of the 20th century the gospel had gained initial entry into many parts of Asia, yet the church remained fragile in many, if not most, places. We've seen the church established in some areas, only to be systematically eradicated through persecution. In those places where the church became more established, God used extraordinary people and events to help the church multiply and stabilize. There is not adequate space to give a full telling of all that God accomplished in just over a century in such diverse and varied parts of Asia. A few stories of revivals, movements, and significant individuals will have to represent the many other stories of God's gracious work throughout the continent.

8.1 Movements of Revival

Revivals broke out all over the world in the first decade of the twentieth century. In Asia, these revivals were crucial to the growth and indigenization of the national church through Asia. Mark Shaw contends that revivals are significant in understanding the global resurgence of Christianity. There are certainly many other vital factors in the spread and establishment of Christianity like bold evangelism, Bible translations into myriad languages, theological shifts, and forces of globalization. However, Shaw contends that revivals served as a delivery system for these other factors.[2] Although revival-like movements have occurred throughout the history of the church, there was a significant series of interrelated revivals occurring all over the world. Ground zero for these revivals, by some accounts, began with the Welsh revival. In 1904, Evan Roberts and a group of young people gathered regularly for prayer, worship and confession of sins. This informal gathering

---

[1] Richard F. Lovelace, *Dynamics of Spiritual Life - An Evangelical Theology of Renewal* (Downers Grove, IL: InterVarsity Press, 1979), 40.
[2] Mark R. Shaw, *Global Awakening: How 20th-Century Revivals Triggered a Christian Revolution* (Downers Grove, IL: IVP Academic, 2010), 12.

soon influenced the established churches and the nation.[3] News of the revival spread in every direction, and churches experienced similar outpourings of the Holy Spirit globally.

Revivals are difficult to capture accurately. The nature and intensity of revivals provoke heightened emotions, which leads to varying eye-witness accounts. Jonathan Edwards described the complex nature of revivals as including muddled motivations and the human tendency to make a mess of even the best things.[4] Here we only highlight a few examples to offer the briefest glimpse of revivals and the geographical diversity of these events. There was a particular increase in revivals in the first decade of the 20th century. Edwin Orr refers to this period as the Fifth Awakening.[5] Previous Awakenings were primarily in North American and Europe, this one was global in its reach. Within a few years, there were revival movements in India, Korea, Wales, and the United States and these revivals encouraged spiritual receptivity in many more nations.

Year	Location	Outcomes
1900	Japan Revival	Total membership of Japanese church doubled
1904-1905	Welsh Revival	100,000+ converted
1905	India Revival	Bombay, Kerala, and other locations
1906	Shantung Revival (1st one)	
1906-1913	Azusa Street Revival (Los Angeles)	Began in LA, but quickly had global impact
1907	Korea Revival	Started in Pyongyang, established the church in Korea
1908	Manchuria (China)	Initiated revival movements in China

Figure 3: Key Revivals in 1900-1910

---

[3] Shaw, 21.

[4] Jonathan Edwards, *Charity and Its Fruits: Christian Love as Manifested in the Heart and Life* (London: Banner of Truth, 1969).

[5] Orr cites the 1st Awakening beginning in mid-18th century, the 2nd Awakening in 1792, the 3rd Awakening in 1830, and the 4th Awakening in 1858-59. J. Edwin Orr, *Evangelical Awakenings in Eastern Asia* (Minneapolis: Bethany Fellowship, 1975), x.

The Korean Revival. The Korean revival that began in Pyongyang in 1907 had significant impact on the whole Korean peninsula and even globally. Revival came during a time when the church was already growing rapidly and members were getting involved in Bible studies.[6] One winter, believers had gathered for a time of preaching and worship. As they were praying on January 6, 1907, Christians began weeping and confessing sin which continued throughout the night. One missionary in attendance, William Blair, commented: "We may have our theories of the desirability of public confession of sin. I have had mine; but I know how that when the Spirit of God falls upon guilty souls, there will be confession, and no power on earth can stop it."[7] The revival spread as attendees returned home and led many churches in revival. Among those present during this powerful event came a generation of Korean pastors who would firmly establish the Korean church. Yun Chi-Ho, Ik Doo Kim, and Kil Sun Ju helped lead the church in becoming deeply Korean without losing the essence of Christianity. Kil, who became the most prominent leader in the post-revival Korean church, died as a martyr in 1935 protesting forced Shintoism.[8]

The Dornakal Revival in India. Christianity in India has been shaped by revivals and ensuing mass movements all over the country. Those events can only be appreciated by hearing about the people and happenings involved in each revival movement. Some movements have the effect of impacting the nation more broadly. Pandita Ramibai (see ch. 7.1) was a vital figure in Indian Christianity. Another was Vedanayagam Samuel Azariah in Telegu country. Azariah left his work with YMCA to pursue a missionary calling in the jungles of Dornakal (in Andrah Pradesh). From his time with the YMCA, Azariah developed a burning passion for evangelism and was equipped by missionaries to be a missionary himself. During his time with YMCA in 1903, Azariah joined with others in forming the Indian Missionary Society in Turunelveli. It was a thoroughly Indian work: Indian missionaries and Indian resources.[9] Across the sub-continent, Indian Christians were taking up responsibility to reach those not yet reached.

---

[6] As in any movement, there were events that prepared the way for the revival that began in 1907. A prayer movement beginning in 1903 and a period of a rapidly growing church. Shaw, *Global Awakening*, 38.

[7] As quoted in John Mark Terry, "The Growth of Christianity in East Asia," *Southern Baptist Journal of Theology* 15, no. 2 (2011): 49.

[8] Shaw, *Global Awakening*, 45.

[9] Sunquist, *Explorations in Asian Christianity*, 67.

Figure 4: Ephiphany Cathedral Dornakal, Andhra Pradesh, India. Photo credit: Jacob Pabbathy, 2010

Azariah's heart for the poor and marginalized took him to Dornakal, where he was appointed as India's first Anglican bishop in 1912. Azariah organized evangelistic preaching in villages through the area. The results were astonishing. Starting in 1921, the church in this region grew by 12,000 converts each month for a decade.[10] From simple beginnings in the midst of Islamic rural India emerged a movement of 250,000 Christians by 1947.[11] Azariah never deviated from preaching the core tenets of the gospel, which resulted in conviction and conversion. At the same time, Azariah worked to translate the church in its Indian context. Construction on the Epiphany Cathedral was begun in 1913 and completed in 1949. This undeniably Christian structure also borrows from indigenous architectural motifs

---

[10] Shaw, *Global Awakening*, 72–73.

[11] This movement was not the first in Telegu country. There was already steady growth of Christians in the area from 1860-1900. G. A. Oddie, "Christian Conversion in the Telugu Country, 1860-1900: A Case Study of One Protestant Movement in the Godavery-Krishna Delta," *Indian Economic Social History Review* 12 (n.d.): 61–79.

(pictured below).[12] Through his leadership, churches and mission societies were able to bring social lift to these low caste Indians. News of what was happening in Dornakal was inspiring ministries in other states of India.[13] Azariah is but one example of Indian leaders throughout the country growing and strengthening the churches through local forms and funding.

Revivals in China. As we have already discovered in previous chapters, the story of Christianity in China is one of immense complexity, with many peaks and valleys along the way. Here we will only highlight three revivals (two in the same place) to trace the basic outline of spiritual awakening in the vast nation of China. We begin in 1908, right on the heels other revivals around the world. Canadian missionaries, Jonathan and Rosalind Goforth, brought revivalist preaching to Northeast China. The couple arrived in Honan, China just prior to the Boxer rebellion and had to escape for their lives via a thousand-mile journey. Upon resettling, the Goforths opened their home to thousands of Chinese to hear preaching. Jonathan travelled widely, preaching the gospel and calling for public confession. His travel included going to Pyongyang to witness the revival happening in 1907. In 1908, revival began in Manchuria (now Liaoning Province in China). Many confessed their sin publicly, weeping together with reports of visions and ecstatic experiences. Thus began revivalism in China. Goforth's ministry saw great response, and, as Ruth Tucker summarizes, "wherever he went, revival followed."[14]

News of the revivals involving Goforth spread quickly throughout the country and inspired others in their ministries. Shaw notes: "Revival has become an indigenous feature as well as an indigenizing force within Chinese Christianity."[15] Powerful Chinese evangelists emerged during this time, including Wang Chang-tai, Ting Li-mei, and Drs. Y. S. Lee and S. S. Yao.[16] In 1910, Ding Limei, launched a student renewal movement in Shantung. Known as the "Moody of China," Ding's student revivals were

---

[12] The pillars of the structure are Dravidian and domes borrow from Saracen heritage. Frykenberg, *Christianity in India*, 239.

[13] Sushil J. Aaron, "Emulating Azariah: Evangelicals and Social Change in the Dangs," in *Evangelical Christianity and Democracy in Asia*, ed. David H. Lumsdaine (Oxford: Oxford University Press, 2009), 100–102.

[14] Tucker, *From Jerusalem to Irian Jaya: A Biographical History of Christian Missions*, 201.

[15] Shaw, *Global Awakening*, 184.

[16] Orr, *Evangelical Awakenings in Eastern Asia*, 39.

effective in reaching Chinese intellectuals who used their intellectual gifts in leading independent churches.[17] The aftermath of this movement resulted in a generation of Christian leaders who would prepare Christians in China for the difficult days of war and persecution.

One revival in a place does not secure spiritual fervency for decades to come. It is human to stray. Some time later, the church in Shantung had grown ill. The reports of local evangelists were bleak, reporting seventy churches already dead and more to come. The feeling was that many had adopted a new religion, but had not been converted to Christ. C. L. Culpepper writes: "they had accepted God's grace as an outside coating of whitewash, but had only 'covered' their sins, not been forgiven for them."[18] Even the foreign missionaries were engaged in debate and slander with each other, until one day in 1927 the missionaries gathered for a meeting in Chefoo. As they worshipped and prayed, the Holy Spirit fell on the group, bringing about confession and reconciliation. Revival soon spread. Seminary students studying the book of Acts experienced an outpouring of the Spirit, which they then took to churches. The impact was manifold. The revival led to a tenfold increase in the churches and a deepening commitment in the churches. In addition, the emphasis on reading the Bible led to increased literacy, particularly among women. This time of renewal led to an increased role for women in ministry in a culture where women had a diminished role in society. "Bible women" began to disciple across the nation with great industriousness.

Revivals in Indonesia. Christianity in Indonesia has grown significantly through revivals. As is always the case, circumstances can create an environment either hospitable or hostile to movements breaking out. God works through such circumstances to effect a movement. In the 1960s, the Indonesian government began to systematically purge all communists by outlawing and punishing all atheists. During this time, about 2 million Indonesians converted to Christianity. Avery Willis concluded: "God prepares peoples and countries for response to the gospel through a confluence of anthropological, political, sociological, economic, cultural, and religious factors."[19]

---

[17] Shaw, *Global Awakening*, 185–86.

[18] C. L. Culpepper, *The Shantung Revival* (Crescendo Book Publications, 1971), https://www.gospeltruth.net/shantung.htm.

[19] Willis, *Indonesian Revival Why Two Million Came to Christ*, 210.

Flames of revival spread in several places—Nias, Java and Timor–beginning in the uncertain days surrounding the attempted military coup on 30 September, 1965. Witnesses saw evidences of revival beginning which burst into unprecedented power in September 1965.

Four days previously, in the eastern Indonesian province of Timor, a rebellious young man had received a vision of the Lord, commanding him to repent, burn his fetishes, and confess his sins in church. He did. On Sunday, 26 September, 1965, he attended a service at the Reformed Church in Soe, a mountain town of about 4,000 people, where the revival broke out. People heard the sound of a tornado wind. Flames on the church building prompted police to set off the fire alarm to summon the volunteer fire fighters. Many people were converted that night. Many were filled with the Spirit, including speaking in tongues, some in English. By midnight, teams of lay people had been organized to begin spreading the gospel the next day. They gave themselves full-time to visiting churches and villages and saw thousands converted with multitudes healed and delivered. In one town, alone they saw 9,000 people converted in two weeks. [20] Throughout Asia, revival movements such as these served to increase the number of Christians as well as deepen the fervency of Christian faith.

Observations of these Revival Movements

Revivals led to indirect church growth. Strictly speaking, revivals actually impact those who are already Christians. The evangelistic fruit reported from times of revival is a consequence of the Holy Spirit's impact on believers first. Sometimes, revivals fuel evangelistic campaigns, as the Korean revival which sparked the "Million Souls for Christ" campaign in 1910-1911.[21]

Revivals deepened the spirituality of both young and maturing churches. People attend church or convert to Christianity for many reasons, not all of them altruistic. Sometimes people–even today–hope for financial gain, others are drawn to the "successful" atmosphere, and many are drawn by

---

[20] George W. Peters, *Indonesia Revival; Focus on Timor* (Grand Rapids, MI: Zondervan Pub. House, 1973), 20–31.
[21] R. E. Shearer, *Wildfire: Church Growth in Korea* (Grand Rapids, MI: William B. Eerdmans, 1966), 57.

hope in miracles of healing.[22] These revivals were instrumental in helping people move from worldly motivations to a deeper conviction of their own sinfulness and need for a savior.

Revivals were so clearly of God, that they accelerated the indigenization of local churches. In part this indigenization happened because revivals moved at the grass roots level, rather than through the ranks of ecclesiastical structures. Mark Shaw draws on the notion of the gospel's translatability as put forward by historians Andrew Walls and Lamin Sanneh.[23] Shaw claims, "The real story of World Christianity starts not from above but from below, with indigenous movements of translated Christianity." [24] He describes revivals as a key time when Christianity is translated culturally to become truly local.

8.2 Growth through Evangelistic Events

Periodically, God raises up individuals with an extraordinary anointing that have far-reaching impact for the sake of Christ. Dr. John Sung was one such individual. Sung was a Methodist pastor's son born in Fujian Province, China in 1901. Showing great academic aptitude, Sung earned multiple degrees, including a Ph.D. in chemistry at Ohio State University in the United States. From there he entered Union Theological Seminary in New York. It was during this time in seminary in 1927 that Sung came under conviction of his sins and beseeched God for forgiveness. On that late September night, John Sung was "born again,"[25] and it ignited within him an evangelistic fervor that would not fade until his last breath.

Sung returned to China in 1927, throwing his doctoral diploma off the ship. He taught chemistry for a short time and then entered full-time ministry. Over the next twelve years he would get married and have five children, set up and train evangelistic bands, and travelled throughout China, Taiwan, and Southeast Asia preaching tirelessly everywhere he went. For example, when Sung visited Vietnam in 1938, preaching three-hour sessions, three times a

---

[22] Shearer, 55–56.

[23] See further in Sanneh, *Translating the Message*; Walls, *The Missionary Movement in Christian History*.

[24] Shaw, *Global Awakening*, 29.

[25] This is the term Sung used to describe his experience in his personal journals. John Sung, *The Journal Once Lost - Extracts From The Diary of John Sung*, ed. LEVI (Singapore: Armour Publishing, 2008), 42–44.

day for a week led to revivals in Danang, Vinh Long, and Saigon. These revivals led to confession of sin, reconciliation between Christians, and deepened the Christian convictions of a yet-young church just prior to the years of war and persecution.[26]

Health problems plagued Sung his entire adult life, stemming from health issues that developed during his college days in America. The rigors of constant travel and an unrelenting schedule taxed his health beyond what it could bear. Sung died in 1944 at the young age of 42. Another significant evangelist, Wang Ming Tao, preached at Sung's funeral. It is estimated that 100,000 people were converted to Christ through his ministry. Historian, John Roxborogh, summarizes his ministry: "He was astonishingly effective in moving people to repent of sin, to turn to Christ, and to give their lives to Christian service—and to stay committed." In some ways, Sung did for Chinese Christians what Sundar Singh did for Indian Christians—remove the Western smell without losing the essence of the gospel.

One outcome of the revivals was an emphasis on large gatherings with evangelistic preaching. The quintessential example of big-event crusades was Billy Graham. This American Southern Baptist evangelist held live evangelistic events where it is estimated that he preached in person to more than 200 million people, more people than any other person in history. He also had a broadcast ministry over six decades which was heard by as many as 2.5 billion people. Once Graham had worldwide recognition, his crusades in countries around the world served as catalytic events, bringing together a wide range of church leaders in a country, forging unity and collaboration for the sake of Christ. For example, in 1973, Graham did four nights in Seoul, South Korea where 3.2 million people came to hear him.[27] Christian leaders in Seoul look back on this event today as a pivotal time for the Korean church. During Graham's years of ministry he made many trips to Asian nations where he has held court with top leaders and held crusades in a number of Asian cities, including Hong Kong, Tokyo, Manila, and Taipei.

Billy Graham's impactful ministry allowed for evangelists across Asia to rise up. Standing beside Billy Graham in the Seoul crusades in 1973 was his

---

[26] Reimer, *Vietnam's Christians*, 33.

[27] "Seoul, South Korea: A Look Back at Billy Graham's Largest Ever Crusade," Billy Graham Evangelistic Association, February 8, 2018, https://billygraham.org/story/seoul-south-korea-a-look-back-at-billy-grahams-largest-ever-crusade/.

translator Billy Kim. Kim began in ministry pastoring a small church of 10 congregants in Suwon, South Korea. During his ministry the church grew to 15,000, and he served a wider role as an evangelist and church statesmen. Large evangelistic events become markers of Christian growth in a nation. Keeping to the example of South Korea, in 1980 the final night of Here's Life Korea crusade drew 2,700,000, the largest single Christian meeting in history. Over the course of several nights, 1.5 million people chose to follow Christ.

Evangelistic crusades and rallies were used with great effect to grow and galvanize the national church across Asia, even in unlikely places. In 2018, Franklin Graham, son of Billy Graham, held a stadium event in Hanoi, the capital of Vietnam. This high-profile event allowed for the scattered church to come together to worship and encourage each other–an occasion especially meaningful to a church which struggled under limited freedoms (as it does to this day). Events like this encourage isolated believers through the larger gathering of believers. Large-scale evangelistic events have played an important role, particularly in countries where Christians are a minority, which is to say all but four Asian countries.[28]

8.3 The Rise of Pentecostalism

In 1900, the number of Pentecostals[29] was barely noticeable and now they number in the hundreds of millions.[30] A quick glance at the largest churches and denominations in every continent would show a significant presence of Pentecostalism. The Pentecostal movement in the twentieth century is "becoming the single most momentous recent missionary movement in Christian history."[31] It is hard to imagine that it is a late-comer to the

---

[28] Four Asian nations that are statistically considered majority Christian nations: Armenia, Georgia, Timor Leste, and the Philippines.

[29] Here we use 'Pentecostal' in the broader sense to include those identifying in Pentecostal and Charismatic movements. There are technical distinctions between these two terms, but there is little agreement on precise definitions. In the broader movement, Anderson includes "all churches and movements that emphasize the working of the gifts of the Spirit, both on phenomenological and on theological grounds." Anderson, *An Introduction to Pentecostalism*, 10–15.

[30] Wes Richards, "An Examination of Common Factors in the Growth of Global Pentecostalism: Observed in South Korea, Nigeria and Argentina," *Journal of Asian Mission* 7, no. 1 (2005): 85.

[31] Frykenberg, *Christianity in India*, 465.

denominational scene.[32] What began in small brush fires in Topeka, Kansas and Azusa Street in California grew to over half a billion by the end of the century.[33] Pentecostal Christianity went from the periphery of Christianity to one its largest stakeholders in a matter of one hundred years.[34] In Asia, Pentecostals account for more than 40% of those adhering to Christianity.

---

[32] Of course, there have been expressions of Christian faith displaying the faith expressions now associated with Pentecostalism. Prior to the twentieth century these individuals or groups remained outliers to their denominations. The shift in the early 1900s was churches fully identifying with Pentecostal faith expressions.

[33] Shaw, *Global Awakening*, 11.

[34] According to Allan Anderson, with an estimated 500 million Pentecostal Christians, it is second only to the Roman Catholic Church in numerical representation. Anderson, *An Introduction to Pentecostalism*, 1.

How did the Modern Pentecostal Movement[35] Begin?

Charles Parham, left the Methodist Church to start a Bible school in Topeka, Kansas, where on 1 January 1901 he challenged students to study the Holy Spirit in the book of Acts and pray for an out pouring. After many hours of devoted prayer, Agnes Ozman had spoken in tongues as did half of the 34 students. Parham took this emphasis as he moved to Kansas City and then to Houston. William J. Seymour, a Negro, studied in Charles Parham's Bible School in Houston.[36] It was Seymour who would take these ideas further in practice and in geography. Of particular note is the Azusa Street revival in Los Angeles. Seymour had begun pastoring a small church in Los Angeles that did not like his teaching on speaking in tongues as a sign of Spirit baptism. He, along with a few church members, gathered in a member's home for worship and prayer in 1906. People began to have different ecstatic experiences leading to a swelling number of those joining in. They rented a storage building on Azusa Street and meetings continued to grow. The group was interracial during a time when it was not accepted, and this ministry became the epicenter for a distinctive Pentecostal movement. Those events have been seen as the beginning of Pentecostalism in America. But these events did much to normalize and institutionalize Pentecostalism as a global phenomenon. Many of the common characteristics of Pentecostalism have appeared throughout Christian history, but the events at the beginning of the

---

[35] Malaysian scholar, Hwa Yung, rightly challenges the history of Pentecostalism originating in America as an oversimplification. While it is without doubt that charismatic practices have been periodically present in church practices throughout the centuries and around the globe, what we seek to describe here is the Pentecostal movement. Although features of Pentecostalism have been present for a long time, what developed out of Azusa Street was an identifiable movement that provided new language and even identity for Christians around the world experiencing similar phenomenon. Bergunder notes that despite attempts to decentralize the beginnings of the Pentecostal movement, historians still the source of organized Pentecostalism in American. Hwa Yung, "Pentecostalism and the Asian Church," in *Asian and Pentecostal: The Charismatic Face of Christianity in Asia*, ed. Allan Anderson and Edmond Tang (Oxford; Baguio City: Regnum Books International, 2005), 41; Michael Bergunder, *The South Indian Pentecostal Movement in the Twentieth Century*, Studies in the History of Christian Missions (Grand Rapids, MI: Eerdmans, 2008), 3.

[36] Parham was beset by accusations and practices that were morally and ethically compromising which disqualified him from providing anything beyond his initial contribution. Anderson, *An Introduction to Pentecostalism*, 34–35.

twentieth century were unique in that the gifts of the Spirit were emphasized as essential to church life.

Over time, the mainstream Pentecostal movement developed and organized as well as splintered and divided. Theological controversies developed over a variety of issues: the finished work of Christ, the role of revelation, ecclesiastical polity, and articulation of trinitarian doctrine, just to name a few. From this came new denominations, each with distinctions. Particularly, in the 1950s and 60s, the larger Pentecostal denominations became increasingly global. It has become common parlance now to speak of the movement in terms of waves.

Accompanying the new Pentecostal movement was an increase of charismatic emphasis and practice in existing Christian denominations. There have been charismatic movements in every major Christian denomination, most of all among Catholics.[37]

How did Pentecostalism Grow in Asia?

Earlier in this book we have described revivals in India, Wales, and Korea that exhibited many of the same characteristics as those found in the Azusa Street event. In fact, the Indian revival involving Pandita Ramabai and the revival in Wales predated the revival in Los Angeles. Thus, the charismatic gifts were not new or unheard of; rather, what developed in America was a distinctive movement with the ongoing emphasis on these gifts of the Spirit.

Charismatic/Pentecostal manifestations have long been a feature of revivals and mass movements. In truth, movements with Pentecostal characteristics occurred in Asia well before Parham and Seymour in America. A revival began in Tirunelveli in 1860, through the ministry of John Christian Arrolappen, featuring the speaking and interpretation of tongues, visions, and confession of sins.[38] In addition, several of those we have already highlighted (Pandita Ramabai, Sadhu Sundar Singh, John Sung) displayed the use of tongues, seeing visions, prophecy, and supernatural healing.

---

[37] David Martin, *Pentecostalism: The World Their Parish* (Malden, MA: Blackwell Publishers, 2002), 156–57.
[38] Yung, "Pentecostalism and the Asian Church," 44.

Asian Christians never distanced themselves from the supernatural in the same ways western Christians did.[39] A supernaturalistic worldview is still intact in much of Asia[40] Thus, supernatural expressions of faith practice did not come as novel or different. It just was. As many converted to faith in Christ, it was not unusual for them to experience visions, tongues, and special healings.

Pentecostalism is a global phenomenon, and Asia is no exception. Nearly every Asian nation has been touched by the movement. In some countries, like Malaysia and Singapore, Charismatic and Pentecostal expression came through contact with transnational church networks (primarily Pentecostal denominations). Although it didn't grow up indigenously in Malaysia, 75% of Malaysia's evangelical Christians are Charismatic/Pentecostal.[41] In many places charismatic practices grew from within older, established denominations. In the Philippines, estimates are 26% of the total population is charismatic, with most of these remaining in the Catholic Church.[42] Many of Asia's Pentecostals have come out of indigenous Christian movements, rather than exported denominations. For example, in Myanmar where international Christian missionaries and organizations had been restricted, Pentecostalism developed with minimal presence of international missionaries, giving it a more indigenous flavor.[43]

Whether through denominations, international missionaries, or indigenous movements, the Pentecostal movement has grown rapidly and put down deep roots in the soils of Asia.

---

[39] Hiebert sheds light on this gap in western Christian theology in this landmark article: Paul G. Hiebert, "The Flaw of the Excluded Middle," *Missiology: An International Review* 10, no. 1 (January 1982): 35–47.

[40] Yung, "Pentecostalism and the Asian Church," 50.

[41] Jin Huat Tan, "Pentecostals and Charismatics in Malaysia and Singapore," in *Asian and Pentecostal: The Charismatic Face of Christianity in Asia*, ed. Allan Anderson and Edmond Tang (Oxford; Baguio City: Regnum Books International, 2005), 281–306.

[42] Lode Wostyn, "Catholic Charismatics in the Philippines," in *Asian and Pentecostal: The Charismatic Face of Christianity in Asia*, ed. Allan Anderson and Edmond Tang (Oxford; Baguio City: Regnum Books International, 2005), 363–84.

[43] Yung, "Pentecostalism and the Asian Church," 38.

Why Has Pentecostalism Thrived in Asia?

Without doubt, Pentecostalism has grown to become a significant presence in Asian Christianity. As any movement does, it began more organically but is now established through strong institutions (churches, Bible schools, and parachurch ministries). In Metro Manila, eight out of ten of the fastest growing churches are Pentecostal. In South Korea, nine of the fifteen largest mega-churches are Pentecostal.[44] Why did this movement grow as it did in Asia?

There has been much research seeking to understand the rapid rise of the Pentecostal churches. Wonsuk Ma suggests three reasons for the appeal of Pentecostalism. First, Pentecostalism, as young movement, has attracted a younger generation. In a continent that weighs demographically heavy on youth, the Pentecostal church has grown rapidly among younger generations that are less tied to traditional practices or institutions. [45] Second, Pentecostalism has a strong appeal to the poor around the world. Asia has been afflicted with severe poverty and physical needs. The prominent religions have not offered much in relief of present difficulties. And some of the religions have even discouraged any concern for the marginalized. [46] Third, Pentecostalism offered a positive message to a hurting world. The message of blessing from a good God has resonated in the hearts of many and been infectious in the spread of its message. Cho Yonggi in Seoul, South Korea, as an example, took this positive message approach which has led to a church of 700,000 members.[47] Keith Hinton, in his study on church growth in Singapore, adds that the Asian preference for pragmatism has made Pentecostal practice more appealing, as it placed more emphasis on changing the present through healings and demonic deliverance.[48]

---

[44] Yung, 40.

[45] Wonsuk Ma, "Asian (Classical) Pentecostal Theology in Context," in *Asian and Pentecostal: The Charismatic Face of Christianity in Asia*, ed. Allan Anderson and Edmond Tang (Oxford; Baguio City: Regnum Books International, 2005), 61–62.

[46] Ma, 64.

[47] Ma, 65, 67.

[48] Keith Hinton, *Growing Churches Singapore Style Ministry in an Urban Context* (O M F Books, 1985), 151.

Christian expression free from tightly controlled liturgies or hierarchies can foster new and empowered expressions of genuine faith. Pentecostalism has served as a powerful contextualizing/indigenizing force for the church[49]

> One of the main reasons for the phenomenal growth of Pentecostalism in the past century has been its remarkable ability to adapt itself to different cultural contexts and give authentically contextualized expressions to Christianity. Pentecostalism is inherently adaptable: the vibrancy, enthusiasm, spontaneity, and spirituality for which charismatics are so well known and their willingness to address the problems of sickness, poverty, unemployment, loneliness, evil spirits, and sorcery has directly contributed to this growth.[50]

This strength of adaptability has also been a challenge for the church in Asia. Freedom can lead to excess and expressions of supernatural power can lead to abuses. Christian expressions tapping into pre-Christian spiritual roots begin to look less distinctly Christian and more shamanistic. Ma notes this proclivity: "No matter how modern a society may look, basically Asian minds are shamanistic in orientation."[51] It is not always easy to distinguish between indigeneity and syncretism which has led to divisions within the Asian Pentecostal movement.

In recent years, emphasis on blessing and pragmatism has led to distortion of Christianity sometimes labeled as the "prosperity gospel." Some high-profile churches espousing this gospel of material gain have found themselves in the midst of controversy and sometimes legal troubles. As the Pentecostal movement has grown, there is increased concern for theological training and setting parameters on charismatic expression. Many of the Pentecostal movements have grown out of reaction to existing churches and therefore are prone to divisiveness and separation.[52]

---

[49] Yung, "Pentecostalism and the Asian Church," 53.
[50] Allan Heaton Anderson, "Pentecostalism and Charismatic Movements in Asia," in *The Oxford Handbook of Christianity in Asia*, ed. Felix Wilfred (Oxford: Oxford University Press, 2014), 168.
[51] Ma, "Asian (Classical) Pentecostal Theology in Context," 69.
[52] Sunquist, *Explorations in Asian Christianity*, 51.

Christianity in Asia has grown significantly since 1900 (doubling twice during the century) and often through these movements of renewal and evangelism.[53] The Pentecostal movement, in particular, has redrawn the map of global Christianity and shows no sign of slowing down. "Not much observation is required to discover that some communities have seemed much more open to the Gospel and more susceptible to turning to the Christian faith than others."[54] In this chapter we have seen how the Asian church has grown through a variety of Christian movements. These movements have not only increased the number of Christians, they have allowed Christianity to develop and mature in each location. While some places have seen dramatic growth of Christianity other places have seen little change. Christianity has grown unevenly through movements throughout its history.

---

[53] Hwa Yung, "Mission and Evangelism: Evangelical and Pentecostal Theologies in Asia," in *Christian Theology in Asia*, ed. Sebastian Kim (Cambridge: Cambridge University Press, 2008), 250.

[54] Frykenberg, *Christianity in India*, 206.

Chapter 9: Multidirectionality of Mission: The Church of Asia Mobilized to New Frontiers

"We rejoice that a new missionary era has dawned. The dominant role of western missions is fast disappearing. God is raising up from the younger churches a great new resource for world evangelization, and is thus demonstrating that the responsibility to evangelise belongs to the whole body of Christ."

–Lausanne Covenant[1]

The 19th century was dubbed "the Great Century" by Kenneth Scott Latourette.[2] Missionaries had taken the gospel far and wide and had seen Christianity become a truly global faith. After a century of unprecedented Protestant missionary movement to the four corners of the globe, a World Missionary Conference was held Edinburgh in 1910. This gathering brought missionary practitioners and statesmen from all over the world in what John R. Mott called: "the most notable gathering in the interest of the worldwide expansion of Christianity ever held, not only in missionary annals, but in all Christian annals."[3] The meeting was filled with optimism about the spread of Christianity in places where there had not been any Christian presence.

The Edinburgh missionary conference would be significant in shaping the 20th century Christian movement. Out of this one conference would develop two streams of global mission thrust. One stream, the ecumenical one, led to the development of the World Council of Churches (WCC) which would become a significant international body, joining many denominational communions in 85 nations. Over time, the WCC became increasingly theologically progressive. The second stream to emerge out of the Edinburgh conference remained Evangelical and gathered in a monumental evangelism

---

[1] "The Lausanne Covenant," The Lausanne Movement, 1974, http://www.lausanne.org/en/documents/lausanne-covenant.html.

[2] Kenneth Scott Latourette, *A History of the Expansion of Christianity* (San Francisco: Harper, 1937).

[3] C. Howard Hopkins, *John R. Mott, 1865-1955: A Biography* (Grand Rapids, MI: Eerdmans Pub Co, 1979), 342.

conference in 1974 called Lausanne. [4] Both of these streams became influential in connecting church leadership across Asia in areas of theology and mission advance.

Another striking feature of the Edinburgh conference was the minimal presence of delegates from non-Western nations, only 17 out of more than 1,200 delegates. Although attendees were focused on the global expansion of the church, much of the world was not represented and there was a subtle (or not so subtle) implication that the mission relied on Western missionaries. [5] One of the few non-Westerners was V. C. Azariah (see previous chapter) from India. Azariah famously challenged the attendees at the conference not to send missionaries, but "to give us friends." One hundred years later, there was a Lausanne gathering in Cape Town, South Africa. At this meeting fewer than 40% of the attendees were from western nations. [6] This change marks the shift in global missions and leadership in the global church.

Little did the organizers of the Edinburgh conference know that the world would undergo significant political changes in the 20th century supported by strong nationalistic movements. In China, the May Fourth Movement and subsequent movements forced Western missionary organizations to turn leadership of the church into local hands. In the 1920s and 30s, many missionary organizations followed suit all over Asia. [7] This was followed by decolonization and the formation of independent nations around the world. Church and denominational leaders in each nation now had increased control over ecclesiastical matters.

The ultimate sign of maturity for the church in any one place is not indigenization or self-governance; it is cross-cultural mission. The church of Christ, imbued with the Great Commission, should never be at rest in one

---

[4] Kim-Sai Tan, *The Great Digression: World Evangelism since 1910: The Ecumenical Digression and the Evangelical Response* (Petaling Jaya, Malaysia: Malaysia Bible Seminary, 1981), 1–23.

[5] Stanley, "Twentieth-Century World Christianity: A Perspective from the History of Missions," 71.

[6] Luis Lugo, ed., "Global Survey of Evangelical Protestant Leaders" (Pew Research Center, June 22, 2011), 17, http://www.pewforum.org/2011/06/22/global-survey-of-evangelical-protestant-leaders/.

[7] Stanley, "Twentieth-Century World Christianity: A Perspective from the History of Missions," 56, 74.

culture. Rather, the church is always crossing cultural boundaries, always translating into new cultures or mixes of cultures.

9.1 As They Go…Diaspora Movement as Gospel Movement

It was persecution that sparked the beginnings of Christian cross-cultural missions. Christians in Jerusalem were dispersed (Greek *diasporan*) throughout Judea and Samaria (Acts 8:1), sharing the gospel along the way (Acts 8:4). People on the move take with them their ideas and beliefs. Christianity moved with people as they moved. Asia was connected through its trade routes known as the silk road.[8] Traders moved from the western edges of Asia to China in the east with the gospel. When Timur (Tamerlane) tore through Central Asia, he destroyed both the church there as well as the Silk Road holding Asia together. In recent years, Asian Christians have begun moving again throughout Asia and taking the gospel with them.

People have always been on the move. Famines and wars drive people to new locations. Empires expand and contract, taking new ideas, languages, and commerce to different lands. These realities are continuing, only in greater numbers than ever before. With 258 million international migrants and another 750 million internal migrants, there are a billion people currently residing outside of their homelands.[9] There are many different motivations for people to move their lives to new lands. Here, we will look at three primary ways in which people move from one place to another and the impact it has had on Christian presence.[10] Some immigrate to another country as personal choice. Others go to another country to work for a specified time. Regrettably, some are compelled to flee their homelands due

---

[8] Moffit calls the silk road routes the "only tangible symbols of continental identity." Moffett, *A History of Christianity in Asia*, 483.

[9] Michael D. Crane, "Urbanizing the Church in an Urbanizing Asia," in *Urbanization: Impacts on the Church, Mission and Society Today*, ed. Lip Siong Chen and Weng Kit Cheong (Kota Kinabalu, Malaysia: Sabah Theological Seminary, 2018), 114.

[10] "A world Christianity approach which divides the world into separate regions may play down the movements between them and the presence of migrant communities everywhere." Kirsteen Kim, "Mission in the Twenty-First Century," *Norsk Tidsskrift for Misjonsvitenskap* 1, no. 2 (2011): 65.

to threats of violence based on their ethnicity, religion, or political affiliations.[11]

Many have moved permanently from one country to another for personal reasons. Commonly, Christians from nations with a Christian minority will move to nations perceived to have more religious freedom and opportunities. For example, embattled Christians from heavily Islamic nations in western Asia have immigrated to Lebanon where Christianity has more liberty and demographic representation. Many Christians from Malaysia and Brunei have immigrated to Australia or New Zealand. These movements shift the religious landscapes of the home countries as well as the destination countries. In the years leading up to complete communist control of China, many thousands of Christians moved to Taiwan, altering the religious landscape of the country. In such cases, the newly settled population then sought to reach out to those around them. Immigrant Christians have brought a lift to the national churches in their destination countries.

One in five people in the city of Dubai is Filipino. There are 1.5 million Indonesians working in Saudi Arabia. More than three million Nepalis are working in Malaysia and Gulf State nations. Economic inequalities have encouraged movements of migrant labor around the world. With millions of Christians going to and returning from other nations, it is creating change across Asia. Francisco notes the impact on churches: "Churches in both places have been changed by multiple forms of diversity due to migration. No longer confined to a religious ethos often rural, Christian communities at places of origin have been transformed by being sources of migrants."[12] Christians finding work in other countries are seeing this as an opportunity to spread the Christian faith in places where there has been restricted gospel witness.

---

[11] Admittedly, this is an oversimplification of complex realities. Motivations are most often mixed and some can fit more than one category. For example, a person may go to another nation to work, and during that time may claim asylum and become a refugee or resettle permanently. For more on refugee movements, see Michael D. Crane, "Refugees in the Urban Wilderness: Plight of Refugees in Landing Cities and Opportunities for Response," *International Journal of Urban Transformation* 1, no. 1 (October 2016): 51–70.

[12] Jose Mario C. Francisco, S. J., "Migration and New Cosmopolitanism in Asian Christianity," in *The Oxford Handbook of Christianity in Asia*, ed. Felix Wilfred (Oxford: Oxford University Press, 2014), 585.

A sad consequence of a fallen world is the forced movement of peoples fleeing homelands because of threats of violence. In many places, Christian-majority ethnic groups live in lands where their Christian faith is not welcomed. Chin, Karen, and Kachin tribes in Myanmar have been forced to flee violence directed at them by the government in a predominantly Buddhist country. Armenian Christians in Muslim-majority Turkey have faced severe persecution and genocidal activities. The violence in these cases is often a mix of ethnic, political, and religious conflict. In other cases, individuals and families coming to faith in Christ have sought refuge outside of their country of origin due to threats on their lives. There are a number of Asian nations that remain hostile to Christian presence.

Persecution has plagued the church in Asia since its earliest days. Sunquist frames it this way: "Christianity is at home in Asia, but it has always been a home as nomadic or refugee existence rather than as in a palace or among royalty." [13] Just as the early church preached the gospel as they fled persecution in Acts 8, the same is happening today. Christians forced to leave Southwest Asian and Central Asian nations have been taken their faith to other parts of Asia, Europe and Australia.

9.2 The Rise of Asian Missions Agencies

In 2007, news about 23 Koreans who had been kidnapped by the Taliban in Afghanistan came as a surprise to the world. The shock was not that they were Koreans, but that they were missionaries. This was no longer the western enterprise of the Edinburgh conference. Asian Christians reaching the rest of the vast continent with the gospel has been referred to as the fourth wave of Christianity in Asia.[14] Non-Western missionaries are on the rise (see Figure 4).

---

[13] Sunquist, *Explorations in Asian Christianity*, 11.
[14] Scott Sunquist calls the Syrian/Persian advance the first wave. The second wave was the Catholic advance. The Protestant advance was the third wave. Now is the time for the Asian Church. Sunquist, 3.

Non-Western Missionaries	Total Missionaries
For 1990: 48,884	35.6% of 137,170
For 1995: 89,160	45.1% of 197,430
For 2000: 164,230	55.5% of 295,952

Figure 5: The Rise of Non-Western Missionaries[15]

A number of scholars have been calling attention to the need to go beyond mere involvement in missions, but to "look ahead and develop a kingdom-centered Asian mission model to ensure the mistakes of past missionary efforts are not repeated."[16] New models are being developed by Christians from nations where missionary activity is still restricted. Older models of mission sending are adapting to include Asian partners. A quick glance at Korea, India and China give us a snapshot of the diverse ways in which the Asian church is sending out missionaries.

Korea
Even with the emergence of Christianity in Korea taking place primarily since 1907, the Korean church wasted no time in sending out their own missionaries around the world. In many respects, the Korean church followed a similar pattern as in the West, sending from denominational mission agencies. With more than 20,000 missionaries sent out, Korea has provided both examples and leadership for the growing Asian mission force.

India
The ancient Mar Thoma Church underwent a modernizing reformation in the late 1800s which spawned the Mar Thoma Evangelistic Association in 1888. The central leader of the Dornakal Revival described in the previous chapters was Anglican bishop V. S. Azariah. Prior to moving to Dornakal, Azariah helped initiate two mission organizations: the Indian Missionary Society (1903) and the National Missionary Society (1905). In the years since then, many more organizations have started. Estimations and definitions vary widely, but there are about 40,000 domestic and international missionaries

---

[15] Smallman, William H., "Missions—Personnel with Purpose," *Missions in a New Millennium: Change and Challenges in World Missions.* W. Edward Glenny and William H. Smallman, eds. (Grand Rapids: Kregel Publications, 2000), 27.
[16] Chin Do Kham, "Partnership Issues and Challenges in Asian Mission," in *Asian Church and God's Mission*, ed. Wonsuk Ma and Julie C. Ma (Manila: OMF Literature, 2003), 45.

of Indian origin. [17] Indian Christians have moved to every corner of India as missionaries and are using every means available to take the gospel to other nations. With so much of the church being from lower and poorer castes, Christians in India have employed a variety of means to support missionaries to the nations.

China

In 1943 on Easter Sunday, the challenge was issued at Northwest Bible Institute in Shanxi Province to take the gospel to western China. The professor who issued the challenge, Mark Ma, and the students that responded began taking short-term trips to western China, calling the group the "Back to Jerusalem Evangelistic Band." The effort was disrupted in 1949 when the Communists took control. It was almost another forty years before another wave of Christian leaders called for the Back to Jerusalem Movement. Their desire to was to trace the Silk Road trade routes back to Southwest Asia (the Middle East), sharing the gospel. [18]

China's Christians are mobilized into missions by extraordinary faith. Paul Hattaway describes a conversation with some of the church leaders in the country: "I have learned not to impose my limited Western thinking on the Chinese church. They believe that part of their mandate from God is to completely evangelize their whole nation and to make China 'the first truly born-again Christian country in Asia.' Don't be surprised if they succeed." [19] Thus, Chinese Christians have once *again* taken up the call to retrace the old Silk Road with the gospel.

Under government leadership, China has been active in large infrastructure projects around the world that will enable an increase of trade and movement of resources. Chinese Christians see this as an opportunity to take the gospel to places where there has been very little Christian witness. [20]

---

[17] Robin Thomson, "Asian Mission Movements from South Asian Contexts," in *Understanding Asian Mission Movements*, ed. Kang San Tan, Jonathan Ingleby, and Simon Cozens (Petaling Jaya, Malaysia: Asia CMS, 2013), 35–36.

[18] Terry, "The Growth of Christianity in East Asia," 47.

[19] Hattaway, *Back to Jerusalem*, 3.

[20] Lip Siong Chen, "Global Urbanization through China's Belt and Road Initiative: Opportunities for Urban Mission," in *Urbanization: Impacts on the Church, Mission and Society Today*, ed. Lip Siong Chen and Weng Kit Cheong (Kota Kinabalu, Malaysia: Sabah Theological Seminary, 2018).

9.3 Multinational Missions Partnerships

With the rise of Asian churches sending cross-cultural missionaries, as well as the increase of diaspora movements of people, missions is increasingly a multi-national endeavor. It is common for missionaries to work closely with other missionaries from different nations, even different continents. Non-denominational mission sending agencies are internationalizing rapidly.

In 1865, J. Hudson Taylor started China Inland Mission in London. The organization has now become Overseas Missionary Fellowship (OMF) International and is headquartered in Singapore. Twenty percent of OMF International's membership is Asian, and Patrick Fung became their first Asian international director in 2006. Many other mission organizations have followed a similar path to internationalization, with offices, recruiting, and training in multiple countries.[21]

With missionaries from diverse backgrounds now collaborating, it is creating challenges in cross-cultural partnership. Mission organizations used to work more autonomously. Now, culturally-informed views of teaming, leadership, fellowship, and even missiological priorities are adding a new level of challenge for missionaries. In the past, western-based organizations wielded the power because they held the resources. This same imbalance exists with Asian-based organizations from wealthier nations. The notion of partnership is proving more complicated than shaking hands over an agreement on the Great Commission.[22] Learning how to partner well regardless of financial resources will be a challenge for missions in the next century.

---

[21] A few internationalized mission organization are listed here as an example: Frontiers International, Pioneers International, Serving in Mission (SIM), Operation Mobilization (OM), and Wycliffe.

[22] Sugden does well to get behind the surface level show of harmony in the missions community: "The context of international partnership is set in the context of different cultural perceptions of a 'global culture' and local cultures.' Tension between these perceptions often emerges in international consultations. Because Western cultures, agencies and churches have networks that span the world, they often present their concerns as spanning the globe, and are perceived by others to be global agencies. This can produce a defensive reaction in Two Thirds World people, or minority groups in the north. They wish to prevent their own identity and contribution from being subsumed under the powerful agendas of others and from being co-opted into a global operation over which they have no control by stressing the integrity of their own national identity.... However, the truth of the matter is that the Western agencies and churches are just as local as the Two Thirds World agencies; they are

9.4 Opportunities and Challenges of Mission in Asia: Negotiating the - isms of the 21st Century

Asian Christianity has rarely been in a place of privilege or political favor. From a minority position, Asian Christians have always been steeped in inter-faith engagement. While this positions the Asian church theologically to relate to other faiths and worldviews, it has been complicated by forces of globalism, tribalism, and consumerism. These forces impact the church in complex ways and impact the church's mission.

Christianity in Asia has grown quickly in the last two centuries, but has had to endure a turbulent existence. While devout faith has sustained millions of Christians through great tribulations, in many places Christianity has not fully engaged with Christians' religious and cultural backgrounds. Malaysian scholar, Tan Kang San urges Asian Christians to move beyond the veneer of Christian faith to full transformation in all aspects of life. Only then does a Christian-shaped worldview begin to take shape.[23]

Christianity is a global faith with universal implications, but this needs to be translated into every cultural milieu. Gambian historian Lamin Sanneh stresses the importance of this translational task: "Missionary adoption of the vernacular, therefore, was tantamount to adopting indigenous cultural criteria for the message, a piece of radical indigenous cultural criteria for the message, a piece of radical indigenization far greater than the standard portrayal of mission as Western cultural imperialism."[24] But the missionary is only the beginning of the process. As the faith is passed from the missionary to the newly established church in a place, the local church then further indigenizes their faith and practice.

However, the church is never fully at rest in a particular culture or place. The essence of Christianity as good news to be heralded to the whole world places on the church an impetus for public engagement. There is a danger of

---

just as shaped by their own local cultures. The global is not the preserve of one culture or agency, it takes place at the intersection of two or more equally local cultures." Sugden, *Seeking the Asian Face of Jesus: The Practice and Theology of Christian Social Witness in Indonesia and India 1974-1996*, 422.

[23] Kang San Tan, "Will Asian Christianity Blossom or Wither," *Mission Round Table: The Occasional Bulletin of OMF Mission Research* 1 (January 2005): 12–13.

[24] Sanneh, *Translating the Message*, 3.

an indigenous form of Christianity becoming inward or static, preventing Christianity from crossing ever-new boundaries. But it must also avoid becoming generic or commodified: "(We lament) the homogenizing pressures of globalization, where the gospel is treated like a hamburger-exactly the same size, shape, and smell everywhere in the world." [25] Christianity as public truth must be taken to the public square.

---

[25] Miriam Adeney, "Trends in Asia: Implications for Mission," *Mission Round Table: The Occasional Bulletin of OMF Mission Research* 1 (January 2005): 2.

Chapter 10: Christianity in Asia: 20th and 21st Century Growth and Status

"We will not hide them from their children,
But tell to the coming generation
The glorious deeds of the Lord, and his might,
And the wonders that he has done."

–Psalm 78:4

The telling of history is not merely an academic exercise; it is rehearsing the acts of God so that others will set their faces towards the God who works in all of history. The historical Psalms of the Bible (cf. 78, 105, 106) recount the faithful works of God in the history of God's people. This history-telling performs several functions. It is an act of worship to remember the "glorious deeds of the Lord, and his might, and the wonders that he has done" (Ps. 78:4). It also offers a warning, as we are reminded in Psalm 78, that we are prone to forget that it was God who has delivered us faithfully (cf. 78:7, 11, 42). Telling the story of God at work through the ages is also part of the discipleship of the next generation. This is so "that the next generation might know them, the children yet unborn, and arise and tell them to their children, so that they should set their hope in God" (Ps. 78:6-7a). In this chapter, we endeavor to give a sweeping picture of the church throughout Asia, so that the next generation should set their hope in God.

It can be conservatively estimated that there are 400 million Christians in Asia today, with the number rising. Only two continents boast more Christians: Africa and Latin America. At the beginning of this book we noted that Asia was the birthplace of Christianity and for a thousand years was its heartland, along with North Africa. Today, Asia has the potential to be the heartland of Christianity once more.

A continent as vast and diverse as Asia is not easy to capture in one glance. In other parts of the book, we have explored selected stories more deeply. Here we change tacks by giving a short summary of recent events throughout the continent. It is impossible to do this without omitting important events and people that were used by God in marvelous ways to spread and establish the church in lands far and wide.[1] It should also be noted that the coverage of countries will not be even for a number of reasons. First, the context differs considerably from country to country. For some countries, the gospel has only arrived recently, while other nations have complex histories involving a variety of Christian traditions. Second, the shear enormity of the nations and different tribes within the nations forces a careful curating process. Third, some nations remain under severe hostility towards Christ and the church and little information is available for publication. It is hoped that these brief descriptions whet the appetite for readers to learn more about God's activity in the nations of Asia. But this brief survey will inevitably oversimplify Christian expression in each context: "Historical trajectories and general impressions may serve to give a first-order survey of the terrains. However they are not reliable guides to the complex realities on the ground."[2]

Growing interest in the history of the church in Asia has resulted in volumes detailing these important stories. This account can only hope to imitate a smooth, flat stone skipping across the waters, never plumbing the depths of the historical record.

10.1 Central Asia

Christianity was once alive and well for centuries in towns and cities across Central Asia. The rise of Islam and the destructive path of conquerors removed any vestiges of ancient Christianity for centuries. As Russian influence across the region brought with it their Orthodox churches. These churches grew along with the population increase of Russians and Ukrainians, but they made few inroads among the predominantly Muslim peoples of Central Asia (with the exceptions of Georgia and Armenia). Communism under the Soviet Union institutionalized atheism for seventy years, which weakened religion of every sort. In 1991 these former Soviet states have become independent nations, but most continue to tightly control

---

[1] Regarding this process of selecting history, Frykenberg captures it well: "So many are the separate stories of distinct Christian communities that, short of producing an encyclopedic work encompassing every tiny element the task of the historian is to develop a strategy or a tactical paradigm by which to determine not so much what to *include* as what to *exclude*." Frykenberg, *Christianity in India*, 6.
[2] Poon, "The Theological Locus of Christian MOvements in Southeast Asia," x.

religious activity. Russians have gradually moved back to Russia, but other Christian groups have begun to establish themselves in the major cities.[3]

Afghanistan

On the southern edge of Central Asia is the land-locked nation of Afghanistan. Its rugged terrain and turbulent politics have prevented consistent Christian witness in the country. Even during its more progressive days, Christian presence was restricted; and it remains one of the least evangelized nations in the world.[4]

Armenia

Armenia is one of the few majority Christian countries in Asia and the oldest Christian kingdom. The Armenian Orthodox Church is the overwhelming majority in the nation, but there are growing numbers of Catholic and Protestant Christians.

Azerbaijan, Kazakhstan, Kyrgyzstan, Turkmenistan, Uzbekistan

These former Soviet states share many cultural similarities and majority Muslim populations. These lands were once home to vibrant churches prior to the violent persecution of Timur the Great in the 14th Century. The Russian Orthodox Church is the most visible Christian presence, but its influence was muted during the seventy years of communist rule. Since these nations gained independence, the Russian communities have grown smaller.

Georgia

Whether Georgia is a part of Europe or Asia is a matter of debate. Going by defined boundaries of the Caucasus mountains, Georgia is a part of Asia. Georgians believe Simon and Andrew first preached the gospel in Georgia. Saint Nino of Cappadocia (290–338) is credited with establishing the church in this nation. Upon King Mirian III's conversion to Christianity in 337, Georgia became predominantly Christian.[5] This small former Soviet state is majority Georgian Orthodox (84%).

---

[3] Sebastien Peyrouse, "Christian Minorities on the Central Asian Silk Roads," in *The Oxford Handbook of Christianity in Asia*, ed. Felix Wilfred (Oxford: Oxford University Press, 2014), 51–54.

[4] Anonymous, "Afghanistan," in *Sejarah Gereja Asia, Volume 1*, ed. Donald E. Hoke (Malang: Yayasan Penerbit Gandum Mas, 2000), 74–75.

[5] Sunquist, *Explorations in Asian Christianity*, 31.

Iran

More than one empire has risen out of the land of Iran. This land where Daniel told of a vision of the Messiah (Dan. 7:13-14) became fertile soil for the early church and bloodied soil during severe periods of persecution. These swings in perception of Christianity have continued to this day. The Islamic Revolution in 1979 closed the door on any open Christian activity, yet there are consistent reports of a rapidly growing Iranian church both within its borders and around the world.[6] Iranian Christians in California are broadcasting Christian television programming and are revitalizing struggling churches in Western Europe.[7]

Turkey

Turkey was once the center of Christendom and has as part of its legacy a great number of theologians and saints. The arrival of the Ottoman Empire did irrevocable damage to Christian presence in the nation. Turkey has a small population of Greek Orthodox Christians as well as Jacobite, Syrian, and Armenian Christians, but in decreasing numbers due to emigration out of the country. A substantial Greek population left during a trade agreement with Greece to bring Muslims from Macedonia into Turkey.[8] There are scattered Turkish churches, but they remain a small minority.

10.2 Southwest Asia

Southwest Asia has commonly been known as the Middle East (a designation oriented to Europe's location), but is more appropriately oriented to the Asian context. Christianity finds its historical roots in this part of the world, where it continued to grow until the emergence of Islam in 629 CE. The Arab church has struggled to establish a settled identity ever since. For most of the intervening period since the rise of Islam, Christians (and Jews) have been forced to live in dhimmis for their "protection." Under dhimmis restrictions, Christians have been subjected to restrictive laws, higher taxation and limited opportunities to rise in either the private or public sector which have weakened the once strong church. Cragg captures this struggle:

---

[6] Krikor Markarian, "Today's Iranian Revolution: How the Mullahs Are Leading the Nation to Jesus," *Mission Frontiers*, October 2008, 6–13.

[7] "Muslim Converts Breathe New Life into Europe's Struggling Christian Churches," Fox News, March 21, 2017, https://www.foxnews.com/world/muslim-converts-breathe-new-life-into-europes-struggling-christian-churches.

[8] Robert B. Betts, *Christians in the Arab East: A Political Study*, Revised edition (London: SPCK, 1979), 110.

Yet 'Christian' was a descriptive of Arabs centuries before Islam, and there has been a Christian Arabism, an Arab Christianity, throughout the Muslim centuries since Muhammad's day. The Muslim dominance of Arabness, however, from the beginning brought a tension and tribulation into that Arab Christian existence under which it has labored and survived.[9]

The rise of independent nations combined with resurgent fundamentalist Islam has made it hard for the church in this part of the world to find any footing. Any traction Christians might have gained has been beset by division between branches of the churches, sometimes holding onto centuries-old feuds).[10] With few exceptions (Lebanon and Israel/Palestine), Christianity still has an uphill climb.

Arabian Peninsula (Saudi Arabia, Kuwait, Bahrain, Qatar, UAE, Yemen, Oman, and Qatar)

These nations are grouped together because they share common geography and minimal Christian presence. Christian communities were established in the Arabian Peninsula from the days of the early church. A sixth-century poet described his travels along the coast of Arabia. Nearing settlements, he could hear the wooden clappers (instead of bells used in other places) calling Christian worshippers. Little was known of Christianity in the Gulf until recently archeological discoveries of church and monastic structures.[11] A church council held in 676 CE indicates there were five sees (bishoprics) along the western side of the Gulf.[12]

With the rise of Islam and its military might, the Christian population was decimated on the peninsula. Christian missionaries came to the Gulf in the late 1800s and early 1900s. Samuel Zwemer and others established medical missions, but also sought to share the gospel and distribute Christian

---

[9] Kenneth Cragg, *The Arab Christian: A History in the Middle East by Kenneth Cragg* (London: Mowbray, 1991), 10.

[10] Herman G. B. Teule, "Christianity in Western Asia," in *The Oxford Handbook of Christianity in Asia*, ed. Felix Wilfred (Oxford: Oxford University Press, 2014), 26.

[11] One church building in Jubail was only discovered in 1986. In 1992, the remains of a Christian monastery was discovered on a small island off the coast of Abu Dhabi. Andrew Thompson, *Christianity in the UAE: Culture and Heritage* (Dubai: Motivate Publishing, 2011), 52.

[12] Thompson, 57.

literature. Today, Christian presence is primarily found among the large numbers of Christians from other parts of the world there to work (including large populations of Filipino and Indian Christians). Local Christians in these lands face tremendous persecution and often relocate to other countries.

Iraq

The Syrian Orthodox Church has been anchored in Selucia-Ctesiphon (near present-day Baghdad) from ancient days. The Chaldean Patriarch is based in Baghdad and has had a long and established tradition in Iraq. In the north, there was some movement of Kurds coming to Christ, even whole villages. But most were displaced by ethnic violence targeted at Kurds. [13] These Christian communities continue until today but have lost numbers during the recent wars due to immigration. In more recent days, Evangelicals have established churches in the cities of Iraq. Volatility in the country has meant instability for the church.

Israel/Palestine

Israel and Palestine have too complex of a history and current arrangement to give it justice in this short paragraph. This biblical heartland remains some of the most religiously contested geography in the world. In this contestation, most of the attention is on Muslim and Jewish relations, but little is said of the significant Christian Palestinian community (10% of the Palestinian population). Palestinian Christianity has existed in a strange zone between historical animosities with Israel while adhering to and worshipping the God of Israel.[14] Jerusalem itself is divided into four quarters (Muslim, Jewish, Christian, and Armenian). As Armenians claim Christianity, in effect, half of the quarters are devoted to Christian presence. There are efforts in reaching the Jewish community with the gospel, but it has been slow work.

Jordan

Like many of the countries in Southwest Asia, Christianity's presence in Jordan dates back to the beginning and continues today. Christians comprise only 4% of the total population and enjoy relative freedom. Although Jordan has a diverse Christian presence, the majority are Eastern Orthodox.

---

[13] Betts, *Christians in the Arab East*, 104.
[14] Cragg, *The Arab Christian*, 11.

Lebanon

Lebanon stands out from most of the Arab majority nations as being openly culturally and religiously diverse.[15] Deep historical roots provide Lebanon with its own identity, and the long-standing Christian presence in the country sets it apart as well. With an estimated 40% Christian population (down from 70% in 1900),[16] Lebanon is a center in the region for Christian Arabic-language materials and institutions.

Kenneth Cragg notes: "The Lebanon of the final quarter of this [20th] century is a scene of infinite tragedy, a desperate indictment of religions and their role in the bankruptcy of politics and strangling of hope."[17] The French made some territorial inclusions to the north and south that made Lebanon more politically and religiously volatile. Muslim Shia and Muslim Sunni populations as well as the Christian community have all been vying for government representation, which broke out into violence in the late twentieth century.

The Maronite church is the most prominent in Lebanon. Leaders of the previously Syrian church made the shift to the Catholic communion in 1736, acknowledge the Roman Pope. Patriarchs became bishops. Latin took over from Syriac.[18] Even with greater religious freedoms and larger percentages of Christian presence, the church was damaged by ongoing feudal tradition of Lebanese history.[19]

Syria

Syria has a long and complex interaction with Christianity. One of Christianity's earliest and most famous converts, the apostle Paul, was confirmed in his Christian faith in Damascus. Since that time, there has been a Christian presence, albeit a complex one. Eastern Orthodox Christians, Jacobites, Nestorians, Armenians, and Catholics have all found a home there.

---

[15] "While the rise of Muslim nationalism greatly diminished the Christian role, Lebanon for some time continued to fulfil a unique function as the only surviving centre of cultural and religious pluralism and of economic and political freedom within the Arab world." Lewis, *The Middle East*, 347.

[16] Sunquist, *Explorations in Asian Christianity*, 84.

[17] Cragg, *The Arab Christian*, 205.

[18] Cragg, 2017.

[19] Cragg, 211.

Many were pushed out of Turkey during a time of ethnic and religious persecution.[20]

10.3 East Asia

At the beginning of the twentieth century, Christianity was barely noticeable in East Asia. The nations on the eastern edge of Asia put up great resistance to each other as well as to the Christian faith. Both China and Japan saw Christianity take root and then suffer under tremendous persecution. Christianity has reentered the region with slow results in some places and significant growth in others.

China

Perhaps no country has seen greater undulations in Christian presence than China. Between the Boxer Rebellion and World War II, the church enjoyed steady growth (particularly until 1920)[21] which produced significant leaders who would walk through the stormy times ahead during the Cultural Revolution. Watchman Nee, Wang Ming Dao, John Sung and countless other women[22] and men faithfully spread the gospel (some called them "gospellers") and discipled masses before freedoms diminished in the decades following World War II. Most scholars estimate there were about one million Christians in China in 1949.[23]

During Mao Tse-Tung's Cultural Revolution, the church went through severe persecution. The Three-Self Patriotic Church and Catholic Patriotic Association were closed for a time and then given some level of allowance,

---

[20] Betts, *Christians in the Arab East*, 94–98.

[21] Latourette, knowing the statistics were open to inaccuracies, placed the number of communicants in 1917 at 312,970 and perhaps 500,000 to 700,000 in 1927. Kenneth Scott Latourette, *A History of Christian Missions in China*, 1st edition (New York: Russell & Russell, 1929), 779–80.

[22] Women came to take on an increased role in evangelism and discipleship throughout China. This coincided with a change in women's roles in society at large. Pui-lan Kwok, "Claiming Our Heritage: Chinese Women and Christianity," *International Bulletin of Missionary Research* 16, no. 4 (October 1992): 150–54.

[23] Philip Yuen-sang Leung, "Conversion, Commitment, and Culture: Christian Experience in China, 1949-99," in *Christianity Reborn: The Global Expansion of Evangelicalism in the Twentieth Century*, ed. Donald M. Lewis, Studies in the History of Christian Missions (Grand Rapids, MI: Wm. B. Eerdmans, 2004), 100.

but only under heavy control of the government. Their freedoms to express Christian truth varied from province to province.

Many Chinese Christians, weary of government control, chose to go underground. Networks of house churches developed and grew exponentially, especially on the eastern side of China. For example, a woman called Mama Kwong boldly preached the gospel and organized an extensive house church network. She did this despite being imprisoned three times and having one of her sons being martyred at the hands of the Red Guard.[24] Kwong is one among many who defied the Cultural Revolution. One publication estimated that ten thousand Chinese became Christians every day. While good statistics are difficult to ascertain; balanced conservative estimates for 2010 are 21 million Catholics and 85 million Protestants among the Chinese.[25] Although government persecution persists, the church continues to grow, giving China the largest Christian population in Asia.

Japan

The church that grew from the original entry of Christianity in Japan in the 16th century was nearly entirely eradicated by 1630 by Japanese authorities. Despite claims that Japan was influenced by Christian practice, leaders rejected an overt Christian practice.[26] Two centuries later missionaries reentered the nation, resulting in steady growth of the church until World War II. The war and the rise up to it was challenging for the church to demonstrate their loyalty to Japan without condoning injustice. Churches that took a stand against the rising militarism paid dearly for it. And churches who supported the militarism shifted increasingly to something Yoshiaki Yui labels "Shintoistic Christianity."[27] The end of the war saw a spike in missionary activity and a time of response, but it was short-lived.[28]

---

[24] Colin Whittaker, *Great Revivals* (London: Marshall Pickering, 1984), 153.

[25] Terry, "The Growth of Christianity in East Asia," 45–46.

[26] Toyohiko Kagawa claims that several religious practices among the Buddhists were borrowed directly from Christian practice. Toyohiko Kagawa, *Christ and Japan*, trans. William Axling (New York: Friendship Press, 1934), 77.

[27] Yoshiaki Yui, "The Church in Japan," in *Church in Asia Today: Opportunities and Challenges*, ed. Saphir Athyal (Singapore: Asia Lausanne Committee for World Evangelization, 1996), 26.

[28] Terry, "The Growth of Christianity in East Asia," 48.

Christians remain less than one percent of the total population, and the aging congregations struggle to gain momentum there.[29]

Korea

Korea remained resistant to Christianity until the end of the 19th century and beginning of the 20th century. Samuel Moffett, whose father entered Korea as missionary in 1890, noted the remarkable growth from a struggling few to ubiquitous signs of Christian presence.[30] As described earlier in the book, missionaries sought to plant indigenous churches in the country. This was then fueled by a revival beginning in 1907 in Pyongyang, which set patterns for the Korean church that continue until today. The church grew rapidly, partly due to the missionary methods of Nevius (described in chapter 4.8). Other important factors included a Bible translation and spiritual practices that were uniquely Korean, allowing Christianity to grow deep in Korean soil.[31] The church again experienced growth in 1919-1931 and 1945-1960.

After the war in Korea, North Korea came under communist rule and become one of the most oppressive nations toward the Christian faith. Pyongyang, once known as the "Jerusalem of the East" suddenly had no visible Christian presence.[32] Since 1988, the Bongsu Church has been permitted to worship, but seemingly under tight government control.

In South Korea, the church grew rapidly in the 1970s and 1980s, to the point that it is home to the world's largest Pentecostal, Presbyterian, and Methodist churches. It is said that six new churches were started every day during the 1980s.[33] Recently, however, the church has plateaued and started declining in the generation coming up in the beginning of the 21st century.

Mongolia

When Communists took control of Mongolia in 1921, there was no known presence of Christianity in the country. When Communism collapsed in

---

[29] Samuel Lee, *The Japanese and Christianity* (Amsterdam: Foundation University Press, 2014), 32.

[30] Moffett, *The Christians of Korea*.

[31] G. Thompson Brown, "Why Has Christianity Grown Faster in Korea Than in China?," *Missiology: An International Review* XXII, no. 1 (January 1994): 84–85.

[32] Bong Rin Ro, "The Church in Korea," in *Church in Asia Today: Opportunities and Challenges*, ed. Saphir Athyal (Singapore: Asia Lausanne Committee for World Evangelization, 1996), 73.

[33] Ro, 56.

1990, Christians reentered Mongolia and planted new churches, which reproduced quickly. Estimations are 45,000 Christians across different denominations today.[34] The church has grown and matured to the point that many missionaries consider their work done.[35]

Taiwan
As with so many countries, the Christian presence took many turns over the centuries. When the Japanese controlled Taiwan starting in 1895, they preferred to minimize the denominations present. As Presbyterians and Catholics were more established, they were given allowance to continue. When Chiang Kai-Shek and his supporters left mainland China, they took up residence in Taiwan. At this time, a number of ministries and Christians fled China and established their ministries in Taiwan. In a matter of fifteen years, Christians went from 13,000 in 1945 to 180,000. Today, about six percent of the population is Christian.[36] The presence of strong Chinese churches and seminaries there have served as a stronghold for Chinese Christians around the world.

10.4 Southeast Asia

Christianity made its first inroads in Southeast Asia through Western colonial powers. The Portuguese, Spaniards, and French introduced Catholicism to the region. The Dutch and British brought Protestantism. "It was not until the latter part of the twentieth century, after most of the Southeast Asian nations gained independence, that indigenous leadership and growth in the churches took place."[37] Although Christianity remains a minority religion in most of the Southeast Asian nations, it has contributed to the modernization of these recently independent nations.[38]

Brunei
Brunei is a small nation sandwiched between two Malaysian states on the island of Borneo. Since gaining independence, the Brunei government has

---

[34] Terry, "The Growth of Christianity in East Asia," 49.
[35] Brian Hogan, *There's a Sheep in My Bathtub: Tenth Anniversary Edition*, 2nd ed. (Fayetteville, AR: Asteroidea Books, 2017).
[36] Terry, "The Growth of Christianity in East Asia," 50.
[37] Goh, *Christianity in Southeast Asia*, 2.
[38] Georg Evers, "'On the Trail of Spices': Christianity in Southeast Asia," in *The Oxford Handbook of Christianity in Asia*, ed. Felix Wilfred (Oxford: Oxford University Press, 2014), 70–71.

privileged the Muslim majority and made it very difficult for the sizeable Christian population (estimated 10%) of Chinese, Filipinos, and indigenous peoples from Borneo.[39] With only a couple of sanctioned churches, most of the Christians are forced to meet discreetly in homes.

Cambodia

Cambodia's story, like many of the other countries, involves rejoicing and heartbreak. This former French colony had early Catholic influences. In the 1920s, Christian and Missionary Alliance missionaries saw a response to the gospel and churches formed. These grew over the next few decades until the devastating time of Pol Pot's Khmer Rouge regime (1975-1979). During this time, when 30% of the population was killed, 90% of the Christians in the country were killed.[40] The targeted slaughter of all who were educated has made it a long road for the country to rebuild as well as for the church to grow. Increased freedom in the country has allowed for the Cambodian church to take root once more in this majority Buddhist land.

Indonesia

The country of Indonesia is spread over an archipelago of thirteen thousand islands, with diverse peoples, cultures, and languages. For most of their history, these peoples have been parts of different kingdoms, each with their own histories. We explored some of the early growth of Christianity in some different parts of Indonesia (see chapter 4.9). Throughout this majority Muslim nation are pockets of Christians across all denominations. In the 1960's, there was a movement on the most populated island of Java of two million coming to faith.[41] Today, parts of Indonesia appear to have almost no Christian presence and other parts claim a Christian majority.

Laos

The land-locked nation of Laos has been under communist rule since 1975 and has been highly restrictive of any Christian activity. Prior to that time, the seeds of the gospel were sown by missionaries and local Christians. Due to the close relationship between Laos and Vietnam, Catholic missionaries ventured from Vietnam into Laos with minimal results. Today, Christians in

---

[39] Goh, *Christianity in Southeast Asia*, 68.

[40] Don Cormack, *Killing Fields, Living Fields* (London; Grand Rapids, MI: Monarch Books, 2001), 182.

[41] Willis, *Indonesian Revival Why Two Million Came to Christ*.

the country must keep a low profile and worship in secret because of government restrictions.

Malaysia

Malaysia had only intermittent exposure to Christianity until the Portuguese entered Malacca in the 1500s along with Jesuit missionaries. During the Dutch and English times of rule, Protestantism entered the country. Mainline denominations, like Anglicans and Methodists, were established early during the British colonial period. Other denominations entered later, particularly after World War II. East Malaysia, on the island of Borneo, saw movements among several of the tribes and has a high percentage of Christians. West Malaysia remains majority Muslim with a small Christian minority.

Myanmar

Myanmar (formerly Burma) was one of the earliest Protestant mission fields. The Buddhist majority nation has a significant Christian population primarily among minority ethnic groups in the country. In the 1920s, the maturing church among the Karen, Chin, and Kachin tribes took on increased independence. The largest known baptismal service happened there at the Kachin Baptist Centennial Convention in 1977 with 6,000 baptized in one day.

After the country gained independence in 1948, the government was overthrown by a socialist regime in 1962. In the ensuring years all foreign missionaries were expelled and limitations were placed on Christians in the country. The government-controlled church practice and even access to Bibles, requiring a registry of all Bibles with the names of who received them. In recent years, the country has gradually loosened restrictions on Christian practice. In some states, Christianity is the majority primarily among minority tribes. Although, restrictions on Christianity have loosened somewhat, the church remains a small minority in the country.

Philippines

The Philippines stands out as an anomaly in the Asian landscape in many ways. It is the only nation colonized by Spanish in Asia and became predominantly Catholic during that time. Catholic institutions are deeply established, including the oldest university in Asia (University of Santo Tomas) established in 1611. Catholic rituals and ceremonies are deeply embedded in Philippine culture. Robbie Goh observes: "Christianity in the

Philippines is no dead colonial legacy, but continues to be a vital part of the national political life, as well as of the daily lives of individual citizens."[42]

The nation then came under the occupation of the United States at the end of the 19th century, which then opened the door for Protestant missionaries to enter, as well as many other religious groups.[43] As a result, the Philippines stands among only a few nations in Asia that are majority Christian (95%). Roughly two-thirds are Catholic, and the remaining third are predominately Evangelical or associated with Christian cults (i.e. Jehovah's Witnesses, Mormons, Iglesia Ni Christo, etc.).

Singapore
Singapore is one of the smallest nations in the world, but due to global connectivity and influence, is able to compete above its weight class. Early interaction with Christianity was with European colonists and not a positive exchange. In the nineteenth century, Catholics, Anglicans, and Methodists established churches through missionaries, but this work focused more heavily on the English-speaking foreigners and elites. Beginning in the 1950s, a number of denominations and parachurch organizations established a presence in Singapore. Some of these were international headquarters (i.e. Overseas Missionary Fellowship, Youth for Christ International and World Evangelical Fellowship).[44] Singapore experienced significant church growth from the 1950s until the 1980s.[45] This city-state is only 14.6% Christian, but as a group they are highly influential in a variety of levels.

Thailand
The majority Buddhist nation of Thailand is unique in Southeast Asia for never having been colonized. Although the country has relative freedom of religion, Christianity has not made significant inroads. Catholic missionaries have had a presence for nearly five hundred years, but communicants remain around two hundred thousand with about one-third being in Bangkok. American Baptists, in part through the work of Dr. Daniel McGilvary, saw growth in Northern Thailand in and around Chiang Mai. There has also been

---

[42] Goh, *Christianity in Southeast Asia*, 19.

[43] Wiliiam McKinley, president of the United States and a Methodist, spoke of the American obligation to "Christianize" the Philippines. Goh, 24.

[44] James Wong, "The Church in Singapore," in *Church in Asia Today: Opportunities and Challenges*, ed. Saphir Athyal (Singapore: Asia Lausanne Committee for World Evangelization, 1996), 301–3.

[45] Hinton, *Growing Churches Singapore Style Ministry in an Urban Context*, 23.

receptivity among the tribal peoples in the hills of Northern Thailand.[46] In Bangkok, the Chinese population has seen more response due to missionaries leaving China and arriving in Thailand to serve. The percentage of Christians in Thailand remains at one percent.

Timor Leste

This small nation on the southern edge of Southeast Asia is the newest recognized nation in the region. It was under Portuguese rule for about two centuries and, during that time, became predominantly Catholic. It was then under Indonesian rule for a tumultuous 25 years, before gaining independence. Claiming a 96% Catholic population, Timor Leste takes company with the Philippines as the only two majority Christian nations in Southeast Asia.

Vietnam

In chapter 3, we saw the Catholic Church established in Vietnam through the initial efforts of Alexander de Rhodes and many thousands of faithful Vietnamese who persevered under heavy persecution. It is estimated that 130,000 were martyred. The Catholic Church in Vietnam gained state support when the French entered as colonial rulers. This was particularly true in South Vietnam. When Vietnam came under complete communist control in 1975, the Catholic Church was subjugated by the government and given little freedom. Even in more recent years when they supposedly had more religious freedom, the government bulldozed Catholic properties and took them as government land. The Catholic Church continues to be a significant presence in the nation, with eight million parishioners, making it the second largest Catholic population in Asia (after the Philippines).[47]

Protestants only entered Vietnam at the end of the nineteenth century. This resulted in slow growth at first, but gained momentum with the publication of the Vietnamese Bible in 1926. Between 1921 and 1940, more than twenty thousand Vietnamese were baptized and a strong, self-supporting church was established.[48] As the nation endured tumultuous decades of war and politics, the church continued steady growth. There was a time of revival in 1971, just prior to another difficult time for the Vietnamese church. When Vietnam

---

[46] Narin Sritandon, "The Church in Thailand," in *Church in Asia Today: Opportunities and Challenges*, ed. Saphir Athyal (Singapore: Asia Lausanne Committee for World Evangelization, 1996), 242–43.

[47] Reimer, *Vietnam's Christians*, xv, 2, 23.

[48] Reimer, 28–30.

was united as a communist nation in 1975, there were 160,000 Evangelical Christians. At this time, the country went "dark" for a decade. Missionaries were forced to leave, and contact with the global church was limited. Another time of revival came to several churches in Saigon (now Ho Chi Minh City). God gave renewed boldness to several pastors (Ho Hieu Ha, Nguyen Huu Cuong and Le Thien Dung), resulting in many thousands coming to faith in Christ from 1978 to 1983.[49] The government arrested the pastors and closed the churches. The result was an Acts-like (cf. Acts 8:4-8) dispersal, resulting in the multiplication of house churches. The Vietnamese government learned that pressing too hard on the church only seemed to make it grow. In more recent years, the government has allowed churches and events, but always with heavy regulation. Nevertheless, during the decades since 1975, the church has seen 900 percent growth, with Evangelicals numbering more than 1.6 million.

10.5 South Asia

South Asia is surrounded by vast ocean and soaring mountains, giving these nations many cultural commonalities. This birthplace of two of the great world religions (Hinduism and Buddhism) has also seen other faiths take root, like Sikhism, Islam, and Christianity. The arrival of Christianity goes back to Christianity's earliest centuries, but other parts of the sub-continent remained untouched by Christian presence until the last two centuries. Though percentages remain low, Christianity has and is making its presence known in this part of the world.

Bangladesh

Bangladesh was formed through a British concession to allow two Muslim majority nations flank India. Christian presence goes back nearly four centuries with Catholic entré. This majority Muslim nation has had a Christian population with various Christian institutions, but has seen little growth for many years.[50] Protestant efforts have seen more results among minority ethnic groups, including a people movement among the Garo

---

[49] Reimer, 60–62.
[50] Warren Webster, "Bangladesh," in *Sejarah Gereja Di Asia, Volume 1*, ed. Donald E. Hoke (Malang: Yayasan Penerbit Gandum Mas, 2000), 86–90.

tribe.[51] In recent years there have been reports of many thousands coming to faith in Christ.[52]

Bhutan

Bhutan is a Buddhist kingdom nestled in the remote Himalayas and has had very little contact with Christianity. A brief time in the 1960's allowed for medical missionaries in the small nation.[53] The land-locked nation officially has freedom of religion but has maintained strict resistance to Christian witness entering. There are churches but they are isolated and bound by strict bands on proselytizing.

India

India is the most populous democracy in the world. "Like India's history, Christianity in India is complex."[54] We've already described the early history of the Mar Thoma churches as well as the Catholic inroads later. Both continued to grow and spread to other parts of India. Although the Protestants arrived late, they made up for lost ground in just two hundred years. India has such large Hindu and Muslim populations that, Christianity remains a minority in most of the country (3% of the population). However, mass movements in different parts of the country have given the church momentum. In the northeast, in Mizoram and Nagaland, Christianity is the majority religion (83% and 70% respectively).[55]

---

[51] Simon H. Sircar, "The Church in Bangladesh," in *Church in Asia Today: Opportunities and Challenges*, ed. Saphir Athyal (Singapore: Asia Lausanne Committee for World Evangelization, 1996), 362–63.

[52] Hazel Torres, "Christianity on the Rise in Bangladesh as Tens of Thousands of Muslims Are Turning Away from Allah to Embrace Jesus," Christianity Today, March 15, 2017, https://www.christiantoday.com/article/christianity-rising-fast-in-bangladesh-as-tens-of-thousands-of-muslims-are-turning-away-from-allah-to-embrace-jesus/105712.htm.

[53] Billy Bray, "Bhutan," in *Sejarah Gereja Asia, Volume 1*, ed. Donald E. Hoke (Malang: Yayasan Penerbit Gandum Mas, 2000), 110–11.

[54] F. Hrangkhuma, "The Church in India," in *Church in Asia Today: Opportunities and Challenges*, ed. Saphir Athyal (Singapore: Asia Lausanne Committee for World Evangelization, 1996), 393.

[55] Hrangkhuma, 418–23.

Maldives
The Maldives are a small group of islands in the Indian Ocean. The Islamic nation strictly prohibits any Christian activity for its citizens. Any Christians in the small nation keep their faith a secret due to persecution.

Nepal
Nepal, boasting some of the most majestic mountains in the world, has ensured stronger control over outsiders bringing religious ideas to the nation. The rugged terrain has created a natural barrier, and the government has sought to protect the predominately Hindu population. Capuchin monks were expelled from the land in 1914.[56] However, globalization has meant that many Nepalis have had opportunities to travel, first through the British military, and then for work across Asia, particularly as security forces. Many Nepalis became Christians while working abroad and returned with the gospel to the cities and villages throughout the nation. In recent years, the Christian population has tripled and is fast developing an established footprint in the nation.

Pakistan
Pakistan was formed as a nation based on religion when the British departed from India. The embattled minority Christian community is well established but has been primarily from a lower caste and thus have had difficulty securing their own religious rights and freedoms. There was a revival in Pakistan beginning in 1905, but the fires of revival have since waned. Freedom for missionary activity is restricted in the country, but the large diaspora of Pakistanis working overseas has opened opportunities for Christian outreach.

Sri Lanka
The predominately Buddhist island nation of Sri Lanka has a population of about 20 million. There is archeological evidence of Christian contact going back to the sixth century. Today, Christians account for about nine percent of the population, due in part to the interactions of the Christian Tamil population in India. Early missionary efforts were seen as too aggressive and offensive, which stirred a revitalization of Buddhism in the land.[57]

---

[56] Frykenberg, *Christianity in India*, 8.
[57] Frykenberg, 8.

Conclusion

Christianity began in Asia and flourished in Asia for a thousand years. Metropolitan bishops were once serving in cities across Asia and actively sending out monks and missionary bishops to places where there was not yet a Christian presence. The church in Asia endured suffering far beyond anything experienced in the West. When the Christian outlook was bleak in much of the world, it was the Asian church that continued to carry the torch, even under the thumb of Islamic rulers.

One violent conqueror after another tore through Central Asia bringing devastation to the church. Changes in imperial rulers in China and Japan brought a virtual end to Christian presence for centuries. Southeast Asia only had the briefest touches with Christianity until recent centuries.

Only a few places have had an ongoing Christian presence since the early centuries. Christian presence in the earliest Christian strongholds in modern day Syria and Iraq are limping from recent wars and religious violence. Armenia underwent centuries of political domination and then became the targets of attempted genocide, nevertheless, they continued to hold onto their faith. India was the one place that maintained a growing Christian presence in Asia from the early centuries until today.

The nineteenth and twentieth century saw the reemergence of Christianity in Asia. Western Protestant missionaries took of the calling to make disciples of all nations and spearheaded efforts in Bible translation, evangelism and church planting. Revivals and people movements took the fruit of these missionaries and brought accelerated growth in some places. In the twentieth century the church gained new footholds in countries long resistant to Christianity and the now established and mature Asian church has sought to reach the remaining parts of Asia lacking a Christian presence. We close with words from Akira Hatori: "Christ seeks you in Asia! Christ seeks you for Asia! Then Asia can with Christ to the world!"[58]

---

[58] Akira Hatori, "Christ Seeks Asia," in *Christ Seeks Asia*, ed. W. Stanley Mooneyham (Hong Kong: The Rock House Publishers, 1969), 267.

Questions for Understanding and Reflection

Chapter One

1. Identify the various ways that the Church of the East grew.

2. One way the Church of the East grew was through the faithful witness of Christian commercial traders traveling along the Silk Road. How might this 'commercial evangelism' work in the modern world?

3. How important is an ascetic life-style in the promoting of Christianity? Are there ways it might harm or help the growth?

4. Summarize the theological affirmations of Aphrahat. Are you comfortable with his theology? If not, why? Do you believe it is important for theological formulations to use the language found in the early creeds? Why or why not?

5. The school at Nisibis was important for the eastward spread of the Church of the East. What about the school helped it to be so effective? How might modern theological education be more effective in preparing Christians for missions?

6. Outline the history of Christianity in India from the earliest times to the present. What lessons can the modern church learn from this history?

7. Identify the various reasons why the Church of the East declined and, in many places, disappeared. Are any of these a present danger for your own church or denomination? If so, how might the church prepare itself to resist decline?

Chapter Two

1. In the early centuries of the spread of Orthodoxy, translating Christian material into native languages proved invaluable. In the modern context of globalization, which might be more helpful: translating scripture into languages that do not yet have an adequate translation or assisting the people to adapt to the modern world by teaching them a more widespread language which would already have a scripture translation?

2. What are the advantages and disadvantages of government assistance in the work of evangelism and missions?

3. What lessons about missions and church growth can we learn from the life of Stephen Khrap?

4. In China, the Russian Orthodox Church had a number of industrial establishments. List them and express your own feelings about a church which promotes industry. Note strengths and weaknesses.

5. Nicolas Kasatkin said, "It [is] inappropriate for a missionary to retire unless he is totally unable to serve." Do you agree or disagree? Why?

Chapter Three

1. Xavier emphasized the importance of children, especially for his work in India. Outline his thoughts and practice. How would you evaluate his emphasis and use of children?

2. Contextualization was an important element in the Roman Catholic missionaries studied in this chapter. Summarize the various ways each of them adapted the Christian Faith to the native culture. Are you uncomfortable with any of these ways? If so, why?

3. Examine the dominant culture around you. How might the church today adapt to that culture for the sake of the Gospel?

4. What are some aspects of the dominant culture around you that are completely incompatible with the Gospel?

5. Several times in this chapter, it was noted that some missionaries sought primarily to promote the Christian Faith among higher castes, nobility, royalty, and/or upper classes. List these attempts. Do you agree or disagree with this strategy? Give reasons for you answer.

6. In order to promote his understanding of the Gospel, Alexander de Rhodes disobeyed the governing authorities both in his own organization and in the local governments. Do you believe he was correct to do so? Justify your answer.

Chapter Four

1. List the reasons suggested for the slowness of Protestants to become involved in missions. Which, if any of these reasons, might be valid grounds for delaying missions?

2. Are any of the reasons suggested for the lack of missions present in the modern church? What are some other reasons that might be suggested today?

3. Illustrate the importance of nationals for the growth of Christianity by describing the work of two mentioned in this chapter.

4. The Serampore Trio and the later Baptist Mission Society had two different understandings of what a mission society was. Describe the two views and indicate which view is closest to your own preference. Justify your preference.

5. Early Roman Catholic missionaries translated material for use in worship and instruction, e.g. the Lord's Prayer, the Creed, the 10 Commandments. Early Protestant missionaries were more inclined to translate the Bible. Which approach do you think may be more effective in the early stages of missionary work? Why?

6. Choose three of the missionaries mentioned in this chapter. Summarize and evaluate their work.

Chapters Five, Six and Seven

1. Describe what is meant by the Three-Self Movement. What are the three emphases? Do you agree or disagree that these are valid goals for a church or Christian organization?

2. What are the responsibilities of wealthy Western churches toward their materially poorer third world sister churches?

3. Do you have any sympathy for those Chinese Christian movements which were attracted to the egalitarian teaching of Communism? Why or why not?

4. Several of the indigenous movements studied in these chapters had charismatic or Pentecostal aspects. One commentator has observed that if these types of churches continue to grow along present trends "within a few decades, such denominations will represent a far larger segment of global Christianity, and just conceivably a majority."[1] Might this be true in your country? How do you feel about that? Why?

5. Note the movements in these chapters that seem to have declined or disappeared in the face of modernity and global changes. How can your church guard itself from the same fate?

6. In considering the Philippine Independent Church, we noticed a wedding of nationalism to a Christian movement. What are the advantages and disadvantages of such a union? Would you like the church to be more or less nationalistic? Why?

---

[1] Jenkins, *The Next Christendom*, 8.

Chapters Eight, Nine and Ten

1. What significant events shaped the Christian movement in Asia during the 20th century?

2. The church grew through both missionaries and revival movements. How does that inform our missions practice today?

3. Where is the church struggling the most in Asia? Where is the church growing and strengthening the most in Asia?

4. As the church of Asia looks forward, how challenges and opportunities lie ahead?

Works Cited

Aaron, Sushil J. "Emulating Azariah: Evangelicals and Social Change in the Dangs." In *Evangelical Christianity and Democracy in Asia*, edited by David H. Lumsdaine, 87–130. Oxford: Oxford University Press, 2009.

Adeney, David H. *China: The Church's Long March*. Ventura, CA: Baker Publishing Group, 1985.

Adeney, Miriam. "Trends in Asia: Implications for Mission." *Mission Round Table: The Occasional Bulletin of OMF Mission Research* 1 (January 2005): 2–11.

Adhav, Shamsundar Manohar. *Pandita Ramabai*. Madras: Christian Literature Society, 1979.

Akkeren, Philip van. *Sri and Christ: A Study of the Indigenous Church in East Java*. London: Lutterworth P, 1970.

Anderson, Allan. *An Introduction to Pentecostalism: Global Charismatic Christianity*. Cambridge, UK: Cambridge University Press, 2004.

Anderson, Allan Heaton. "Pentecostalism and Charismatic Movements in Asia." In *The Oxford Handbook of Christianity in Asia*, edited by Felix Wilfred, 158–70. Oxford: Oxford University Press, 2014.

Anderson, Allan, and Edmond Tang. "Independency in Africa and Asia." In *The Cambridge History of Christianity, Vol. 9: World Christianities c. 1914-c. 2000*, edited by Hugh McLeod, 116. Cambridge: Cambridge University Press, 2006.

———. "Independency in Africa and Asia." In *A World History of Christianity*, edited by Adrian Hastings, 121. Grand Rapids, MI: Wm. B. Eerdmans, 2011.

Anonymous. "Afghanistan." In *Sejarah Gereja Asia, Volume 1*, edited by Donald E. Hoke, 73–83. Malang: Yayasan Penerbit Gandum Mas, 2000.

———. "Life of Mar Aba: English Translation with Introduction." Edited by Roger Pearse, 2013. http://www.tertullian.org/fathers/life_of_mar_aba_0_intro.htm.

Appasamy, A. J. "A Biographical Introduction." In *The Real Life*. Madras: Christian Literature Society, 1968.

Astrain, Antonia. "Francis Xavier." In *The Catholic Encyclopedia*. Vol. 7. New York: Robert Appleton Company, 1909. www.newadvent.org/cathen/06233.htm.

Austin, Alvyn. *China's Millions*. Grand Rapids, MI: Wm. B. Eerdmans Publishing, 2007.

Bailey, Betty Jane, and J. Martin Bailey. *Who Are the Christians in the Middle East?* Grand Rapids, MI: Wm. B. Eerdmans, 2003.

Barraclough, Geoffrey, and Geoffrey Parker, eds. *The Times Atlas of World History*. 4th edition. Maplewood, N.J: Hammond Incorporated, 1993.

Barrett, David B., George Thomas Kurian, and Todd M. Johnson, eds. *World Christian Encyclopedia: A Comparative Survey of Churches and Religions in the Modern World Volume I: The World by Countries: Religionists, Churches, Ministries*. 2nd ed. Oxford: Oxford University Press, 2001.

Bays, Daniel H. *A New History of Christianity in China*. Chichester, West Sussex ; Malden, MA: Wiley-Blackwell, 2011.

Beaver, R. Pierce. "Anderson, Rufus." In *Concise Dictionary of the Christian World Mission*, edited by Stephen Neill, Gerald H. Anderson, and John Goodman, 21. London: Lutterworth Press, 1971.

Bergunder, Michael. *The South Indian Pentecostal Movement in the Twentieth Century*. Studies in the History of Christian Missions. Grand Rapids, MI: Eerdmans, 2008.

Betts, Robert B. *Christians in the Arab East: A Political Study*. Revised edition. London: SPCK, 1979.

Boyd, Robin. *An Introduction to Indian Christian Theology*. Madras: Christian Literature Society, 1977.

Bray, Billy. "Bhutan." In *Sejarah Gereja Asia, Volume 1*, edited by Donald E. Hoke, 107–19. Malang: Yayasan Penerbit Gandum Mas, 2000.

Brody, Dimitri. "Nicolas Kasatkin." In *The Blackwell Dictionary of Eastern Christianity*, 343. Malden, MA: Blackwell Publishers, 1999.

Broomhall, A. J. *The Shaping of Modern China: Hudson Taylor's Life and Legacy: Volume One*. Carlisle: Piquant Editions, 2005.

Brown, G. Thompson. "Korea." In *A Dictionary of Asian Christianity*, edited by Scott W. Sunquist, 448. Grand Rapids, MI: Wm. B. Eerdmans, 2001.

———. "Why Has Christianity Grown Faster in Korea Than in China?" *Missiology: An International Review* XXII, no. 1 (January 1994): 77–88.

Brunner, Emil. "A Unique Christian Mission: The Mukyokai (Non-Church) Movement in Japan." In *Religion and Culture: Essays in Honor of Paul Tillich*, edited by Walter Leibrecht. New York: Arno Press, 1979.

Burkitt, F. Crawford. *Early Eastern Christianity St. Margaret's Lectures, 1904 on the Syriac-Speaking Church.* Pascataway, NJ: Gorgias Press, 2002.

Butler, Rex, Ken Cleaver, Rodrick K. Durst, Lloyd A. Harsch, James Lutzweiler, and Stephen Presley. *Churchfails: 100 Blunders in Church History.* Edited by David K. Stabnow. Nashville, Tennessee: Holman Reference, 2016.

Cabillas, Dionito M. "The Distinctive Contribution of the Church [IFI] on Church Unity and Mission." *Iglesia Filipina Indepentiente* (blog). Accessed October 29, 2018. http://ifi.ph/?page_id=106.

Chan, Simon. *Grassroots Asian Theology: Thinking the Faith from the Ground Up by Simon Chan.* Downers Grove, IL: IVP Academic, 2014.

Chen, Lip Siong. "Global Urbanization through China's Belt and Road Initiative: Opportunities for Urban Mission." In *Urbanization: Impacts on the Church, Mission and Society Today*, edited by Lip Siong Chen and Weng Kit Cheong. Kota Kinabalu, Malaysia: Sabah Theological Seminary, 2018.

China Group. "Xu Guangqi." In *A Dictionary of Asian Christianity*, edited by Scott W. Sunquist, 913. Grand Rapids, MI: Wm. B. Eerdmans, 2001.

Coakley, J. F. "Church of the East." In *The Blackwell Dictionary of Eastern Christianity*, edited by Ken Parry, 122–23. Oxford: Blackwell Publishers, 1999.

Comnemo, Maria Adelaide Lala. "Nestorianism in Central Asia during the First Millennium: Archaeological Evidence." *Journal of the Assyrian Academic Society*, n.d., 20–53.

Cormack, Don. *Killing Fields, Living Fields.* London; Grand Rapids, MI: Monarch Books, 2001.

Covell, Ralph. "Ricci, Mateo." In *A Dictionary of Asian Christianity*, edited by Scott W. Sunquist, 705. Grand Rapids, MI: Wm. B. Eerdmans, 2001.

Cragg, Kenneth. *The Arab Christian: A History in the Middle East by Kenneth Cragg.* London: Mowbray, 1991.

Crane, Michael D. "Refugees in the Urban Wilderness: Plight of Refugees in Landing Cities and Opportunities for Response." *International Journal of Urban Transformation* 1, no. 1 (October 2016): 51–70.

———. "Urbanizing the Church in an Urbanizing Asia." In *Urbanization: Impacts on the Church, Mission and Society Today*, edited by Lip

Siong Chen and Weng Kit Cheong, 101–44. Kota Kinabalu, Malaysia: Sabah Theological Seminary, 2018.

Culpepper, C. L. *The Shantung Revival*. Crescendo Book Publications, 1971. https://www.gospeltruth.net/shantung.htm.

DeWaard, Nellie. *Pioneer in Sumatra: The Story of Ludwig Nommensen*. London: OMF International, 1962.

Dixon, Roger L. "The Major Model of Muslim Ministry." *Missiology: An International Review* 30, no. 4 (October 2002): 443–54.

Donaldson, James, and Alexander Roberts, eds. *Ante Nicene Fathers: The Writings of the Fathers Down to Ad 325: Volume 8*. 2nd edition. Peabody, MA: Hendrickson, 1999.

Dwe, Clifford Kyaw. "Tha Byu, Ko." In *A Dictionary of Asian Christianity*, edited by Scott W. Sunquist, 829–30. Grand Rapids, MI: Wm. B. Eerdmans, 2001.

East, W. Gordon. *The Geography Behind History*. Revised and Enlarged. New York: W. W. Norton & Company, 1965.

Edwards, David A. "The Legacy of Francis Thomas McDougall." *International Bulletin of Missionary Research* 31, no. 4 (October 2007): 204–8.

Edwards, Jonathan. *Charity and Its Fruits: Christian Love as Manifested in the Heart and Life*. London: Banner of Truth, 1969.

England, John C. "Reclaiming Our Christian History." *Inter-Religio* 19 (Summer 1991): 21–38.

England, John C., Jose Kuttianimattathil, John Mansford, Lily A. Quintos, David Suh Kwang-Sun, and Janice Wickeri, eds. *Asian Christian Theologies: A Research Guide to Authors, Movements, Sources: Volume 1: Asia Region, South Asia, Austral Asia*. Delhi; Quezon City; Maryknoll, N.Y: Orbis Books, 2005.

England, John C., Jose Kuttianimattathil, John Mansford Prior, Lily A. Quintos, David Suh Kwang-Sun, and Janice Wickeri, eds. *Asian Christian Theologies: A Research Guide to Authors, Movements, Sources, Vol. 2: Southeast Asia*. Delhi: ISPCK, 2003.

England, John C., John M. Prior, and Jose Kuttianimattathil, eds. *Asian Christian Theologies: A Research Guide Authors, Movements, Sources: Volume 3: Northeast Asia*. Delhi; Quezon City; Maryknoll, N.Y: Orbis Books, 2004.

Evers, Georg. "'On the Trail of Spices': Christianity in Southeast Asia." In *The Oxford Handbook of Christianity in Asia*, edited by Felix Wilfred, 65–79. Oxford: Oxford University Press, 2014.

Foster, John. *First Advance: Church History 1: AD 29-500.* London: SPCK, 1972.

Francisco, S. J., Jose Mario C. "Migration and New Cosmopolitanism in Asian Christianity." In *The Oxford Handbook of Christianity in Asia*, edited by Felix Wilfred, 575–92. Oxford: Oxford University Press, 2014.

Frykenberg, Robert Eric. *Christianity in India: From Beginnings to the Present.* Oxford History of the Christian Church. Oxford; New York: Oxford University Press, 2008.

George, Timothy. *Faithful Witness: The Life and Mission of William Carey.* Birmingham, AL: New Hope, 1991.

Goh, Robbie B. H. *Christianity in Southeast Asia.* Southeast Asia Background Series 7. Singapore: Institute of Southeast Asian Studies, 2005.

González, Justo L. *A History of Christian Thought: Volume 1: From the Beginnings to the Council of Chalcedon.* 2nd ed. Nashville: Abingdon Press, 1987.

Gorder, A. Christian, van. *Muslim-Christian Relations in Central Asia.* Central Asian Studies Series. London; New York: Routledge, 2008.

Guinness, M. Geraldine. *The Story of the China Inland Mission.* London: Morgan and Scott, 1893.

Hatori, Akira. "Christ Seeks Asia." In *Christ Seeks Asia*, edited by W. Stanley Mooneyham, 259–67. Hong Kong: The Rock House Publishers, 1969.

Hattaway, Paul. *Back to Jerusalem: Three Chinese House Church Leaders Share Their Vision to Complete the Great Commission.* Carlisle; Waynesboro, GA: Piquant; Gabriel Resources, 2003.

Hedlund, Roger E., ed. *Quest for Identity: India's Churches of Indigenous Origin.* Delhi: ISPCK, 2000.

Herrmann, Georgina. "A Central Asian City on the Silk Road: Ancient and Medieval Merv." *Archaeology International* 1 (1997): 32–36. https://doi.org/10.5334/ai.0110.

Hiebert, Paul G. "The Flaw of the Excluded Middle." *Missiology: An International Review* 10, no. 1 (January 1982): 35–47.

Hill, Graham. *GlobalChurch: Reshaping Our Conversations, Renewing Our Mission, Revitalizing Our Churches.* Downers Grove, IL: IVP Academic, 2016.

Hill, James Hamlyn. *The Earliest Life of Christ Ever Compiled From the Four Gospels, Being the Diatessaron of Tatian.* Edinburgh: T & T Clark, 2001.

Hinton, Keith. *Growing Churches Singapore Style Ministry in an Urban Context*. O M F Books, 1985.

Ho, Chee Sin. "Oldham, William Fitzjames." In *A Dictionary of Asian Christianity*, edited by Scott W. Sunquist, 616. Grand Rapids, MI: Wm. B. Eerdmans, 2001.

Hogan, Brian. *There's a Sheep in My Bathtub: Tenth Anniversary Edition*. 2nd ed. Fayetteville, AR: Asteroidea Books, 2017.

Hopkins, C. Howard. *John R. Mott, 1865-1955: A Biography*. Grand Rapids, MI: Eerdmans Pub Co, 1979.

Hrangkhuma, F. "The Church in India." In *Church in Asia Today: Opportunities and Challenges*, edited by Saphir Athyal, 393–434. Singapore: Asia Lausanne Committee for World Evangelization, 1996.

Tan, Jin Huat. "Pentecostals and Charismatics in Malaysia and Singapore." In *Asian and Pentecostal: The Charismatic Face of Christianity in Asia*, edited by Allan Anderson and Edmond Tang, 281–306. Oxford; Baguio City: Regnum Books International, 2005.

Hunt, Robert A. "The Legacy of William Shellabear." *International Bulletin of Missionary Research* 26, no. 1 (January 2002): 28–31.

Hutauruk, J. Raplan. "Nommensen, Ludwig Ingwer." In *A Dictionary of Asian Christianity*, edited by Scott W. Sunquist, 608. Grand Rapids, MI: Wm. B. Eerdmans, 2001.

Innocent, Archimandrite. "The Russian Orthodox Mission in China." *The Chinese Recorder*. Accessed June 15, 2017. www.orthodox.cn/history/1610romc_en.htm.

Irvin, Dale T., and Scott Sunquist. *History of the World Christian Movement*. Maryknoll, NY: Orbis Books, 2001.

Jacob, Adai. "Jacobite Syrian Orthodox Church, India." In *A Dictionary of Asian Christianity*, edited by Scott W. Sunquist, 406. Grand Rapids, MI: Wm. B. Eerdmans, 2001.

Jenkins, Philip. *The Lost History of Christianity: The Thousand-Year Golden Age of the Church in the Middle East, Africa, and Asia--and How It Died*. New York, NY: HarperOne, 2008.

———. *The Next Christendom: The Coming of Global Christianity*. Oxford University Press, USA, 2002.

Jennings, Raymond P. *Jesus, Japan, and Kanzo Uchimura: A Study of the View of the Church of Kanzo Uchimura and Its Significance for Japanese Christianity*. Tokyo: Kyo Bun Kwan, Christian Literature Society, 1958.

Johnson, Todd M. "Contextualization: A New-Old Idea, Illustrations from the Life of an Italian Jesuit in 17th-Century India." *International Journal of Frontier Missions* 4 (1987): 9–20.

Jonge, Christian G. F. de. "Kruyt, Albertus Christian." In *A Dictionary of Asian Christianity*, edited by Scott W. Sunquist, 458. Grand Rapids, MI: Wm. B. Eerdmans, 2001.

Kagawa, Toyohiko. *Christ and Japan*. Translated by William Axling. New York: Friendship Press, 1934.

Kham, Chin Do. "Partnership Issues and Challenges in Asian Mission." In *Asian Church and God's Mission*, edited by Wonsuk Ma and Julie C. Ma, 43–60. Manila: OMF Literature, 2003.

Kim, Kirsteen. "Mission in the Twenty-First Century." *Norsk Tidsskrift for Misjonsvitenskap* 1, no. 2 (2011): 56–73.

Kinnear, Angus I. *Against the Tide, the Story of Watchman Nee*. Wheaton, IL: Tyndale House Publishers, 1973.

Koschorke, Klaus, Frieder Ludwig, and Marian Delgado, eds. *A History of Christianity in Asia, Africa, and Latin America, 1450-1990: A Documentary Sourcebook*. Grand Rapids, MI: Wm. B. Eerdmans, 2007.

Koshy, T. E. "Brother Bakht Singh--A Saint of God: An Overview of His Life and Ministry." Brother Bakht Singh: A Servant of God, 2007. http://www.brotherbakhtsingh.org/briefbio.html.

Kwok, Pui-lan. "Claiming Our Heritage: Chinese Women and Christianity." *International Bulletin of Missionary Research* 16, no. 4 (October 1992): 150–54.

Latourette, Kenneth Scott. *A History of Christian Missions in China*. 1st edition. New York: Russell & Russell, 1929.

———. *A History of Christianity: Volume I: Beginnings to 1500*. Rev. ed. New York: Harper & Row, 1975.

———. *A History of the Expansion of Christianity*. San Francisco: Harper, 1937.

———. *A History of the Expansion of Christianity: Vol. 2: The Thousand Years of Uncertainty 500 A.D. to 1500 A.D.* Grand Rapids, MI: Zondervan Publishing Company, 1970.

———. *A History of the Expansion of Christianity: Vol. 6: The Great Century: North Africa and Asia: 1800 A.D. to 1914 A.D.* Grand Rapids, MI: Zondervan Publishing Company, 1944.

———. *A History of the Expansion of Christianity: Volume 3: The Centuries of Advance, 1500 A.D. to 1800 A.D.* Grand Rapids, MI: Zondervan Publishing Company, 1967.

Lawrence, Carl. *The Church in China: How It Survives and Prospers Under Communism*. Minneapolis, MN: Bethany House Publishers, 1985.

Lee, Samuel. *The Japanese and Christianity*. Amsterdam: Foundation University Press, 2014.

Lemercinier, Geneviève. "The Effect of the Caste System on Conversions to Christianity in Tamilnadu:" *Social Compass* 28, no. 2–3 (1981): 237–68.

Leung, Philip Yuen-sang. "Conversion, Commitment, and Culture: Christian Experience in China, 1949-99." In *Christianity Reborn: The Global Expansion of Evangelicalism in the Twentieth Century*, edited by Donald M. Lewis, 87–107. Studies in the History of Christian Missions. Grand Rapids, MI: Wm. B. Eerdmans, 2004.

Lewis, Bernard. *The Middle East : 2000 Years of History from the Rise of Christianity to the Present Day*. London: Phoenix Giant, 1995.

Lovelace, Richard F. *Dynamics of Spiritual Life - An Evangelical Theology of Renewal*. Downers Grove, IL: InterVarsity Press, 1979.

Lugo, Luis, ed. "Global Survey of Evangelical Protestant Leaders." Pew Research Center, June 22, 2011. http://www.pewforum.org/2011/06/22/global-survey-of-evangelical-protestant-leaders/.

Ma, Wonsuk. "Asian (Classical) Pentecostal Theology in Context." In *Asian and Pentecostal: The Charismatic Face of Christianity in Asia*, edited by Allan Anderson and Edmond Tang, 59–92. Oxford; Baguio City: Regnum Books International, 2005.

MacCulloch, Diarmaid. *Christianity: The First Three Thousand Years*. New York: Penguin Books, 2009.

Maggay, Melba Padilla. "Early Protestant Missionary Efforts in the Philippines: Some Intercultural Issues." In *Asian Church and God's Mission*, edited by Wonsuk Ma and Julie C. Ma, 29–42. Manila: OMF Literature, 2003.

Mangalwadi, Vishal. *The Legacy of William Carey: A Model for the Transformation of a Culture*. 1st US ed. Wheaton, IL: Crossway Books, 1999.

Markarian, Krikor. "Today's Iranian Revolution: How the Mullahs Are Leading the Nation to Jesus." *Mission Frontiers*, October 2008, 6–13.

Martin, David. *Pentecostalism: The World Their Parish*. Malden, MA: Blackwell Publishers, 2002.

"Martyn, Henry." In *The Oxford Dictionary of the Christian Church*, 866, n.d.

Matthew, Samuel. "Sundar Singh." In *A Dictionary of Asian Christianity*, edited by Scott W. Sunquist, 43. Grand Rapids, MI: Wm. B. Eerdmans, 2001.

McAmis, Robert Day. *Malay Muslims: The History and Challenge of Resurgent Islam in Southeast Asia*. Grand Rapids, MI: Wm. B. Eerdmans Publishing Co., 2002.

McCallum, Dennis. "Watchman Nee and the House Church Movement in China: Unpublished Paper," 1986. https://www.xenos.org/essays/watchman-nee-and-house-church-movement-china.

McKean, Laura. "The Narrative of Chiengmai." In *Historial Sketch of Protestant Missions in Siam 1828-1928*, edited by George Bradley McFarland, Reprint. Bangkok: White Lotus Press, 1999.

Miura, Hiroshi. *The Life and Thought of Kanzo Uchimura, 1861-1930*. Grand Rapids, MI: Wm. B. Eerdmans Publishing Co., 1997.

Moffett, Samuel Hugh. *A History of Christianity in Asia: Beginnings to 1500*. San Francisco: HarperSanFrancisco, 1992.

———. *A History of Christianity in Asia, Vol. II: 1500-1900*. Maryknoll, N.Y: Orbis Books, 2005.

———. *The Christians of Korea*. Friendship Press, 1962.

Moore, Charles E. "Introduction." In *Sadhu Sundar Singh: Essential Writings*, 9–29. Modern Spiritual Masters Series. Maryknoll, NY: Orbis Books, 2005.

"Mukti Mission US | About." *Mukti Mission* (blog), 2018. http://muktimission.us/.

Mursell, Gordon. *English Spirituality: From 1700 to the Present Day*. London: Westminster John Knox Press, 2001.

"Muslim Converts Breathe New Life into Europe's Struggling Christian Churches." Fox News, March 21, 2017. https://www.foxnews.com/world/muslim-converts-breathe-new-life-into-europes-struggling-christian-churches.

Nee, Watchman. *The Normal Christian Church Life*. 2nd ed. Living Stream Ministry, 1980.

———. *The Normal Christian Life*. Reprinted edition. Wheaton, IL.; Fort Washington, PA: Tyndale House Publishers, Inc., 1977.

———. *The Spiritual Man*. New York: Christian Fellowship Publishers, 1968.

Neill, Stephen. *A History of Christian Missions*. 2nd edition. History of the Church 6. Penguin Books, 1991.

————. *A History of Christianity in India: The Beginnings to AD 1707.* Cambridge: Cambridge University Press, 1984.

Nevius, John. *The Planting and Development of Missionary Churches.* Reprint of the 4th ed. Nutley, N.J: P & R Pub., 1973.

"Nicholas of Japan." *Orthodox Wiki* (blog), 2007. http://orthodoxwiki.org/Nicholas_of_Japan.

Noort, Gert. "The Road from Magic to Faith: Life and Work of Alb. C. Kruyt (1869-1949), Missionary in Central Celebes Indonesia." Dissertation, Utrecht University, 2006.

Norihisa, Suzuki. "Uchimura Kanzo." In *A Dictionary of Asian Christianity*, edited by Scott W. Sunquist. Grand Rapids, MI: Wm. B. Eerdmans, 2001.

Nyhus, E. "An Indonesian Church in the Midst of Social Change: The Batak Protestant Church 1945-1957." Dissertation, University of Wisconsin-Madison, 1987.

Oak, Sung-deuk. "Presbyterian Mission Methods and Policies in Korea, 1876-1910." In *Korean Church, God's Mission, Global Christianity*, 32–47. Regnum Edinburgh Centenary Series 26. Oxford: Regnum Books International, 2015.

Oddie, G. A. "Christian Conversion in the Telugu Country, 1860-1900: A Case Study of One Protestant Movement in the Godavery-Krishna Delta." *Indian Economic Social History Review* 12 (n.d.): 61–79.

Olson, Roger E. *The Story of Christian Theology: Twenty Centuries of Tradition & Reform.* Downers Grove, IL: IVP Academic, 1999.

Orr, J. Edwin. *Evangelical Awakenings in Eastern Asia.* Minneapolis: Bethany Fellowship, 1975.

Palmer, Martin. *The Jesus Sutras: Rediscovering the Lost Scrolls of Taoist Christianity.* New York: Ballantine Books, 2001.

Partonadi, Sutarman Soediman. *Sadrach's Community And Its Contextual Roots. A Nineteenth-Century Javanese Expression of Christianity.* Amsterdam: Rodopi Bv Editions, 1988.

Payaslian, Simon. *The History of Armenia: From the Origins to the Present.* New York: Palgrave Macmillan, 2007.

Pedersen, Paul B. *Batak Blood and Protestant Soul: The Development of National Batak Churches in North Sumatra.* Grand Rapids, MI: Eerdmans, 1970.

Peters, George W. *Indonesia Revival; Focus on Timor.* Grand Rapids, MI: Zondervan Pub. House, 1973.

Peyrouse, Sebastien. "Christian Minorities on the Central Asian Silk Roads." In *The Oxford Handbook of Christianity in Asia*, edited by Felix Wilfred, 52–63. Oxford: Oxford University Press, 2014.

Phan, Peter C. "Rhodes, Alexandre De." In *A Dictionary of Asian Christianity*, edited by Scott W. Sunquist, 699–701. Grand Rapids, MI: Wm. B. Eerdmans, 2001.

Phillips, Tom. "China on Course to Become 'world's Most Christian Nation' within 15 Years." *The Telegraph*, April 19, 2014. http://www.telegraph.co.uk/news/worldnews/asia/china/10776023/China-on-course-to-become-worlds-most-Christian-nation-within-15-years.html.

Pierson, Paul E. "The New Context of Christian Mission: Challenges and Opportunities for the Asian Church." In *Asian Church and God's Mission*, edited by Wonsuk Ma and Julie C. Ma, 11–28. Manila: OMF Publishers, 2003.

Poon, Michael. "The Theological Locus of Christian MOvements in Southeast Asia." In *Christian Movements in Southeast Asia: A Theological Exploriation*, edited by Michael Nai-Chiu Poon, ix–xxxv. Singapore: Trinity Theological College, 2010.

Preston, Diana. *The Boxer Rebellion: The Dramatic Story of China's War on Foreigners That Shook the World in the Summer of 1900.* New York: Walker Books, 2000.

Ranche, Apolonio. "An Introduction to the Iglesia Filipina Endependiente (Philippine Independent Church)." *Iglesia Filipina Indepentiente* (blog). Accessed July 10, 2008. http://www.ifi.ph/history.htm.

Reimer, Reg. *Vietnam's Christians: A Century of Growth and Adversity*. Pasadena, CA: William Carey Library, 2011.

Reimer, Reginald E. "Ancestor Worship." In *A Dictionary of Asian Christianity*, edited by Scott W. Sunquist, 18–24. Grand Rapids, MI: Wm. B. Eerdmans, 2001.

Richards, Wes. "An Examination of Common Factors in the Growth of Global Pentecostalism: Observed in South Korea, Nigeria and Argentina." *Journal of Asian Mission* 7, no. 1 (2005): 85–106.

Ro, Bong Rin. "The Church in Korea." In *Church in Asia Today: Opportunities and Challenges*, edited by Saphir Athyal, 50–80. Singapore: Asia Lausanne Committee for World Evangelization, 1996.

Sanneh, Lamin. *Translating the Message: The Missionary Impact on Culture.* Maryknoll, NY: Orbis Books, 1989.

Schaff, Philip, and Henry Wace, eds. *A Select Library of Nicene and Post-Nicene Fathers of the Christian Church, Second Series*. Vol. Vol. 13. Grand Rapids, MI: William B. Eerdmans, 1956.

Schreiner, Lothar. "The Legacy of Ingwer Ludwig Nommensen." *International Bulletin of Missionary Research* 24, no. 2 (April 2000): 81–84.

"Seoul, South Korea: A Look Back at Billy Graham's Largest Ever Crusade." Billy Graham Evangelistic Association, February 8, 2018. https://billygraham.org/story/seoul-south-korea-a-look-back-at-billy-grahams-largest-ever-crusade/.

Shaw, Mark R. *Global Awakening: How 20th-Century Revivals Triggered a Christian Revolution*. Downers Grove, IL: IVP Academic, 2010.

Shearer, R. E. *Wildfire: Church Growth in Korea*. Grand Rapids, MI: William B. Eerdmans, 1966.

Shenk, Wilbert R. "Rufus Anderson and Henry Venn: A Special Relationship?" *International Bulletin of Missionary Research* 5, no. 4 (October 1981): 168–72.

Singh, Bakht. "How I Got Joy Unspeakable and Full of Glory." Brother Bakht Singh: A Servant of God, 2007. http://www.brotherbakhtsingh.org/webtestimony.html.

Sircar, Simon H. "The Church in Bangladesh." In *Church in Asia Today: Opportunities and Challenges*, edited by Saphir Athyal, 361–78. Singapore: Asia Lausanne Committee for World Evangelization, 1996.

Sng, Bobby E. K. *In His Good Time: The Story of the Church in Singapore 1819-2002*. 3rd edition. Singapore: Singapore Bible Society, 2003.

Somaratna, G. P. V. "Ashram Movement." In *A Dictionary of Asian Christianity*, edited by Scott W. Sunquist, 43. Grand Rapids, MI: Wm. B. Eerdmans, 2001.

Sritandon, Narin. "The Church in Thailand." In *Church in Asia Today: Opportunities and Challenges*, edited by Saphir Athyal, 238–65. Singapore: Asia Lausanne Committee for World Evangelization, 1996.

Stanley, Brian. "Christian Missions, Antislavery and the Claims of Humanity, c. 1813-1873." In *World Christianities c. 1815-c. 1914*, edited by Sheridan Gilley and Brian Stanley, Vol. 8. The Cambridge History of Christianity. Cambridge: Cambridge University Press, 2006.

———. "Twentieth-Century World Christianity: A Perspective from the History of Missions." In *Christianity Reborn: The Gloabl*

Expansion of Evangelicalism in the Twentieth Century, edited by Donald M. Lewis, 52–86. Studies in the History of Christian Missions. Grand Rapids, MI: Wm. B. Eerdmans, 2004.

Streeter, B H, and A. J. Appasamy. *The Sadhu: A Study in Mysticism and Practical Religion*. London: Macmillan Co, 1921.

Sugden, Chris. *Seeking the Asian Face of Jesus: The Practice and Theology of Christian Social Witness in Indonesia and India 1974-1996*. Oxford: Regnum Books, 1997.

Sumartana, Th. *Mission at the Crossroads: Indigenous Churches, European Missionaries, Islamic Association and Socio-Religious Change in Java 1812-1936*. Jakarta: Pt BPK Gunnung Mulia, 1991.

Sung, John. *The Journal Once Lost - Extracts From The Diary of John Sung*. Edited by LEVI. Singapore: Armour Publishing, 2008.

Sunquist, Scott W. *Explorations in Asian Christianity: History, Theology, and Mission*. Downers Grove, IL: IVP Academic, 2017.

Swanson, Herbert R. *Khrischak Muang Nua*. Bangkok: Chuan Printing Press, 1984.

Tan, Jin Huat. *Brookes, the British, and Christianity: Christian Missions and the State in Sarawak, 1841-1963*. STM Series. Seremban: Seminari Theoloji Malaysia, 2012.

Tan, Kang San. "Will Asian Christianity Blossom or Wither." *Mission Round Table: The Occasional Bulletin of OMF Mission Research* 1 (January 2005): 11–16.

Tan, Kim-Sai. *The Great Digression: World Evangelism since 1910: The Ecumenical Digression and the Evangelical Response*. Petaling Jaya, Malaysia: Malaysia Bible Seminary, 1981.

Tang, Li. "A History of Uighur Religious Conversions (5th-16th Centuries)." Asia Research Institute, National University of Singapore, June 2005.

Terry, John Mark. "The Growth of Christianity in East Asia." *Southern Baptist Journal of Theology* 15, no. 2 (2011): 42–51.

Teule, Herman G. B. "Christianity in Western Asia." In *The Oxford Handbook of Christianity in Asia*, edited by Felix Wilfred, 17–30. Oxford: Oxford University Press, 2014.

"The Lausanne Covenant." The Lausanne Movement, 1974. http://www.lausanne.org/en/documents/lausanne-covenant.html.

Thompson, Andrew. *Christianity in the UAE: Culture and Heritage*. Dubai: Motivate Publishing, 2011.

Thompson, Phyllis. *Sadhu Sundar Singh: A Biography of the Remarkable Indian Disciple of Jesus Christ*. Singapore: Genesis Books, 1994.

Thomson, Robin. "Asian Mission Movements from South Asian Contexts." In *Understanding Asian Mission Movements*, edited by Kang San Tan, Jonathan Ingleby, and Simon Cozens, 35–50. Petaling Jaya, Malaysia: Asia CMS, 2013.

Tiedemann, R. G. "China and Its Neighbors." edited by Adrian Hastings, n.d.

Torbet, Robert. *Venture of Faith: The Story of the American Baptist Foreign Mission Society and the Women's American Baptist Foreign Mission Society*. Valley Forge, PA: Judson Press, 1955.

Torres, Hazel. "Christianity on the Rise in Bangladesh as Tens of Thousands of Muslims Are Turning Away from Allah to Embrace Jesus." Christianity Today, March 15, 2017. https://www.christiantoday.com/article/christianity-rising-fast-in-bangladesh-as-tens-of-thousands-of-muslims-are-turning-away-from-allah-to-embrace-jesus/105712.htm.

Tucker, Ruth A. *From Jerusalem to Irian Jaya: A Biographical History of Christian Missions*. 2nd ed. Grand Rapids, MI: Zondervan, 2004.

Tung, Sie Kwan. "The Waves of the 'Local Church': Watchman Nee's 'Little Flock' in China." *Bridge* 56 (2-23): 1992.

Vischer, Lukas, ed. *Christian Worship in Reformed Churches Past and Present*. Grand Rapids, MI: Wm. B. Eerdmans Publishing Company, 2002.

Walls, Andrew. "The Mission of the Church Today in the Light of Global History." *Word & World* XX, no. 1 (Winter 2000): 17–21.

———. *The Missionary Movement in Christian History: Studies in the Transmission of Faith*. Maryknoll, NY: Orbis Books, 1996.

Ward, William. *The First Hindoo Convert: A Memoir of Krishna Pal*. Philadelphia: American Baptist Publication Society, 1852.

Ware, Timothy. *The Orthodox Church: An Introduction to Eastern Christianity*. London: Penguin Books, 1964.

Warneck, Gustav. *Outline of a History of Protestant Missions*, 1906.

Webster, Warren. "Bangladesh." In *Sejarah Gereja Di Asia, Volume 1*, edited by Donald E. Hoke, 85–103. Malang: Yayasan Penerbit Gandum Mas, 2000.

Wells, Kenneth Elmer. *History of Protestant Work in Thailand, 1828-1958*. Bangkok: Church of Christ in Thailand, 1958.

White, Keith J. "Jesus Was Her Guru." *Christian History | Learn the History of Christianity & the Church* 87 (2005): 16–21.

Whittaker, Colin. *Great Revivals*. London: Marshall Pickering, 1984.

Willis, Avery T. *Indonesian Revival Why Two Million Came to Christ.* William Carey Library Pub, 1977.

Wiyono, Gani. "Ratu Adil: A Javanese Face of Jesus?" *Journal of Asian Mission* 1, no. 1 (1999): 65–79.

Wong, James. "The Church in Singapore." In *Church in Asia Today: Opportunities and Challenges*, edited by Saphir Athyal, 299–323. Singapore: Asia Lausanne Committee for World Evangelization, 1996.

Wostyn, Lode. "Catholic Charismatics in the Philippines." In *Asian and Pentecostal: The Charismatic Face of Christianity in Asia*, edited by Allan Anderson and Edmond Tang, 363–84. Oxford; Baguio City: Regnum Books International, 2005.

Wright, Arthur F. "Changan." In *Cities of Destiny*, edited by Arnold Toynbee, 143–49. New York: McGraw-Hill, 1967.

Yates, Timothy. "Venn, Henry." In *A Dictionary of Asian Christianity*, edited by Scott W. Sunquist, 872. Grand Rapids, MI: Wm. B. Eerdmans, 2001.

Ye'or, Bat. *The Decline of Eastern Christianity under Islam: From Jihad to Dhimmitude; Seventh-Twentieth Century*. English Translation. London: Associated University Presses, 1996.

Yeung, Timothy. "The Chinese Expression of Pentecostalism." *Cyberjournal for Pentecostal Charismatic Research*, no. 16 (2007). http://www.pctii.org/cyberj/cyberj16/yeung.html.

Young, Richard Fox. "East Asia." In *World Christianities*, Vol. 9. The Cambridge History of Christianity. Cambridge: Cambridge University Press, 2014.

Yui, Yoshiaki. "The Church in Japan." In *Church in Asia Today: Opportunities and Challenges*, edited by Saphir Athyal, 20–49. Singapore: Asia Lausanne Committee for World Evangelization, 1996.

Yung, Hwa. *Mangoes or Bananas?: The Quest for an Authentic Asian Christian Theology*. Oxford: Regnum Books, 1997.

———— "Mission and Evangelism: Evangelical and Pentecostal Theologies in Asia." In *Christian Theology in Asia*, edited by Sebastian Kim, 250–70. Cambridge: Cambridge University Press, 2008.

————. "Pentecostalism and the Asian Church." In *Asian and Pentecostal: The Charismatic Face of Christianity in Asia*, edited by Allan Anderson and Edmond Tang, 37–58. Oxford; Baguio City: Regnum Books International, 2005.

Index